First Be Reconciled

Polgylossia: Radical Reformation Theologies

Edited by Peter Dula, Eastern Mennonite University; Jennifer L. Graber, College of Wooster; Chris K. Huebner, Canadian Mennonite University; and J. Alexander Sider, Bluffton University

A series intended for conversation among academics, ministers and laypersons regarding knowledge, beliefs and the practices of the Christian faith. *Polyglossia* grows out of John Howard Yoder's call to see radical reformation as a tone, style or a stance, a way of thinking theologically that requires precarious attempts to speak the gospel in new idioms. It is a form of theological reflection that blends patient vulnerability and hermeneutical charity with considered judgment and informed criticism. The books in this series will emerge out of conversations with contemporary movements in theology, as well as philosophy, political theory, literature, and cultural studies.

A Precarious Peace: Yoderian Explorations on Theology, Knowledge, and Identity by Chris K. Huebner, 2006

The Purple Crown: The Politics and Witness of Martyrdom by Tripp York, 2007

States of Exile: Visions of Diaspora, Witness and Return by Alain Epp Weaver, 2008

First Be Reconciled: Challenging Christians in the Courts by Richard P. Church, 2008

First Be Reconciled

RICHARD P. CHURCH

Foreword by Thomas L. Shaffer

Challenging Christians in the Courts

Herald Press
Scottdale, Pennsylvania
Waterloo, Ontario

Library of Congress Cataloging-in-Publication Data
Church, Richard Patrick.
  First be reconciled : challenging Christians in the courts / Richard P. Church ; foreword by Thomas L. Shaffer.
    p. cm.—(Polyglossia ; 4)
  Includes bibliographical references (p.   ) and index.
  ISBN 978-0-8361-9410-4 (pbk.)
  1. Christianity and law—History of doctrines. 2. Reconciliation—Religious aspects—Christianity—History of doctrines. 3. Mennonite Church. General Assembly. Use of the law. 4. Reconciliation—Religious aspects—Mennonites. 5. Mennonites—Doctrines. I. Title.
  BR115.L28C49 2008
  261.5—dc22
                                        2008028604

Unless otherwise indicated, the Bible text is from the *New Revised Standard Version* Bible, copyright © 1989, by the Division of Christian Education of the National Council of the Churches of Christ in the USA, and is used by permission.

FIRST BE RECONCILED
Copyright © 2008 by Herald Press, Waterloo, Ont. N2L 6H7
  Published simultaneously in the United States of America by Herald Press, Scottdale, Pa. 15683. All rights reserved
Library of Congress Control Number: 2008028604
International Standard Book Number: 978-0-8361-9410-4
Printed in the United States of America
Cover design by Judith Rempel Smucker

14 13 12 11 10 09 08   10 9 8 7 6 5 4 3 2 1

To order or request information please call 1-800-245-7894 or visit www.heraldpress.com.

To Stanley Hauerwas, for complicating everything

Contents

Foreword by Thomas L. Shaffer 9
Author's Preface 13

1. Litigation as Theological and Ethical Topic 15
2. A Hopeful Story 25
3. The Corinthian Context 37
4. Reading 1 Corinthians 6 45
5. Litigation and Reconciliation in the Early Church 57
6. Litigation and Reconciliation During the Reformation 67
7. Early Anabaptist Challenges to the Use of the Law 83
8. The Use of the Law 91
9. The Practice of Reconciliation 109
10. Conclusion 133

Notes 141
Index 225
The Author 231

Foreword

Richard P. Church deals with Anabaptists and the law by practicing what the great modern teacher of biblical theology Walter Brueggemann once called "the mark of discernment and maturity," which is "to strip life down to one compelling loyalty." Church shows here how the children of the Radical Reformation have stripped their lives in and under the law to one compelling loyalty. John Howard Yoder once called this "the cohesion of the believing community in the face of the pressures working against its identity."

Church's focus is primarily historical, among Anabaptists as they have coped with the government—from their resolute refusal in the 16th century to let the local government in Zurich control their faith (a refusal routinely leading to martyrdom), to their dispersion in Europe and the new world.

Mennonites in North America are no longer persecuted (and do not persecute), but they do talk to one another a lot as they exercise among themselves their one compelling loyalty. Meanwhile, we lawyers, who yearn for questions to be settled and put away in the file cabinet, marvel at the Mennonites' endless and mostly unresolved conversations on what John Calvin called "the uses of the law."

Church, an unusual American lawyer and farmer, rejoices in the endless conversations. He hears "multiple voices with different emphases," as his neighbors explore and then explore again and then revise what they thought they had decided on the classic issues—pacifism, conscription, the lawsuits St. Paul seemed to have in mind when he wrote to the Christians in Corinth that they should avoid the courts.

The endless conversations spend as much time on what believers should do instead of going to law when they disagree with their neighbors. And not only about the lawsuits they do not file but about adventures in the law that are not lawsuits—hearings before administrative agencies (zoning boards, county commissioners, city councils), decisions submitted to arbitrators (e.g., over unpaid wages), counter-claims in the face of lawsuits the defendants would never have filed for themselves, negotiated disputes among corporations; divorce, child support, "friendly" suits to resolve unsettled questions; law reform motivated by social justice, legal action to protect exploited poor people.

The endless conversations include a question I once put to my late friend Yoder: whether a bright Mennonite college student should apply for admission to law school. (Richard Church did that, and now he is a lawyer; but he also farms.) The Mennonite answer to that question was, of course, "Let's talk." An addition to the endless conversations.

These conversations are held, as Yoder put it, "where the redeemed individual and the social structure are both present, namely, in the Christian community . . . the primary social structure with which the gospel works." The reason it has been important not only to preserve and protect such a community (almost inevitably local among the Anabaptists) is that its communal business is, as Yoder puts it, "less with what we should decide and do than with how we think about deciding and doing," less with arriving at final answers and using force to give them effect (as the civil courts do) than with bearing witness to an agenda that focuses on compassion, forgiveness, and, if need be, as St. Paul said, giving in rather than litigating: "Rather take wrong," he said, "rather suffer yourselves to be defrauded" (1 Cor 6:7).

The endless conversations are full of the old questions of the Christian tradition and of the story of Israel. They were not invented in the 16th century. Church traces them part of the way back—to the Emperor Constantine. He shows how St. Augustine dealt with them by himself becoming a within-the-community judge who sought not so much justice as reconciliation among the faithful; how the Lutheran Reformation emphasized suffering wrongs (except when litigating on behalf of neighbors rather than against them); how Calvinist thought led instead to "a clear ordination" of the civil courts; and how the Radical Reformation, with its refusal of "the sword," was led both to decline civil litigation as a matter of witness and to figure out an agenda that was more positive than trying to submit love of neighbor to the courts. (Declining litigation may only turn a debate into an alley fight, as I was told the day I was admitted to the Bar.)

What was the more positive agenda? Church shows how the positive Anabaptist agenda is not only love of neighbor but also a demonstration to the rest of the civil community on how love of neighbor works: He quotes John Yoder, who said the "very existence" of the church, "the fraternal relations of her members, their way of dealing with their differences and their needs are, or rather should be, a demonstration of what love means in social relations."

A call, as Church puts it, "to new forms of power in the midst of deep disagreement."

Thomas L. Shaffer
Robert and Marion Short Professor of Law Emeritus
University of Notre Dame
July 2008

Author's Preface

One of my Christian brothers who has also sojourned in the law, once wrote, "Stanley Hauerwas ruined my legal career." This book is the outworking of that statement in my own life. I went to Duke University in the summer of 1995 to be a lawyer. I left ten years later (with several breaks to engage in the practice of law) with both a JD and PhD in theological ethics in hand. While I have practiced and continue to practice law, I was scarred by those courses with Hauerwas, which introduced me to John Howard Yoder and were populated by the editors of this series. They created a level of discomfort about my work as a lawyer that remains to this day.

As I have struggled to articulate the various concerns that being a Christian and a lawyer should raise, it seemed obvious to me that the place to start was the uncritical embrace of the courts by all Christians and the loss of church as a discerning body in which disputes are reconciled. In this book, I have sought to bring the church's practices in these regards back into the forefront of the church's collective conscience. As will be clear in the end, I am not seeking for new rules for Christians to follow regarding litigation. Rather, my hope is to remind the church to what it is called to witness when it is christened in Acts 1. To be a witness to the kingdom of God come in the cross and resurrection of Jesus Christ has everything to do with the manner in which Christians resolve disputes. As I looked at the historical record, it seemed only the Anabaptists had maintained any consistent set of reflections on this point. Thus, this project became an attempt to locate how Christians resolve disputes by placing that question within the Mennonite context.

Although this book is written for a wider audience (see the discussion in particular in chapter 1 regarding ecclesial stance), it could not have been completed without the assistance of many within Mennonite church circles. In particular, Dennis Stoesz and others with the Mennonite Church USA Historical Committee and the staff at the Goshen College's

Harold and Wilma Good Library provided invaluable assistance in locating various archival resources related to Mennonite reflection on litigation, particularly as found in *The Use of the Law*, discussed in chapter 8.

In addition, a host of conversation partners and teachers have been essential to this project in its preparation as a dissertation or in its current form. Although all of the conversation partners that have contributed to the betterment of this book cannot be listed (or likely even remembered), the book is better in particular for my friendships with Alex Sider and Peter Dula, who have both provided key insights and guidance in its drafting. In addition, Dula edited the book and has graciously nudged it toward greater clarity. Gary Eichelberger has been a constant conversation partner over the past thirteen years regarding what it means to be a lawyer and a Christian. H. Jefferson Powell at the Duke Law School was also instrumental to the development of this book, which he oversaw at various stages as independent study projects or as a dissertation committee adviser.

Finally, Stanley Hauerwas has been a faithful mentor and friend since my arrival at Duke. His entry into my life marks a point in which all things changed. His encouragement has been unceasing. It was his commitment that this book was worth writing and that I was capable of the task that has led to its creation. Despite this wonderful cadre of friends and supporters that have led to betterment of this book, I am certain that there is still more to learn. Any errors that remain are my sole responsibility.

Much has changed in my life since I arrived at Duke. Most importantly, my wife, Kristy, and her two daughters, Sierra and Zoe, and now our two sons, Jonas and Ezra, grace my days. Each of them pitched in as late-night and early-morning hours were stolen to complete this project. I am grateful for their patience and assistance, without which this book could not have been completed.

Richard P. Church
Siler City, North Carolina
June 2008

1

Litigation as Theological and Ethical Topic

> So if anyone is in Christ, there is a new creation: everything old has passed away; see, everything has become new! All this is from God, who reconciled us to himself through Christ, and has given us the ministry of reconciliation; that is, in Christ God was reconciling the world to himself, not counting their trespasses against them, and entrusting the message of reconciliation to us.
> —*2 Corinthians 5:17-19*

Reconciliation in Lieu of Nonviolence

No one has written with more clarity and force than John Howard Yoder regarding the connection between the church's stance toward violence and its witness to the gospel. Yet Yoder's peace witness is often viewed as merely securing the absence of violence. This reading of Yoder and the Anabaptist witness is inaccurate, however, for Yoder suggests "our task as Christians in this world [is] to bring a ministry of reconciliation to our fellowman."[1] Such radical peacemaking is more than nonviolence; it is the bringing about of reconciliation, which is both the work of the church in the world and an anticipation of the fulfillment of the kingdom inaugurated in Christ's reconciling death and resurrection. Therefore, the church rejects not only violence, but also "the compulsiveness of purpose that leads the strong to violate the dignity of others. . . . Our readiness to renounce our legitimate ends whenever they cannot be attained by legitimate means constitutes our participation in the triumphant suffering of the Lamb."[2] Such peace is not possessed, but is ever elusive and almost always a momentary and fragmented achievement.

First Corinthians likewise makes clear that reconciliation is at the heart of the gospel. Paul argues there that the church is constituted by its unity.[3] The suggestion in 1 Corinthians 6 that litigation should be forgone or disputes resolved within the church, the topic at the heart of this book, is part of Paul's larger project of bringing about and restoring the unity of the body of Christ in Corinth. Living in a reconciled manner is the church's witness to the inauguration of the kingdom of Christ.[4] On the other hand, conflict that fails to produce reconciliation renders the church incapable of coherent witness to the power of the resurrection. Such failure denies within the church's own communal life the reconciling work of Christ that, according to 1 Corinthians 11, the eucharist makes materially evident.

If peace is then more determinative than the absence of violence, if the reconciliation of God to human *and* human to human is at the heart of the good news, what then of litigation? This book is an exploration of that question. I take this particular claim—that the peaceable church is not only marked by its refusal to have recourse to physical violence, but also by its participation in a ministry of reconciliation—and locate it in relationship to participation in civil litigation. I pursue this task by viewing the church's history of discernment on participation in litigation with a particular focus on the peace church tradition. I conclude that participation in at least many forms of modern litigation renders the church's witness to the ministry of reconciliation unintelligible, a conclusion amplified when both litigants are members of the church.

Litigation in the Church

This project is particularly pressing because if participation in litigation is problematic, the church's witness is in jeopardy. While a variety of statistics regarding the litigiousness of American society and Christians in particular might be cited,[5] nothing illustrates the church's acceptance carte blanche of civil litigation as an appropriate mode of adjudicating disputes more dramatically than the recent crisis within the American Catholic Church. Catholic laypersons sued their own dioceses to the brink of bankruptcy, putting the continued existence of the body charged with bearing and living out the gospel witness itself in question.[6] Church leaders themselves have adopted litigation as a tactic, as sister dioceses and church bodies brought suit against other dioceses in regard to priests transferred without full disclosure of their sexual misconduct.[7] The cases highlighted the manner in which the culture of litigation (and capital) has come to predominate in the church. The Archbishop of San Bernadino acknowledged, "It's like a family member taking another family member to court," but concluded, "I have a responsibility to protect the finances of the diocese."[8] Absent from the discussion was the potential of using church-constituted canon law courts to resolve these legitimate grievances.

It is not that Roman Catholics are the only ones of various catholic churches[9] that have minimized the potential implications of the church's ministry of reconciliation and the particular challenge to litigation found in 1 Corinthians 6. It is just the most dramatic recent example. Likewise, it is not that the actions of church leaders in their abuse and cover-up of abuse within the church must not be rightly named sin. It was the canon law itself that was betrayed in the process of covering those sins over in lieu of addressing them within the structures of discipline established within the Catholic community.[10] Yet sin—and likewise conflict—is not a surprise to the church; it is the norm. What is surprising is that the church addresses sin through the practices of forgiveness and reconciliation or, as a worst case, through the gracious act of excommunication. This gracious response to sin is the church's embodiment of the reality narrated in the life and death of Jesus Christ.

The argument of this book is that much is at stake theologically in regard to litigation: the peaceable kingdom—which Christ preached and inaugurated in his life, death, and resurrection and which is being brought to eschatological fulfillment in and through the church—is a reconciled peace in which Jew and Gentile, wolf and lamb, litigant and litigant are reconciled to one another to become one body in Christ. Therefore, if modern litigation fails to produce reconciliation and yet is still used with ubiquity by Christians, the church's witness to that peaceable kingdom is at risk.

With this said, it is essential to note the limited scope of the claims made herein. Some forms of litigation lead to division instead of reconciliation; insofar as they do, they make incoherent the church's witness and its distinctive mode of being in the world. However, some forms of litigation and/or some modes of engaging in litigation may lead to reconciliation. Determining the nature of and the church's appropriate relationship to any particular mode of civil dispute resolution is thus a prudential decision that must be made in light of the concrete set of practices the church finds itself offered by the wider society. To aid in this process, this book traces the historical trajectory of some of the church's prudential reasoning on litigation, beginning with the biblical record of that discernment in 1 Corinthians 6 and proceeding through various key historical theological moments with a particular focus on Anabaptist reflection on litigation. Yet none of this work will produce a "position" on "litigation." All of it, however, is fruitful for churches today as they continue the work of discernment regarding participation in modern litigation—or, for many, take up the question of litigation for the first time. Thus, I do not make an argument against "litigation" in the abstract. Rather, I present a challenge to the church to take up anew the task of discernment regarding its relationship to civil adjudication mechanisms and to determine the analogies or disanalogies between those practices and the word of 1 Corinthian 6, other relevant biblical texts, the gospel witness as a whole, and the church's memory and practice. The recovery of these texts, witness, and memory is the task of this book.

On Litigation as Ethical Topic

While of particular interest to Christians, the project is also relevant to the field of legal ethics because it challenges certain core assumptions that have limited the questions asked and answered by most legal ethicists. First among those assumptions is that legal ethics is only for lawyers, that is, legal ethics is about what it is that lawyers should and should not do. Although Thomas Shaffer has argued compellingly that lawyers and clients must be considered co-actors in legal enterprises,[11] even he has yet to give sustained attention to the logical conclusion of his argument that legal ethics ought then to have significant implications for clients as well as attorneys. The assumption in legal ethics remains that lawyers are the only moral actors in litigation.

Legal ethicists have also assumed that litigation ethics is about the appropriate tactics one may use in litigation, that is, litigation ethics sets the boundaries for the proper conduct of litigation. What has remained unaddressed and unchallenged is litigation itself. While a large body of literature has grown up around modes of alternative dispute resolution (ADR),[12] advocating the benefits of ADR over litigation, these arguments have been couched in the language of self-interest. ADR is less costly, less time consuming, can sustain necessary business relationships, and so on. Legal ethicists have not seen that the arguments for ADR may not only relate to benefits to the parties but also speak to the moral appropriateness of more and less adversarial modes of resolving disputes. Overcoming this assumption opens the possibility that the question ought not be "Is this tactic appropriate in the pursuit of litigation?" but rather "Is litigation appropriate as a mode of resolving this dispute?"

That the arguments for ADR have been couched only in the language of self-interest to the parties, however, highlights a final assumption of legal ethics—and most modern ethics for that matter: "ethics" must be the same for all lawyers or persons. Legal ethicists have assumed that ethics may be done and, in fact, should be done in abstraction from the particular communities and places that claim the moral agent. Alasdair MacIntyre's work detailing the breakdown of modern ethical discourse in light of this unhinging of ethical reflection from communities that shared a substantive set of institutions, practices, and discourses is well known.[13] However, in the area of legal ethics, the implications of MacIntyre's work are, for the most part, ignored. Legal ethics is written for all lawyers, regardless of the particularity of the traditions, practices, and places that shape them.[14] The cost of making legal ethics applicable to all lawyers is that the shared moral content sustaining them is razor thin.

The arguments to be made for ADR are made in the language of self-interest, for this, it is at least hoped, will be a shared commitment of all. Other arguments for ADR or against litigation must be forgone, for such arguments necessarily rely on assumptions about the good of a human life, the availability and authority of practices to foster reconciliation and forgiveness, and a host of other shared practices, institutions, and discourses not available to the pluralist "all" for whom ethics in modernity is written.[15]

I offer a challenge to each of these assumptions by asking the question, ought Christians to litigate disputes? In doing so, I attempt to follow Stanley Hauerwas's work on medical ethics—which shifted the focus from medical professionals to patients and their demands on medicine[16]—by focusing not on lawyer's ethics, but on what clients ask of lawyers. Further, such clients are limited to those in dispute that claim Jesus as Lord. Thus, unlike abstract modern ethical theories, the project has the very particular scriptural and historical witness and memory at its disposal. Finally, because this question is asked in the context of the peculiar people called the church, who know already that they have been called out of the world in service to that world, the question of litigation ethics can be asked with an openness to the possibility that Christians' participation in something as foundational to the modern nation state as litigation—as with war—must be rejected.

On Method: Running, Remembering, and Word Care

The method undertaken in exploring the appropriateness of litigation to the Christian life is a looping back to the church's catholic history and practices in their denominational and theological diversity as a means of seeking guidance in the church's going forward. This work follows the pattern outlined by John Howard Yoder for theological reflection, for he suggests that the theologian is called to three central tasks: (1) to be an ecumenical runner between varying traditions within the church, (2) to be an agent of communal memory, and (3) to be an agent of word care regarding the church's witness.[17] Accordingly, I take up litigation in the light of the church's catholic memory, practice, and witness. Nonetheless, I pay particular attention to the Mennonite tradition, insofar as this tradition has found ways to keep litigation in critical question more effectively than any of the other of the plurality of churches in the post-Reformation era. With this said, the project's aims are catholic, not in suggesting that each denomination must embody the Mennonite "position" and practices in relationship to litigation, but rather in suggesting that Mennonite reflection and praxis make clear that ethical resources are available for an imaginative and counter-cultural community to forgo litigation, even in modern America.

In attempting to make clear the argument's ecumenical significance, I begin by retelling the story of one particular Mennonite church's discernment regarding participation in litigation. The remainder of the book is a working out of the history necessary to make sense of the questions raised and actions taken in that story, beginning with a reading of 1 Corinthians 6, a text that all denominations must also take up. However, Scripture does not read itself nor speak without an interpretative community. The work of chapters 3 and 4 is therefore not only a reading of the text, but also location of the text in the light of recent historical-critical scholarship regarding the dispute resolution options available in the Greco-Roman world of the early first century.[18]

As other texts also bear on litigation and resolving disputes within the church, the choice to focus on 1 Corinthians 6 should be defended.[19] It is noteworthy that several of these other texts address not only litigation within the church, but the pursuit of litigation at all. As will become evident in the exploration of Anabaptist understandings of litigation, 1 Corinthians 6 is not the only nor the determinative text, but rather the Sermon on the Mount[20] and 2 Corinthians 5[21] play essential roles in Anabaptist reflection on the proper relation to the law. Litigation within the church is seen as particularly problematic, but litigation is the main concern. This book focuses on 1 Corinthians 6, nonetheless, because Paul presents not only a challenge to litigation, but also the outlines of the theological support for that position. As alluded to above, in exploring 1 Corinthians 6 and Paul's overarching themes in that letter, one gains insight not only into a "prohibition" on litigation, but also into the nature of the church as a unified and thereby witnessing body. A central concern of the book is to make evident how litigation within the church renders the church's claims regarding Christ unintelligible. First Corinthians 6 provides unique resources for this project.

The book continues the project of deepening the church's memory regarding participation in litigation by exploring the reception and embodiment of this text in the life of the church historically. I begin with an ad hoc survey of three essential theological figures—Augustine of Hippo, Martin Luther, and John Calvin—in three of the church's great traditions, Catholic, Lutheran, and Reformed. For each, I explore not only their reading of 1 Corinthians 6, which will in some instances raise challenges to the Anabaptist theology that will follow—not only surrounding litigation but around the proper understanding of the state—but also place their lives and historical contexts. These explorations will begin to draw links explored throughout the remainder of the book between church discipline, litigation among believers, and the relationship of the church to the civil authority.[22] This history-telling in chapters 5 and 6—like the exegetical reflection in chapters 3 and 4—reports on historical scholarship regarding these figures and periods, with the hope of deepening theological memory in service of present reflection on Christian participation in litigation. This limited task means none of these chapters purports to be a comprehensive history. The defined task is to take up the historical content most important to illuminating litigation discernment.

The task of the ecumenical runner is then taken up by focusing on the particular story of the Anabaptist tradition and its historical discernment and praxis regarding litigation. The ongoing discernment of this witness is unearthed in chapters 7 and 8 by locating the Anabaptist tradition's understanding of litigation beginning with consideration of such founding saints and confessions as Michael Sattler and his Schleitheim Confession, and continuing through the most recent theological reflection, discernment, and witness in regard to litigation, *The Use of the Law*. This guiding document, approved by the Mennonite Church General Assembly in 1981, concludes that (1) litigation within the church is presumptively prohibited and (2) litigation against others is to be pursued only in the light of communal reasoning regarding its appropriateness within the framework of a presumption against litigation.[23]

Finally, chapter 9 takes up Yoder's third theological task of word care, by considering litigation within the church in light of his arguments regarding ecclesiology. The brief theological introduction set forth above in regard to the church's peace witness and the role of reconciliation within the body is explored in detail in this chapter. The question of discipline is also taken up, for in eschewing internal modes of dispute resolution the church not only forfeits its call to reconciliation, but also abandons disciplining the brother and sister. This renunciation of discipline likewise bears a theological cost.[24] The constructive theological work, therefore, takes up not only what is lost in regard to the church's peace and reconciliation witness, but also what is lost and ceded to modernity's limited construction of religion in the failure of discipline that accompanies the abandonment of internal modes of church discernment.

On Schism and Ecclesial Stance

Unavoidably, this book is written in the midst of schism by a non-Mennonite for an audience called "the church" that entails groups and traditions as diverse as Eastern Orthodox and Pentecostal. Nonetheless, it is construed as catholic. It begins with 1 Corinthians 6, a text that each denomination, even in the midst of schism, must take into account. With that said, however, one must immediately acknowledge that the text does not read itself. The interpretative lenses through which the author reads the text are never neutral, but entail a constructive and creative project of focusing light and receding shadows. Yet the text is the common bond that links the various churches to the problems raised by 1 Corinthians 6, equally raising an exegetical if not an ethical challenge to those churches.

From an exegetical and historical enquiry, however, I move to a particular focus on the Anabaptist vine growing out of the Reformation turmoil and in particular to the Mennonite sprout of that vine. That the book has in some ways stacked the deck for the Mennonite position cannot be denied. The author believes that the Mennonites have—with many failings as described herein—continued to ask and reflect on a set of questions regarding litigation that for the most part are simply no longer asked in the mainstream denominations. While the deck is in some way stacked, however, as in every theological enquiry, this fact does not mean that the project is unconcerned to remain catholic. A postmodern context does not preclude ecumenical dialogue; it merely mandates one be more forthright in locating oneself.[25]

If there is a benefit of schism, however, it must be the theological diversity schism spawns. While diversity spawned by schism may cause disunity, on which 1 Corinthians is most focused, this theological diversity within the various denominations may also be a gift to the catholic church if it is used to offer diverse denominational traditions new resources to locate their lives faithfully. Ecumenical dialogue reflects the church's call to Matthew 18, to listening to the other in lieu of ignoring or killing her, so that the church might hear its story told back to it and discern its own voice in the voice of the other. As noted above, Yoder suggests that one of the tasks of the theologian is to serve as "ecumenical runner" between traditions in facilitating this project. The value of this task is grounded in an understanding of the positive benefit that may be derived by the theological and practical diversity spawned by schism.[26]

Thus, this book focuses on the Mennonites for this particular purpose of setting forth an embodiment of the litigation witness that may be required by the gospel of reconciliation. This benefit of denominational diversity, it is hoped, suggests why one is justified in looking at such a peculiar denomination as the Mennonites, for in their distance from the broader culture I locate an openness to an ethic as radical as 1 Corinthians 6 might require. Their alleged "cultural irrelevance" enables the Mennonites to be the best possible "test case" for considering if the church's witness might actually require an ethic as extreme as forgoing some forms of litigation altogether.

With this said, the purpose of this project is in service of the catholic churches. Accordingly, if the project is to remain catholic, it must go on to interrogate this particularly Mennonite witness in the light of other denominational traditions, for stacking the deck does not entail a lack of commitment to critical theological enquiry, but rather acknowledges the impossibility of not stacking the deck. For this reason, conversations with Augustine, Luther, and Calvin are undertaken in the hopes that locating challenges to and resources for supporting the Mennonite reading proposed here can at least demonstrate the necessity of beginning a dialogue surrounding the challenge litigation may pose to the Catholic, Lutheran, and Reformed traditions. This does not cover all of the diversity present in the current state of schism, but it is hoped that each of the other traditions, absent the Eastern Orthodox, who remain beyond the scope of the project for no other reason than the limits of the author's theological and practical knowledge, can trace their roots to one of these four major branches coming out of the Reformation.

The project does not, however, go on to suggest how these denominations would begin to discern regarding litigation today. To do so would require, first, the type of detailed historical enquiry regarding each of these traditions as is performed on the Mennonite tradition in this book. The task of imagining creative ways to make such an ethic "realistic" would then have to begin.[27] This task would necessarily rely on the practical resources available in each of these traditions. To suggest otherwise, that is, to suggest that these traditions must embody a litigation witness in exactly the same manner as the Mennonites, would be to mistake Paul's word on litigation in 1 Corinthians 6 as a moral rule. Further, each of these denominational traditions will bring different resources to that project. It would be neither possible nor appropriate to suggest that this book could narrate how each of these rich and diverse traditions would embody a litigation ethic in the particular context of its own denomination's history. The book's essential argument is for the necessity of reflection on the relationship of participation in civil litigation to the task of being the church. Insofar as other denominations conclude that the challenge presented here is accurately stated, the imaginative task of finding resources within any given tradition to live into this ethic must be taken up.

2
A Hopeful Story

In this chapter, I explore a particular story of conflict and the manner in which a family, church, and community responded to that conflict both outside and within the legal system. The story is found among other stories of conflict in the book *When Good People Quarrel: Studies of Conflict Resolution* by Robert S. Kreider and Rachel Waltner Goossen. The book itself is significant because the authors question the appropriateness of litigation as a means to resolving at least some disputes. The collection of stories, which Kreider and Goossen explain "are based on one or more actual experiences,"[1] suggest that forgoing litigation is a relevant option for an imaginative people willing to be formed by the gospel.

The value of retelling one of these stories of dispute resolution in this book is twofold. The first crucial reason for hearing this story is to make evident that conflict is normal. I argue in chapter 9 that it is in fact beneficial.[2] Life in community will lead to conflict. Acknowledging this truth is the church's great strength. Or, as Ron Kraybill concludes in the foreword to *When Good People Quarrel*, "If you want to have less conflict, invite disagreement!"[3] Stories of conflict are important insofar as they present the church fulfilling its task of discernment, which always requires a stance of openness to conflict as both normal and beneficial to that process.

When Good People Quarrel begins with a second assumption that is also central to the argument of *First Be Reconciled*. In Kraybill's words, "This volume holds great promise for readers as well as grave responsibility. There is promise here because storytelling is the beginning of hope."[4] The connection between vision, storytelling, and hope is essential to the embodiment of Christian ethics in general and in regard to litigation. As the apocalyptic reading of 1 Corinthians 6 in the next chapter will demonstrate, to live as a Christian requires that the world be rightly seen. Right vision is developed via the telling and hearing of new stories through which one begins to imagine the new reality revealed in the Gospels. Storytelling is, therefore, a hopeful activity insofar as one learns that the world can be other than it is.[5] For this reason, storytelling is essential to this book as well. Simply setting forth the exegetical and theological grounds for the priority of reconciliation over divisive litigation is not enough. I must also display lives that embody these accounts. It is the connection between vision, storytelling, and hope, therefore, that dictates the outline of the book itself, in which the story of this chapter is set forth, followed by the exegetical, historical, and constructive theological work necessary to make sense of that story.

However, I must be clear that storytelling alone is not enough, for not any story will do. Kraybill concludes:

> Healing in the end must take us beyond our own stories. We need new ways of thinking about ourselves and new skills for communicating with others. . . . Perhaps most importantly, this volume places before us selections from what Christians hold as the Original Story. Rarely have we viewed the Bible as a study in conflict resolution. Yet the struggle for reconciliation amid brokenness recurs in virtually every chapter. Reconciliation is the center of God's purpose. Thus the promise of ultimate healing springs from encounter with the Original Story.[6]

All of theology as well as this book is the explication of this Original Story. The point now, however, is simply to note that storytelling alone is inadequate to the specific claims of this book. The questions and story presented here make sense only in light of the Original Story of cross and resurrection.

Telling this story well means displaying from where persons like those described in *When Good People Quarrel* come. In other words, what background makes intelligible the questions asked and actions taken in the story. A central claim that I put into historical context in the chapters that follow is that the impetus to ask and answer these questions in the manner displayed in this chapter can only be understood in light of the actors' and authors' particular location within the catholic church. While seeking to display an ecumenical ethic, the stories are grounded in Mennonite theology and praxis.

It is significant that both authors are Mennonites. At the time of writing, Kreider was a professor of history and peace studies at Bethel College, a Mennonite college in North Newton, Kansas. Goossen was a doctoral student in American history at the University of Kansas and a graduate of Bethel College, which, like many Mennonite colleges, has a major in peace studies. The final contributors to the book, along with the many students and colleges Kreider and Goossen attribute the stories themselves to, were David Brubaker, who wrote the study questions, and Ron Kraybill, who drafted the foreword. Both Kraybill and Brubaker at the time were part of the staff of Mennonite Conciliation Service, a denominationally sponsored institute for training mediators and facilitating the mediation of disputes. Finally, the characters in the story themselves find their lives within Faith Mennonite Church in Minneapolis. Thus, the particular questions raised and openness to hearing answers that potentially require absenting oneself from civil legal process are deeply embedded within a Mennonite context.[7]

Before proceeding, however, it must be noted that, while the story poses questions regarding how reconciliation might be reached, litigation was an available option for those in the story. The authors of *When Good People Quarrel* are not suggesting that litigation should be avoided in every instance. Instead, the litigation praxis proposed is a process of discernment informed by a set of gathered reflections on the sense of the biblical texts involved and the memory of a particular tradition's historical practices in regard to litigation. These gathered texts and memories in the book do not answer questions regarding litigation, but rather open up the necessity of ongoing discernment regarding participation in the next potential form of dispute resolution. A rule is not set forth, but a community is called to discernment regarding these matters. In a manner that will be suggested by Richard Hays in the next chapter, the story invites a community to discover "imaginative analogies" between the biblical stories and the world within which they live, such that they might "thereby learn to see [their] own lives in strange and challenging new ways."[8]

A Lawyer Forgoes the Courts

The story I consider in detail here is complicated. Nonetheless, it displays what the church might hope for in its calling together a community of discernment and reconciliation even in the midst of a fractured ending. It is a hopeful story in its witness to the power of the cross, while still acknowledging that power may be seen only in a partial and fragmentary manner in the "now but not yet" that names Christ's lordship over the wider world.

The story begins with an unlikely relationship. Alberto Quintela, the son of Pentecostal migrant farm workers in New Mexico and a gifted student, found his way to Fresno Pacific College, a Mennonite Brethren college. From Fresno Pacific, he enrolled in a master's program in the School of Education at Harvard University. While there, he met Helen, a white South Carolina Methodist, also enrolled in the program. They married and graduated. Alberto then turned down offers to the Harvard Law School and Divinity School to attend law school at the University of Minnesota. At the completion of his degree, he took a job at the Minnesota Attorney General's office, and he and Helen made a decision to purchase their first home in a mixed Hispanic-white inner-city neighborhood on Minneapolis's West Side.[9]

With this introduction, Kreider and Goossen allow Alberto to tell the rest of the story in first-person narrative. I supplement Alberto's story with his wife's account in her book, *Out of Ashes*.[10] As Alberto and Helen moved into their new home, pregnant with their first child, they discovered their immediate neighbors to be a family in crisis. Of most importance for Alberto and Helen were repeated family fights in the yard and late-night parties. In the face of these initial disturbances and while never specifically placing his actions in the context of Matthew 18, Alberto narrates a series of attempts to conciliate the matter directly with his neighbor in a manner remarkably similar to the pattern of Matthew 18, embodied at a neighborhood level.[11] Alberto first went to the neighbor by himself; he was summarily run off his neighbor's property with cursing and threats. Next he discussed the issue with other neighbors and a local community organization, which led to a neighborhood meeting that the disruptive neighbors, although invited, did not attend.[12]

These initial attempts to address the situation and the addition of a party house in the neighbor's back yard led to increasing tensions. Helen makes clear that these tensions were increasingly laced with racial overtones.[13] The neighbor and his children began harassing Alberto as he entered and left his home. In the midst of this deteriorating situation, Alberto and Helen joined Faith Mennonite Church, solidifying a set of commitments that had begun to develop at Fresno Pacific regarding the nature of the Christian life and the centrality of the Sermon on the Mount to that life. After a quiet winter (the cold of Minnesota is apparently capable of quelling all activity), a major incident occurred:

> In April 1981 the turmoil boiled over. A gang of kids decided to crash a party next door. They banged on the door and were refused entry. A riot almost took off. I awoke about 1:00 a.m. and saw three people in our backyard. I turned on our backyard lights.

> There was my neighbor and others in a fistfight. Two police cars pulled up and two policemen attempted to break up the fight. More police arrived. Our garden was trampled and the fence we had built that spring was smashed to bits. One of the kids with a knife had attempted to stab a police officer. A police officer pulled a gun and the riot was quieted. An officer knocked on the door and inquired, "Any damages done here? We're going to arrest these individuals for disorderly conduct and assault. You could also charge them with criminal destruction of property. Do you want to sign a complaint?" I looked out on our backyard and said, "Officer, no." Our neighbor came home at this point and started yelling at me: "You—talking to the police! You're not going to charge my kids with anything because if you do, I'm going to bash your head in the next time I see you." The police officer said, "We could arrest him too." I answered, "No, that's okay. We'll try to handle this in our own way."[14]

This incident led to another direct confrontation between Alberto and his neighbor and further threats being made against the Quintelas. Yet resolutely Alberto narrates a conviction that as Christians, they must continue to seek peace with their neighbors, to "handle this in our own way." The resonances of a people of reconciliation called out of the world are clear.

As tensions and their fear of their neighbors continued to increase, Alberto and Helen enlisted a critical resource for maintaining this witness: "We finally turned to our church for help in April, saying, 'We've got a problem that we can't handle on our own. We're going to be true to what we believe in. We need your help and support.'"[15] The alternative to violence or civil suit, in this case, was not an alternative procedure (in which the neighbors could not have been be forced to participate), but a community to share the cost, measured not only in dollars but also in the emotional toll of the Quintelas's witness. Helen specifically locates this movement in the context of John Howard Yoder's work, quoting Yoder's *Nevertheless* in describing the experience of the church's solidarity at this moment:

> When we speak of the pacifism of the messianic community, we move the focus of ethical concern from the individual asking him [her] self about right and wrong in concern for his [her] own integrity, to the human community experiencing in its life a fore-

> taste of God's kingdom. The pacifistic experience is communal in that it is not a life alone for heroic personalities but for a society. It is communal in that it is lived by a brotherhood of men and women who instruct one another, forgive one another, bear one another's burdens, reinforce one another's witness.[16]

Strengthened with a wider community to bear the cost and to discern regarding the situation, Alberto and Helen continued in their attempts to live at peace with their neighbors.

The results for the church's witness in living together in this manner were dramatic not only in the situation, but also as a witness before the watching world. Following another incident in which the neighbor's son physically attacked Alberto, he records,

> Our church decided to have Sunday vigils in our home. This brought the church and our family together. We shared meals and prayed together. As we heard the commotion outside we'd try to find peace with ourselves, in Christ, in the Word. In July our church decided to have a twenty-four hour, seven-day-a-week candlelight vigil and worship service in our home as an expression of nonviolent response to violence. Not only did church members participate but also members of our community and other acquaintances. The local newspaper got wind of it. People signed up for eight hour shifts to live with us, 8:00 a.m. to 3:00 p.m., 3:00 to 11:00 p.m., 10:30 p.m. to 8:00 a.m. People were coming in all the time. Others would ask, "What's going on here? What are all these cars doing in front of your house?" "Our friends are Mennonites," we explained. "They believe in nonviolence. They believe we can conquer." During all this our church became one.[17]

The response to block parties in the back yard is worship next door. Such action calls forth witness. One church's commitment to live peaceably apart from violence and litigation demanded an explanation from the community at large. Such action, grounded in an understanding that the church must look different from the world, is evangelism.

In August, as the situation continued to deteriorate, the Quintelas's garage was burned down while Alberto was out of town. In the twelve-hour period after the fire, Alberto records more than two hundred people arriving from "all sections of the community" to support their family.[18] Yet the story does not have a fairytale ending. In the face of these escalating threats, ultimately, Alberto and Helen decided to leave the home:

We moved out of our home, our first home. We're still a part of the neighborhood and have become a symbol in our community. Love can conquer all. The community knows me as the lawyer who believes in nonviolence and, whenever I have been asked to intervene in a situation, a nonviolent unit has been created in my community. Faith Mennonite Church, my church, has decided to do evangelism in the community because we have such a residue of people who have read newspaper accounts of our story. I wouldn't be where I am without having a supportive group of people. They say, "We believe in what you believe. The trouble and turmoil we went through served as an inspiration to families in our church to take their own steps and stand up for what they believe in. Trust in the Lord and he will see you through."[19]

That the process ended in this manner points to the ambiguity and incompleteness of the hope to which I am pointing here. The hope for the kingdom of God is more than moving away from violent neighbors, but the transformation of lives together.

While the story ends in Kreider and Goossen's treatment at this point, Helen continues the story. After moving out, the Quintelas considered and ultimately filed a civil suit against their neighbors. This would seem a failure if this book's conclusion was that all litigation is problematic. Without determining if litigation may well have been problematic in this particular case, their description of the process of discernment regarding the choice to litigate is of most importance. Helen describes their decision to sue:

> The lawsuit asked for monetary retribution for property damages and for emotional suffering. After our experience on Baker [Street], Alberto and I felt strongly that an offender must be nonviolently confronted by his or her victim in a safe setting. We believed an offender must be confronted with the victim's emotional struggle to live on with the losses and fears that accompany any victimization. . . .
>
> Alberto and I felt we had tried to confront the Robinsons peacefully. We had attempted first to confront the Robinsons alone. We had tried a neighborhood meeting. Finally we worked through various agencies, such as the Crime-Victim Center, the department of Human Rights, and a police liaison officer.
>
> No attempt had been successful. We believed that the civil court system should be a final resort for nonviolent conflict resolution and administration of justice.[20]

As noted above, there is an implicit reference, made explicit by Helen later, to the outline of Matthew 18 having been followed. The decision to sue was a last resort only appropriate after these other means had been exhausted. Even so, it was made within a continuing context of a commitment to peaceable conflict resolution. As I note in chapter 9, the ability of civil courts in America to end disputes nonviolently, though less than the kingdom-hope of reconciliation, is a real good.

Yet more importantly, Alberto and Helen's choice to sue was only partially their own. Prior to instigating the suit, Faith Mennonite Church, who had participated in their struggle, discerned regarding their decision to sue:

> About thirty-five people gathered at Faith Mennonite for the July 11 meeting. Alberto began the meeting by restating our commitment to nonviolent confrontation of the Robinsons.
>
> Next Myron Schrag, our pastor, spoke on the biblical principles of nonviolence and on our ministry to the city. He quoted Jeremiah 29:7, which calls the exiled people to "seek the peace and prosperity of the city to which I have carried you."
>
> He referred to Matthew 5:14-16 [the church as a city on a hill]. . . .
>
> Myron also reviewed Christ's teachings concerning a brother or sister who sins against you. The steps for reconciliation from Matthew 18:15-20 are ones Alberto and I truly believed we had tried to follow with the Robinsons.[21]

The church's discernment focused on two issues: would the Quintelas' suit spark their former neighbors to more violence, and was the suit itself an appropriate response to harm?

> During the discussion that followed our attorney's presentation, it was evident that many of our church members, as we had anticipated, had questions and concerns. Mennonites have traditionally avoided using the courts. . . .
>
> The July 11 meeting ended at 11:00 p.m., after four hours, and concluded on an uncertain note. Many of our brothers and sisters were not convinced the lawsuit was the best possible alternative. Many discussed the possibility of visiting or writing letters to the Robinsons. Alberto felt it was too late for this.
>
> The week following the meeting was especially hard for Alberto. We knew many members of our church family might have doubts about our legal action.[22]

In the face of this resistance, the pastor ultimately assured the Quintelas of the appropriateness of filing suit based on their stated goals for the litigation:

> Our lawsuit was a public statement on various levels. First, it was a public affirmation of our belief in nonviolent conflict resolution. Second, it would serve notice on individuals who oppress others—due to their beliefs, ethnicity, or background—that the justice system would not condone such behavior. Third, we hoped it would empower other families and individuals similarly abused.[23]

With this assurance the Quintelas proceeded to file suit. In this regard, it would be worthwhile for the Quintelas and Faith Mennonite Church to reflect on this story and ask if they did enough, if their witness required yet more or if enough time was taken to discern this question. Both the Quintelas and Kreider and Goossen are open to this process of continued questioning. Alberto notes in concluding his description of the story:

> We had mixed feelings as to whether we should bring suit against our neighbors. When we calculated the financial costs of leaving the house, we found that we had suffered costs which ran into tens of thousands of dollars. We discussed what we should have done differently. We know that we had made many mistakes. We asked for prayers of other that we might learn and grow from this terrible and beautiful experience.[24]

Brubaker's follow-up questions to Kreider and Goossen's chapter pose similar issues:

1. What key values underlie Helen and Alberto's actions?
2. Was Alberto's decision to confront his troublesome neighbor wise? Would there have been other ways of dealing with the neighbor family?
3. Should the Quintelas have moved out of the neighborhood when the situation became difficult, instead of waiting and trying to deal with it?
4. Did the Quintelas' commitment to nonviolence fail or succeed?[25]

So, while acknowledging that this is perhaps not the transformation of witness for which one might hope—that is, the neighbors do not ultimately see the beauty of Alberto and Helen's life and the suit ultimately ensues—the case is, nonetheless, significant.

Its importance lies in the fact that Alberto and Helen's actions and descriptions are largely incomprehensible to the modern mind and particularly to the legal-trained mind. Alberto is an attorney, and a state Attorney General at that. Yet he and Helen make litigation a last resort and pause with their church to discern before bringing to bear the power of the state through civil legal process. While one might consider whether their proceeding with the suit in the midst of what may have been a lack of consensus within their church was appropriate, Alberto and Helen's failure to turn immediately to the power of the state, even while Alberto is working as an agent of the state, is significant. Yet the Quintelas appear to understand that their lives are not their own. They must share their struggles with Faith Mennonite Church, which rallies around them, just as they must share their decision to sue. In the midst of violence and aided by the wider church community, Alberto and Helen lived as powerful witnesses to reconciliation. This witness should not be viewed as "ineffective" simply because it did not immediately bring reconciliation with their neighbors; judged eschatologically it may look different. Alberto and Helen find both communion and reconciliation with their wider community as they bring a nonviolent witness to bear on their neighbors.

In a broken manner, Alberto and Helen perhaps even find reconciliation with their neighbors, for Helen's book, after dealing in detail with the struggle over the decision to institute suit, takes the topic up once more. Her narrative continues with the story of an ulcer that almost kills Alberto, the emergence of a Hispanic Mennonite ministry in their neighborhood, and Helen's call to lead that ministry and return to seminary. In the midst of this hopeful story, a rather different light is shed on the conclusion of their litigation:

> Our civil lawsuit, filed in July 1982, was finally settled in an out-of-court agreement in December 1986. As time wore on and the legal process unfolded, Alberto and I lost heart for a face-to-face confrontation with the disturbed Robinson family.
>
> Time itself was a factor in this reluctance. After four years, the wounds of our experience were beginning to heal in the context of our church community and the growing fellowship on the West Side. We were hesitant to enter a situation that might reopen our wounds. Our focus had already shifted to learning to live on with the scars we bear. The fellowship had been planted and was thriving. We did not want to turn our energy away from its life-giving growth.[26]

Conclusion

This story offers an example of how disputes may be resolved in a manner that reflects the power of reconciliation ushered into the world in Christ's death and resurrection. It offers an example of how the essential uniqueness of the church in its life together and in interacting with the wider world can be maintained. Producing a people capable of embodying such examples is the task of any community intent on witnessing to the gospel of reconciliation. Furthermore, in stories such as those of Alberto and Helen Quintela, the potential for living into that reconciliation by a community willing to make great sacrifices together is made evident, even in the modern context. Their story makes clear that an imaginative, counter-cultural people can find ways to begin to transform their thinking and praxis regarding disputes both within and outside the church. This chapter is not a template for how to do this in every setting or denomination. The story itself may offer grounds for further reflection and discernment in regard to the actions taken and the witness demanded. What it is, however, is a witness to the potential of the gospel of reconciliation to shape and call a set-apart people.

The chapters that follow argue that the fact that these cases are deeply embedded within the Mennonite context is not surprising, but is rather an outworking of Mennonites' historical reflection on the essential relationships between peace and reconciliation to the message of Jesus and the role of Christian discipleship in the formation of the church. In other words, Alberto and Helen Quintela do not appear from nowhere, but they are trained explicitly and implicitly in a community that has taught them to re-envision the world. The task of the next chapters is to develop the history that makes the questions, descriptions, and actions of this chapter intelligible.

3

The Corinthian Context

> When any of you has a grievance against another, do you dare to take it to court before the unrighteous, instead of taking it before the saints? Do you not know that the saints will judge the world? And if the world is to be judged by you, are you incompetent to try trivial cases? Do you not know that we are to judge angels—to say nothing of ordinary matters? If you have ordinary cases, then, do you appoint as judges those who have no standing in the church? I say this to your shame. Can it be that there is no one among you wise enough to decide between one believer and another, but a believer goes to court against a believer—and before unbelievers at that?
>
> In fact, to have lawsuits at all with one another is already a defeat for you. Why not rather be wronged? Why not rather be defrauded? But you yourselves wrong and defraud—and believers at that.
>
> Do you not know that wrongdoers will not inherit the kingdom of God? Do not be deceived! Fornicators, idolaters, adulterers, male prostitutes, sodomites, thieves, the greedy, drunkards, revilers, robbers—none of these will inherit the kingdom of God. And this is what some of you used to be. But you were washed, you were sanctified, you were justified in the name of the Lord Jesus Christ and in the Spirit of our God.
>
> —*1 Corinthians 6:1-11*

The Task of Exegesis

As noted in the introduction, the benefit of addressing a biblical text to begin understanding the Quintela's story is that its aims are ecumenical, and, despite wide variation on the particulars, there is a unity among denominations in acknowledging a commitment to read the biblical texts as meaningful. I might put this unity as such: all the diverse churches are stuck with the text of 1 Corinthians 6, which appears to suggest Christians ought not litigate at all or use church bodies to reconcile disputes if doing so. As Richard Hays notes, the text is so difficult and challenging to modern Christians that it may explain why 1 Corinthians 6:1-11 is not found in years A, B, or C of the common lectionary.[1]

Further, it is a particularly difficult ethic for the church to hear after the fourth century because it is heard in the wake of Constantine's absorption of the church into civil authority.[2] Although much of the Western world is now post-Christian, having apparently left at least this most direct form of Constatinianism behind, certain elements of the church still appear to long for a return to the civil power of the medieval church. Noting this helps locate why 1 Corinthians 6 is so difficult; it seems to contradict Paul's suggestion that the church be obedient to the state in Romans 13, a text that has been foundational for Christians in understanding their relationship to the state, at least since Constantine. This dichotomy is the frame through which Bruce Winter suggests one approach 1 Corinthians 6:

> Paul's teaching about the attitude of the Christians toward the state is well known in Rom 13. There the rulers are God's vicegerents, God's deacons for the praising of those who do good and for the punishing of evil-doers. . . . Does Paul espouse a contradictory view of the state in 1 Cor 6? Here they are not God's λειττουργοί, but οἱάδικοι, the unrighteous, v. 1. They are those least esteemed in the ἐκκλησία, v. 4, and appearing before them is plainly wrong for Christians, v. 6. The Corinthians were not called upon to honour them by Paul in 1 Cor 6, if they are indeed the same persons mentioned in Rom 13.[3]

As I discuss in a later chapter, it is the text of Romans 13 that convinced John Calvin, perhaps the most important theological forefather to the Christianity that prevails in North America, that Christians simply cannot avoid the secular courts, the text of 1 Corinthians 6 notwithstanding.

But while all churches share this text, agreement on its canonicity just begins the process of understanding what it says to the church today. How is it that the church might read Scripture together? First, as is undertaken in chapters 3 and 4 of this book, the church uses the tools of exegesis to deepen its understanding of original context of the message to the fledgling church at Corinth. Accordingly, I work in this chapter and the next reporting on recent scholarship in regard to 1 Corinthians 6 so as to deepen and expand theological memory. The task of these chapters is not one of determining "what Paul really meant,"[4] but of excavating the historical, social, and ideological context of the 1 Corinthians such that the church might better project 1 Corinthians 6 into the modern world and seeking appropriate analogies in its practice.[5]

In particular, I use Dale Martin's book *The Corinthian Body*, as well as several other conversation partners, to develop the context of the letter to the Corinthians as a whole in this chapter. In chapter 4, a close reading of 1 Corinthians 6 follows, informed by both Martin's work and other recent exegetical work on this passage. In both chapters, while searching for emerging consensus, the work proceeds with an openness to discovering multiple meanings for the church today. Projecting this text into a different context is best conducted with a reticence to name any "literal" or "historical-critical" meaning, all of which are necessarily influenced by theological interpretative frameworks.

Subverting the Body

Martin identifies two key themes in the text of 1 Corinthians: (1) subverting the standard hierarchies regarding the body, the body of Christ, and the polis, so as to restore unity in the Corinthian church/body and (2) addressing the "pollution" of the Corinthian bodies/body by the world and/or sin as a result of the inherent permeability of the body and the body of Christ.[6] Understanding these issues turns on properly understanding the Greco-Roman commonplaces surrounding the body as a metaphor for the polis and the nature of the boundaries between the body and the world.

In regard to hierarchy and disunity, a variety of causes of disunity within the body of the Corinthian church are identified, including rhetoric/philosophy, eating meat sacrificed to idols, prostitution, sexual desire, marriage, speaking in tongues, the resurrected body, and the veiling of women. Martin suggests that each of these causes of division can be understood within the context of two competing groups within the Corinthian church: (1) the "Strong," who, although not from the upper classes of Roman society, would have been upper-middle-class merchants and had some familiarity with the standard commonplaces of Greek and Roman philosophy, rhetoric, and medicine, and (2) the "Weak," who would have made up the majority of the church and would have been from the lower classes.[7] The fact that the Strong and the Weak were both found in the Corinthian church itself is significant, for what is most surprising about the early church was that it was not a homogenous group as most voluntary social groups in the Greco-Roman would have been.[8] This radical reconception of social groupings that included diverse genders, races, and classes was not without friction, however. In Corinth, the upper-class members were operating under the assumption that class distinctions would and should remain within the church's life together. Accordingly, Anthony Thiselton concludes, "The surprise comes not from the emergence of difficulty and conflict over social diversity . . . ; the surprise is, rather, that the transformative power of the gospel could provide a new common status and identity to all believers as 'one body . . . whether Jews or Gentiles, whether slave or free' (12:13)."[9] Martin agrees, suggesting that in every case, except gender, Paul subverts the standard hierarchies that would have prevailed in the Greco-Roman understanding of the ordered body and polis, and concludes that the strong must give up their higher status for the sake of the weak.[10]

What should be immediately surprising to modern Christians versed in the language of individual rights is the assumption that (a) the individual body and the polis or (b) the individual body and the body of Christ are to be equated. Nonetheless, grasping this conflation of individual and community is essential, Martin suggests, to understanding 1 Corinthians. Martin traces in detail the manner in which "in the ancient world, the human body was not like a microcosm; it was a microcosm—a small version of the universe at large,"[11] rendering "as 'natural' what seems to us bizarre: the nonexistence of the 'individual,' the fluidity of the elements that make up the 'self,' and the essential continuity of the human body with its surroundings."[12]

In this Greco-Roman cultural context, issues of disunity were understood as issues of social disease. Martin notes that the commonplace "cure" would have assumed "that illness or social disruption occurs when hierarchy is disrupted. Moreover, the particular form taken by social disruption is class conflict."[13] Under this prevailing wisdom, the disunity in the Corinthian church was the result of the breakdown of hierarchy, that is, of the failure of the Weak to maintain their proper subservient role to the Strong.[14] The theme of the letter, unity, is traditional, but the standard paradigms are subverted therein. Martin suggests,

> Whereas Platonism—indeed, practically all upper-class philosophy and ideology—uses the body analogy to exclude any questioning

of the prevailing hierarchy by attributing status differentiation to nature and arguing for its necessity, Paul argues on the contrary that the normal status hierarchy is only "apparently" unproblematic and that it is actually the lesser members those who are weaker and seemingly less honorable, who are "really" the most honored.[15]

Paul's answer to disunity is not the maintenance of "natural" hierarchical understandings of the body, but the undoing of those hierarchies in such a manner that the Strong submit to the needs of the Weak for the maintenance of unity.[16]

Likewise, the disunity between the Strong and the Weak was also being manifest in the pursuit of litigation within the Corinthian church. Martin argues, "It is the Strong at Corinth who are making use of the courts to settle their differences."[17] Noting that Roman courts were biased toward those with large amounts of wealth, Martin suggests that in litigation between the Strong and the Weak, the Strong almost always prevailed. Paul's advice regarding litigation, Martin concludes, is again about subverting the social hierarchy. "By insisting that disputes be settled within the church, however, Paul has taken away much of the advantage the higher-class Christians would have enjoyed in the courts. . . . In other words, by changing the venue for settling disputes, Paul changes the dynamics of power at work."[18]

Polluting the Body

The second theme Martin traces is also closely related to Paul's particular arguments in 1 Corinthians 6. Throughout 1 Corinthians Paul is raising questions regarding the boundaries between the body, that is, the church, and the world and the possibility of corruption of the body via the breach of those boundaries.[19] Relying on standard Greco-Roman language regarding the body and disease, Martin notes two competing accounts of disease in Corinth. The less dominant but philosophically preferred account of the Hippocratic physicians and the Strong in Corinth suggested that the body was constituted by various humors, the imbalance of which resulted in disease. The lower-class "superstitious" belief of the Weak in Corinth, on the other hand, suggested that disease represented an attack on and invasion of the body, leading to corruption and disease.[20] Martin argues that the dominant, though not uniform, view of the early church and of 1 Corinthians was that the invasion/corruption metaphor is the proper means by which to construe disease and health within the community. The repeated references to the corruption of the Corinthian church via participation in sin, according to Martin, express this lower-class commonplace that the body is subject to corruption or disease via breach of its boundaries.[21]

Martin traces this theme throughout 1 Corinthians, but, critically for understanding 1 Corinthians 6:1-11, he suggests that this idea is exemplified in both 1 Corinthians 5, which addresses a Corinthian Christian having sexual relations with his stepmother, and 1 Corinthians 6:12-20, which addresses Corinthian men consorting with prostitutes. The latter passage concludes as follows:

> Do you not know that your bodies are members of Christ? Should I therefore take the members of Christ and make them members of a prostitute? Never! Do you not know that whoever is united to a prostitute becomes one body with her? For it is said, 'The two shall be one flesh.' But anyone united to the Lord becomes one spirit with him. Shun fornication! Every sin that a person commits is outside the body; but the fornicator sins against the body itself. (1 Cor 6:15-19)

Martin argues that the sin of any one member of the body becomes the point of corruption or invasion of the social body, which is the body of Christ. Yet worse, apocalyptically construed, individuals serve as representative figures for the cosmos and the body of Christ. In the passage set forth above, Martin concludes,

> The two realms represented by the body of Christ and the cosmos [the prostitute] constitute two different worlds of meaning, contrary axiological systems of signification, different "texts." Copulation between representatives of these two cosmic bodies enacts a collision of worlds of meaning: intertextual intercourse. The Christian man penetrating a prostitute constitutes coitus between two beings of such different ontological status that Paul can hardly contemplate the consequences.[22]

As such, Paul is deeply concerned throughout 1 Corinthians and in the passages immediately surrounding 1 Corinthians 6:1-11 with the maintenance of necessary boundaries between the church and the world because the breaking down of these boundaries represents the entry point for disease into the body and makes unintelligible Paul's apocalyptic vision of the reality of the kingdom of Christ, which is a distinct social and economic structure from that of the cosmos.[23]

While Martin does not follow up on this point in his work, a reasonable conclusion is that Paul is similarly concerned with boundaries between the church and the world when he takes up Corinthian Christians engaged in secular litigation in the passage sandwiched between 1 Corinthians 5 and 6:12-20. Following this suggestion, Anthony Thiselton relates 1 Corinthians 6:1-11 to Paul's discussion of the wisdom/foolishness of the cross in chapters 1–4:

> For the issue which now emerges resolves into a general principle: are the "insiders" within the congregation to draw not only their assumptions about "wisdom" and "rhetoric" (1:10-4:21) but also their standards of self-gratification, morality, and manipulation from the secular culture of "outsiders" at Corinth? How distinctive (not how ghetto-like) is the community to be which is founded not on human wisdom or "religion" but on the centrality of Christ and the cross, within the framework of the interpretative and moral tradition of the Scriptures? The case study of initiating litigation brings this universal issue to a sharp focus.[24]

With this said, I should conclude this section and chapter by noting that Martin does not suggest that Paul is counseling the Corinthian Christians to withdraw from society, if such a stance were possible. Rather, he argues that Paul is advocating a "modified sectarianism":

> Although he insists on maintaining firm boundaries between those inside and outside the church, socially those boundaries are permeable. Paul is not afraid that social contact between a Christian and non-Christian will pollute the church; but he does think that the disguised presence within the church of a representative from the outside, from the cosmos, that should be "out there," threatens the whole body.[25]

The church's maintenance of necessary boundaries with the world must be properly seen as the church's participation in the world. Living out this alternative ethic is the church's service to the world insofar as the church locates for the world its relationship of disobedience to the apocalyptically revealed and eschatologically assured reign of Christ. Victor Paul Furnish argues that Paul's point in each of the issues addressed in chapters 5–11 of 1 Corinthians is to make clear the church's task to live in the world as an eschatological community:

Although the coming age, which is "God's reign" (4:20), has been inaugurated in the cross where God's saving power is already at work, the Corinthians would be quite wrong to regard it as somehow fulfilled already (4:8). This "already but not yet" of life in Christ means that the believers in Corinth must reckon for the time being with a dual identity. Fundamentally, in their belonging to Christ and to God they belong to God's reign. Thus, as *God's church* they comprise an eschatological community, a community of the end-time. However, as God's church *in Corinth* they also comprise a "present-time" community with a special social location and continuing social identity.[26]

4

Reading 1 Corinthians 6

With these twin themes in mind—reconciliation of the body and maintenance of the boundary between the church and the world—in this chapter, I conduct a close reading of the text of 1 Corinthians 6. By looking at the text closely, exegetical issues can be highlighted that are relevant to understanding the potential implications of the text as the church reads it today. I conclude the chapter by asking, is there evidence that modern litigation practice raises similar concerns to those flushed out in this and the previous chapter?

The Boundary Between the Church and the World

> [1] When any of you has a grievance against another, do you dare to take it to court before the unrighteous, instead of taking it before the saints?

Paul first challenges the Corinthians regarding suits between believers that are being heard by the *adekoi*, that is, "the unrighteous." The issue for the Corinthians is both injustice in the civil courts and the use of civil courts, which results in the breaking down of the boundaries between the church and the world. Paul's use of *unrighteous* might be construed in one of two ways: (1) the unrighteous are corrupt secular judges in Corinth, in particular, or (2) the unrighteous are all nonbelievers (referred to in verse 6).[1]

The evidence that judges were corrupt in Corinth is significant. Bruce Winter notes that Corinthian civil cases would have been heard by elected magistrates and juries of citizens (in lieu of possibly more reputable appointed Roman proconsuls who heard criminal cases) and cites extensive evidence for corruption in the Roman courts.[2] Likewise, as noted above, the rich in Corinth would have enjoyed advantages in the Roman courts.³ Juries would have only included those from the highest classes, increasing the likelihood of decisions in favor of upper-class litigants. Winter notes Seneca's famous line, "Am I a poor man, to accuse a rich man?" to which the rich man responds, "What would I not be ready to do to you if you impeached me, I who saw to the death of a man who merely engaged in litigation with me?"⁴ Couple this with further evidence of the extensive use of bribes in the civil courts, and Winter concludes that Paul is focused on unjust judges and juries in his use of "the unrighteous."⁵

However, to suggest that Paul is concerned only with the use of unjust judges understates the issue, particularly in light of verse 6 ("but brother goes to law against brother, and that before unbelievers?" RSV) and the broader Jewish context in which Paul is writing. In counseling against the use of civil courts, Paul is following rabbinical law.⁶ Further, the practice of internal dispute resolution would have been standard for other voluntary mutual benefit and religious societies in the Roman world.⁷

In light of the fact that rabbinical law also required avoidance of litigation, the passage might also be read in light of the early church's difficulties, reflected most clearly in Acts 15, of determining when Jewish law would be applicable to Gentile converts. Markus Bockmuehl suggests this reading, concluding that the question of Gentile obedience to Jewish law is at stake throughout 1 Corinthians 5–10. Without specifically addressing 1 Corinthians 6:1-11, he argues that Paul follows Jewish custom by making only the Genesis/Noachide law applicable to Gentiles.⁸ Bockmuehl notes, "With a bit of clever midrash, the idea of six commandments given to Adam was commonly rooted in Genesis 2:16-17: the prohibition of idolatry, blasphemy, adjudication, homicide, illicit sex, theft."⁹ In 1 Corinthians 6:1-11, Paul is negotiating a dispute regarding Gentile observance of Torah. He suggests that Gentiles obey the Genesis/Noachide law (no suits) within the new Christian context (via taking the cases to the church in lieu of Jewish courts).¹⁰

With this particularly Jewish context in mind, it seems more likely than not that the admonition of 1 Corinthians 6 would have been heard as not merely related to the use of unjust judges to resolve disputes, but rather the use of nonbelievers at all. This conclusion is consistent with the broader theme in the letter related to pollution of the Corinthians' bodies/body. In the configuration of the body noted above, issues of pollution, corruption, and boundaries take on much greater importance.¹¹ Add to this Paul's "apocalypticism," which Martin defines as "attention to imminent eschatology and its own system of values and status,"¹² and one begins to understand why the location and manner of resolving disputes, regardless of the quality of secular judges, could take on such significance.

This conclusion is supported by Winter's suggestion that Roman litigation was likely to be particularly factious insofar as personal attack was a standard method by which to proceed in litigation.[13] Focusing on another Roman political structure, the family, Winter notes that Paul's challenge to brother going to law against brother is similarly contrary to Roman understandings of the family as a refuge from acrimony and faction.[14] Finally, Winter notes that litigation itself was a means by which social hierarchies, which Paul was challenging, were created and maintained.[15] Litigation, whether before corrupt or just judges, was a breach of boundaries with the world insofar as Corinthian values were predominating in the church. Richard Hays concludes it was "a failure of the church to be the church."[16]

The Apocalyptic Context

> [2] Do you not know that the saints will judge the world? And if the world is to be judged by you, are you incompetent to try trivial cases? [3] Do you not know that we are to judge angels—to say nothing of ordinary matters?

Verses 2 and 3 provide an eschatological framework to the prohibition in verse 1. Much has been written recently in regard to the apocalyptic nature of Paul's writing.[17] Described most simply, he repeatedly suggests that the true nature of the world is revealed in Christ. This hidden reality will soon be made manifest in and to the broader world. Therefore, much of Paul's discourse in the first four chapters of 1 Corinthians, regarding the wisdom of the world versus the wisdom/foolishness of the cross, can be read within this apocalyptic dualism.[18] The foolishness of the cross is the wisdom of God himself made manifest in Christ, but not yet seen for its true wisdom until the eschatological unveiling occurs.[19]

Hays's commentary on 1 Corinthians 6 is perhaps most helpful in locating this apocalyptic framework. Hays argues:

> Paul tries to show the scandalous absurdity of this practice by reframing the present situation in light of the eschatological reality. He draws on the idea, standard in Jewish and early Christian apocalyptic texts, that God's elect will have a part in the judgment of the world and in ruling it in the age to come (Dan 7:18, 22; Wisd Sol 3:8; Matt 19:28; Luke 22:30; Rev 3:21). . . . His

immediate aim is to highlight the ridiculous contrast between the church's glorious eschatological destiny and its present failure to exercise jurisdiction over minor property disputes.[20]

Understanding the eschatological context in which the Corinthians live should lead to "a conversion of the imagination" in which they see themselves as "the eschatological people of God, called out of their previous social world, like Israel called out of Egypt."[21] Being called out and understanding the true nature of the world means that "they must modify their former ways of life."[22]

The Despised in the Church

[4] If you have ordinary cases, then, do you appoint as judges those who have no standing in the church?

The nature of the "least esteemed" in this verse has given rise to great debate and led to competing translations in the major English versions of the Bible. The NIV suggests this verse be read as an imperative: "Therefore, if you have disputes about such matters, appoint as judges even men of little account in the church!" This reading suggests that the question of to whom the disputes should be taken and the importance of the disputes is at stake.[23] The NRSV, on the other hand, translates the verse as a question, suggesting that Paul is continuing to emphasize the problems with taking litigation to nonbelievers. While the first reading is not wholly implausible, the latter is preferable. Paul has already begun to address who should hear disputes within the body in the first verse and there he calls those persons "saints." It would be surprising if he would immediately turn around to call those saints "men of little account" in the church, as suggested in the NIV translation.

Further, as Hays notes, if Paul were to call those in the church deciding such disputes "men of little account in the church," he would be reinforcing and creating status divisions that the letter as a whole is directly concerned to undercut.[24] Accordingly, in 1 Corinthians 1:26-28, Paul argues that those who are "least esteemed" by the world have been chosen by God. In 1 Corinthians 6:4 Paul returns to this theme, flipping the ironic turn and noting that those outside the church, the unrighteous and nonbeliever, are the ones who should be properly least esteemed by the church.[25] This turn of phrase continues to reiterate both the essential boundary between the church and the world that Paul is drawing throughout the letter and the essential subversion of divisive hierarchies for which he is arguing. Those who are least esteemed by the church are to be those who are held in highest esteem by the world and vice versa.[26]

The Alternative to Civil Litigation

> [5] I say this to your shame. Can it be that there is no one among you wise enough to decide between one believer and another, [6] but a believer goes to court against a believer—and before unbelievers at that?

Paul reiterates the concern first set forth in verses 1-3, of litigating suits outside the body. The rebuke is particularly sharp, suggesting the Corinthians should be ashamed of their behavior. The intensity of the rebuke in this fifth verse tracks closely with the first, in both of which Paul suggests not simply that the individuals in the Corinthians church err in having suits, but the whole church is implicated and made shameful by this action. Furthermore, he adds particular rhetorical bite to this rebuke by challenging whether there is no one with *sophos*, that is, wisdom, enough to discern cases within the Corinthian church. Throughout the letter to the Corinthians it is clear that one of the dividing lines separating the Strong in Corinth from the Weak is the Strong's claim of philosophical wisdom. Repeatedly throughout the letter, including in this verse and in verses 7-8, Paul throws this claim up in the face of the Strong at Corinth, suggesting that their behavior fails to meet not only Christian standards but their own standards of philosophical wisdom.[27]

Further, verse 5 now squarely raises the issue: what was the alternative to civil litigation that Paul had in mind? Is he suggesting the appointment of Christian judges and the formation of Christian courts along the lines of Jewish courts available in Palestine, some Diaspora communities, and later in the Christian tradition in Catholic canon law courts? Or is he suggesting a much less formal means of resolving disputes via ad hoc internal proceedings that are not part of an ongoing and formalized institutional structure? Alan Mitchell, who has written the most extensively on this question, rejects claims that Paul is calling for the creation of Christian courts.[28] This option is untenable according to Mitchell simply because Corinth was likely not one of the Diaspora communities that had Jewish courts as an available dispute resolution option.[29] On the other hand, various groups established internal arbitration procedures within the Roman context. Therefore Mitchell concludes that these forms of private arbitration would have been the preferred option for Paul in developing an alternative mode of dispute resolution within the Christian community.[30]

The Nature of Paul's Eschatology

> [7] In fact, to have lawsuits at all with one another is already a defeat for you. Why not rather be wronged? Why not rather be defrauded? [8] But you yourselves wrong and defraud—and believers at that.

This section of the passage focuses on the most difficult exegetical question regarding 1 Corinthians 6:1-11: how are the first six verses related to the last five? Is Paul's suggestion in the first six verses that members of the Corinthian church judge disputes internally contradicted by his conclusion in the seventh and eighth verses that having lawsuits and disputes at all is a defeat? Should the church forgo litigation altogether? These questions require consideration of whether these texts are to be read through an essentially social or individual lense.

According to an individualistic reading, in conversion an existential change occurs, which renders litigation unnecessary.[31] As Mitchell summarizes it, "Paul is able to bring about the desired effect of communicating the difference Christianity makes in the life of the individual by emphasizing how the baptismal state has eradicated the need for justice as the world understands it."[32] This reading of Paul's apocalypticism follows Rudolf Bultmann's construction of an individualistic and existentially viewed apocalyptic. In his words, "The real point of myth is not to give an objective world picture; what is expressed in it, rather, is how we human beings understand ourselves in our world. Thus, myth does not want to be interpreted in cosmological terms but in anthropological terms—or, better, in existentialist terms."[33] Therefore, Bultmann suggests that eschatology has a profoundly personal rather than communal dimension: "Eschatological existence has become a possibility for us through the fact that God has acted and made an end of the world as 'this world,' by making us ourselves new. 'If anyone is in Christ, he is a new creation; the old has passed away; behold, the new has come' (2 Cor 5:17). So it is according to Paul."[34] Bultmann's eschatological existentialism leads to freedom from desire.[35] It is easy to see how this existentialist eschatology would produce a laissez-faire attitude toward wrongs against oneself. Read through this interpretative lense, Paul suggests that Christians will no longer have disputes in an eschatologically realized context because all desire for the addressing of wrongs will itself be abandoned.

In contrast to this view, Paul's apocalypticism might be read as having cosmological and epistemological importance as well. This cosmological reading requires that the apocalyptic context not be limited to the individual. As summarized by Alexandra Brown,

> The coming Day of the Lord will reveal God's sovereignty not only in the subjective experience of the believer but in the whole creation. The parousia, then, keeps Paul's gospel from a one-sided emphasis on salvation as a subjective human experience at the expense of its universal, cosmological scope. God's saving activity has to do with more than human beings here and now. It has to do with the future redemption of God's whole creation.[36]

In other words, the importance of eschatology is the transformation not merely of the self, but of the cosmos, which likewise involves the creation of a new community, the church, that lives outside the norms of any other given community.

There are structural reasons to prefer this latter reading. To read the last half of 1 Corinthians 6:1-11 as rejecting dispute resolution altogether is to conclude that Paul is contradicting himself in the latter half of the passage. Reaching this conclusion regarding any passage is obviously an unhappy one and should be resisted unless necessarily forcing itself on the exegete. Following this basic hermeneutic insight, the first six verses can be read consistently with the seventh and eighth by concluding that Paul is suggesting that the Corinthian church use an internal method of arbitration to settle their disputes and only suggesting in verses 7-8 that if they are unwilling or unable to do this, they would be better off to forgo litigation altogether.[37]

Further, the nature of the apocalyptic moment itself may also render coherence to this passage. According to Wayne Meeks, the essential distinction is between an individually realized eschatology (à la Bultmann's reading summarized above) and a futurist eschatology or eschatological reservation. The latter emphasizes the imperfection of the present status of Christians, necessitating mutual responsibility.[38] Meeks argues that Paul cannot be arguing for a realized eschatology, for it was exactly this eschatological view that was motivating the Strong at Corinth "to transcend some norms of ordinary behavior and support their conviction that their status is superior to that of persons still concerned with the fleshy world, whom they call 'weak' and 'psychic' Christians."[39] Rather, Meeks argues that Paul's future-oriented eschatology would "emphasize the imperfection of the present status of Christians and the necessity for mutual responsibility."[40]

These two differing eschatological views produce two different ethics: forgo litigation or adjudicate within the body. If Meeks is right, the latter is to be preferred as it implies that verses 7-8 are also addressing the question of boundaries.[41] In other words, the eschatological thrust is not on the individual existential experience, but in the "already but not yet" of the eschatological moment in which "all merely human values and behavior have already been judged by God in Christ; already the present age is passing away (1:26-28; 7:31). Thus believers must exercise internal judgments in the present (5:12-13); the church must cleanse out the old leaven so that it may be a new loaf (5:7-8)."[42]

I address these ecclesiological issues in further detail in chapter 9, but outline them now because the eschatological thrust of the passage has already been raised. As noted already, the church's reconciled life together is not merely an individual existential accomplishment, but is the community's means of making evident the nature of the eschatological kingdom proclaimed and made possible via the work of Christ himself. When divisions in Corinth remained and Paul again felt compelled to write to the Corinthians, he made explicit the connection between the reconciled life of the church and its witness to the new eschatological kingdom:

> From now on, therefore, we regard no one from a human point of view; even though we once knew Christ from a human point of view, we know him no longer in that way. So if anyone is in Christ, there is a new creation: everything old has passed away; see, everything has become new! All this is from God, who reconciled us to himself through Christ, and has given us the ministry of reconciliation; that is, in Christ God was reconciling the world to himself, not counting their trespasses against them, and entrusting the message of reconciliation to us. So we are ambassadors for Christ, since God is making his appeal through us; we entreat you on behalf of Christ, be reconciled to God. (2 Cor 5:16-20)

Reconciliation is made possible via the work of Christ. Insofar as the church lives in a reconciled manner, it witnesses to that reconciling work.[43] Or, God's presence on earth, made possible by Christ's reconciling work, is made evident in the church's life together. As Paul concludes 1 Corinthians, Christ crucified and resurrected continues to be physically present to the world insofar as the church, in its reconciliation to one another, reveals the body of Christ itself.[44] The witness of reconciliation is at stake in 1 Corinthians 6.

A Baptismal Reminder

> [9] Do you not know that wrongdoers will not inherit the kingdom of God? Do not be deceived! Fornicators, idolaters, adulterers, male prostitutes, sodomites, [10] thieves, the greedy, drunkards, revilers, robbers—none of these will inherit the kingdom of God. [11] And this is what some of you used to be. But you were washed, you were sanctified, you were justified in the name of the Lord Jesus Christ and in the Spirit of our God.

While verses 9-11 may appear to be properly returning to the issues of sexual purity and boundaries that surround 1 Corinthians 6:1-11, they contain significant links to the passage's litigation context. As noted above, insofar as all of chapters 5 and 6 focus on the boundaries between the church and the world, be they regarding sexual behavior or litigation, verses 9-11 are part and parcel of this message. The eschatological dichotomy between the unrighteous and the saints, outsiders and insiders, continues to be pursued in these verses. Further the verses are directly related to Paul's heightened concerned in verses 7-8 that the Corinthians are acting in the manner of the world insofar as they were using their suits to defraud their brothers in Christ.[45] The baptismal allusion in verse 11 ("you were washed") is particularly important, for it is the believer's baptism that is the seminal event marking his or her crossing over from the world into the kingdom of Christ.[46] Paul's baptismal reminder is an eschatological reminder of the Corinthian Christians' location in the cosmos. As members of the body of Christ, the ways of the world are to be put behind them, be they litigation or sexual mores.[47] As Margaret Mitchell describes it:

> Since all share the same sanctification in Christ, all now share a common identity (notice the repetition of the name of the Lord in 6:11; cf. 1:10, and the spirit of God, cf. 2:12, over and against their past sinful identities). By carrying out lawsuits in civil courts, Paul argues, the Corinthians are retaining old understandings of their community allegiances which are no longer appropriate. The Corinthians have not fully understood that their identity as

Christians should now be their primary frame of social and even civil reference.[48]

First Corinthians 6 and Modern Litigation

Some have argued that as one of Paul's most practical letters, 1 Corinthians may have little to say to modern America unless a "theological" message can be parsed out of his argument.[49] This suggestion is built on the assumption that a "theological" message must be universal and nonparticular.[50] It implies that there is a significant gap between ethics and theology and, further, that locating our historical distance from the Corinthians renders the text ethically irrelevant.[51] The assumption, however, is in error. While biblical counsels must not be heard uncritically, those ethical counsels can be applied imaginatively in the present moment.[52] Accordingly, I have sought a deeper understanding of 1 Corinthians 6 in its ideological context to better determine the analogies between the present moment and Paul's advice to the young Corinthian church.

In beginning this task, it is appropriate at this point to ask whether the potential for 1 Corinthians 6 to challenge the church's modern litigation choices remains. In other words, is the present situation so entirely different from what Paul describes in 1 Corinthians that one need not go further? Or, can analogous concerns to modern litigation be located such that one must continue to explore how the church might embody this text? In the work of Martin, I located two essential concerns underlying 1 Corinthians and now traced in particular in 1 Corinthians 6: (1) the unity of the body in the subverted hierarchy of the church, and (2) the maintenance of essential boundaries between the body of Christ and the cosmos. Seeking for analogies, we might then ask the questions, is modern litigation inherently or unnecessarily divisive, threatening the unity of the body of Christ; does modern litigation still serve the Strong in the church in a manner that class distinctions are reinforced rather than overcome in the body; and does modern litigation muddle the distinction between the church and the world, threatening the clarity by which the eschatological community, the church, is to be defined?

Even an uninformed observer of American litigation practice can see how frequently it does not serve the purpose of reconciliation of the parties. The enmity-driven and enmity-producing power of litigation is seen perhaps most clearly in the types of litigation that matter most to the day-to-day lives of Christians: family law, real estate law, and small-business disputes. In these most personal suits, even more than suits between large corporations, litigation often is not a reconciling project, but rather leads to enmity and the destruction of relationships.[53]

My most contentious case as a practicing attorney was that of two small-town doctors splitting up a similarly small general practice. What was most noteworthy in the case was the lawyers' ability to reach amicable arrangements as to the dissolution of the partnership, interim working conditions, and the distribution of assets. The parties themselves were then unable to live up to these arrangements, which met their own stated goals for negotiating the dissolution. It became apparent that the litigation served as a means not to seek a fair and just resolution of a dispute, but as a means of warfare in an attempt, at a minimum, to harass severely the other party. In the end, I was fired from the case, apparently for my failure to undertake sufficiently aggressive and confrontational tactics. I was replaced by a medical malpractice lawyer, who had formerly sued the client and been particularly egregious in his attacks during depositions on the physician. It was this level of personal attack and affront that the litigation was meant to serve. This anecdotal evidence suggests that at least some forms of American litigation within and among members of the church would destroy the unity of the body of Christ and fail to produce reconciliation.[54]

Furthermore, litigation has become ubiquitous within the culture of America. Litigation is big business, not only the business of lawyers, but also the business of business, attracting investors, TV dramas, and reality-show makers.[55] It is the standard for how to respond to injury, real or perceived, in American culture, and the response to that injury is not simply to seek just resolution of a dispute, but to seek all that one can from the system. Lawyers are taught not to look to the responsible party, but to the potential party with the deepest pockets. The impact of this practice is felt throughout the culture, and perhaps nowhere more than in the lives of lawyers themselves, who experience higher rates of substance abuse, depression, and a variety of other mental health issues than the general population.[56] While a variety of reasons why lawyers appear to be less healthy than the general population are evident, one suspects at least one reason is that so many lawyers started with hopes of participating in the project of justice and find themselves deeply removed from this project, perhaps even with the disquieting awareness that they are subverting justice.

Finally, as in Corinth, litigation in America favors the Strong against the Weak. Researchers continue to find that the "Haves" fair better than "Have Nots" in American courts. State governments fair better than city governments, which fair better than large corporations, which fair better than small business, all of which are more likely to prevail in litigation than individuals. Researchers posit a number of reasons to explain this data: advantages and experience as "repeat players" in the legal system, financial advantages enabling the "Haves" to deal with the expense of trial and obtain better legal counsel, and the accumulated effect of this advantage as the "Haves" obtain favorable legal precedents.[57] More subtle biases toward the Strong are also evident. For example, Tali Schaefer notes the manner in which parents employing paid nannies are credited by courts for care provided by such nannies in family law cases, while poor parents relying on traditional unpaid kin and community caregivers or daycare centers are not.[58] Further, the anecdotal and statistical evidence of bias within the American court system along racial and gender lines is also significant.[59] Just one example of this phenomenon is recent revisions to the U.S. Sentence Guidelines correcting a long-recognized bias in drug sentencing regimes that broke along racial lines.[60] As in Corinth, litigation often serves to reinforce the status quo, which is to say it serves those with power.

If all this is true, litigation in the churches is participation in one of the dominant institutions of modern American culture and may threaten the essential distinction between the church and the world and may continue to serve the interests of the Strong against the Weak. The goals of winner-take-all American litigation simply are not the goals of Christian dispute resolution. This evidence is sufficient to justify continuing the present inquiry.

5

Litigation and Reconciliation in the Early Church

In the preceding chapters, I have focused on one example of modern Mennonite practice as it relates to litigation and a biblical text that is central to that practice. Yet, for the most part, the reason these chapters are significant is that litigation is entirely unquestioned in the mainstream denominations. In contrast to what would appear to be the importance of Paul's words in 1 Corinthians 6, it is not merely that the presumption has swung in favor of litigation among and outside the church. It is that the question—is litigation appropriate to Christian dispute resolution?—is no longer asked.

The purpose of the next two chapters, which focus on the broader development of the Catholic and Protestant theological traditions, is twofold. First, they locate the Mennonite theological reflection that follows as I trace the roots and theological resources that have sustained Mennonite litigation practice. Second, they locate the politico-theological changes that were stepping-stones to our modern acceptance of litigation carte blanche. With this said, in exploring the theology of Augustine of Hippo, Martin Luther, and John Calvin with regard to dispute resolution, it will become evident that our modern attitude, while perhaps the product of certain shifts evident in these authors, is deeply out of step with their own practice.

While any survey of such a broad expanse of time must be selective, each of the theologians considered here are critical to the theological inheritance of the modern church. Augustine remains foundational for both Catholic and Protestant theology in general and political theology. Martin Luther and John Calvin are similarly seminal figures in the history of Protestant theology. Luther, without the systematic focus of Calvin, set the terms for modern theological debate. Of most importance in the present context, Luther's two-kingdom doctrine (explored in detail in chapter 6) is foundational for Lutheran, Reformed, and Anabaptist understandings of civil government and Christians' participation therein. Even more influential in the particular context of America is Calvin. While the distance between Calvin and the Anabaptist litigation witness will be the greatest, Calvin is still remarkably close to the Anabaptists in theological and practical terms.

Several notes on method are appropriate at this point. I look primarily but not exclusively in these chapters to Augustine, Luther, and Calvin's exegesis of 1 Corinthians 6.[1] I do not stop with exegesis, however, for texts cannot be understood abstracted from the unique social context in which they were formulated and received. Accordingly, I also attempt to place the current state of litigation and church discipline in the broader culture and in the church at the time of Augustine, Luther, and Calvin's writing. In other words, one cannot understand the church's relationship to civil forms of dispute resolution in Augustine, Luther, or Calvin without understanding the changes that had occurred in Roman litigation between Paul's writing to the Corinthians and Augustine's response to those questions three hundred years later, or, even more importantly, the full-fledged development of canon law courts alongside imperial and territorial courts in the late Middle Ages. Likewise, one cannot propose to understand the nature of church discipline in Augustine, Luther, or Calvin without understanding the fledging penitential practice in the church of North Africa in the fourth and fifth century or its full-blown development in the late medieval European church.

This enquiry is deepened with consideration of the broader context of church discipline to which the questions of dispute resolution are inexorably tied. Exegetes and historians have emphasized that the nature of early Christianity (and perhaps all distinct sociopolitical movements) required that the church maintain boundaries with the broader culture while at the same time remaining permeable enough to attract new members. For this reason, H. A. Drake suggests that the paradigmatic characters in the early church were martyr and apologist. These characters are the embodiment of this dichotomy of exclusivity and accommodation.[2] Further, Drake notes that successful organizations that attract new converts in the manner of the early church will necessarily become heterogeneous and require measures "to resolve amicably the differences that inevitably come with such heterogeneity."[3] Accordingly, dispute resolution and discipline structures are the integrated practices by which the church negotiates the boundary maintenance necessary to a growing heterogeneous social organization.[4]

The Later Roman Empire and Constantine

The change in the church's political landscape from Paul's writing of 1 Corinthians to the birth of Augustine in 354 CE was revolutionary. With Constantine's conversion to Christianity, traditionally dated to his vision of 312 CE, the fledging and persecuted Christian movement faced a new set of political challenges as a state-sanctioned and officially privileged religious organization. While the extent of Constantine's "conversion" can be challenged, it is clear that the church moved into a different cultural moment with that conversion.[5] The early church's unique identity came under threat as much of the Roman world espoused Christianity at least nominally. One hundred years after the death of Christ, the author of the "Letter of Diognetus" would suggest, "[Christians] live in their own countries, but only as aliens. They have a share in everything as citizens and endure everything as foreigners. Every foreign land is their homeland, and yet for them every homeland is a foreign land."[6] After Constantine, Christians began to look more and more like natives of imperial Rome.

Likewise, with Constantine's conversion, the success of the Christian emperor and the survival of the empire became a marker of God's providential control over the world.[7] In this new politico-theological matrix, when the Goths overran Rome in 410 CE it sparked not only a military and political crisis, but a theological one as well. Enter Augustine of Hippo with his magisterial *City of God*, which was written as an answer to Christianity's pagan critics for whom the destruction of Rome was evidence of the failure of the Christian God to provide the military support that the pagan gods had evidenced in the building of the Roman Empire.[8] Out of this particular context, *City of God* became a foundational text for Christian political theology in the two millennia that would follow. Augustine "calls us, not to perfection, but to relative peace" in Jean Bethke Elshtain's words, "meaning there is work to be done in the name of peace,"[9] such as killing and war. Regardless, Augustine inherited a theology one step removed from the deity of the Roman emperor,[10] yet Elshtain notes he "was subversive, shifting the center of earthly gravity away from the political order to the 'solid rock' of the *civitas Dei* on pilgrimage."[11] Even in sanctioning Christian's participation in the violence of the earthly city, Augustine uses the language of "alien sojourner"[12] to locate Christians in relationship to the city of man.[13]

Still, a fundamental shift had occurred with Constantine. Augustine's life and ministry were deeply embedded within imperial Christendom. According to Peter Brown, Augustine was willing to "break down the barriers, firmly fixed in the imagination of the average early Christian, between the 'sacred' and the 'profane,' between the purely spiritual sanctions exercised by the Christian bishop within the Church, and the manifold (and at time, horrific) pressures of Roman society, as administered by the Emperors."[14] Even in demythologizing Rome, Augustine sets forth as the model ruler in *City of God* Theodosius, who "reaffirm[ed] all previous legislation suppressing non-Catholics" at the moment that the Goths were sacking Rome.[15] In the end, Jeremiah's image of the resident alien remains foundational for Augustine's political theology, but a distinctly *resident* emphasis drives *City of God*.[16]

As for the Roman imperial courts, much and little had changed for Christians like Augustine and his parishioners. The church had established bishop's courts that regularly heard disputes among Christians and perhaps even among non-Christians.[17] These courts, before, during, and even after Constantine's attempt to bring them into the imperial legal structures via the first Sirmondian Constitution, marked out a limited form of resistance to imperial Christianity. Nicene writers repeatedly distinguished between the law of Christ and the law of Caesar.[18] The former law, embodied in the bishop's courts, rested on a nonjuridical model of adjudication, privileging healing and reconciliation with the coercive force of such courts limited to penance.[19] Accordingly, Jill Harries argues that the early church rejected juridical models of discipline and reconciliation:

> The language employed is healing, not judgement. The bishop is the physician of his flock and, if disputes arise, the bishop's first task is to act as mediator or go-between, and seek to reconcile the conflicting parties, a role, as we have seen to be sharply distinguished from that of judge, or even arbiter. Only if his negotiations and warnings against the dangers of anger had no effect, was the bishop to allow the case to go to him as judge. His authority extended, of course, only over Christians and his powers to enforce a decision concerning a dispute over, for example property or some other 'civil' matter depended on the consent of the disputants, who, as members of his congregation, had implicitly accepted his right to hand down decision on such matters. The sanctions open to him in disciplinary hearings were limited and effective only because regarded as serious by Christians themselves: these were,

for the clergy relegation and, for laymen, penance or, at worst, expulsion from the group (excommunication), a penalty regarded by believing Christians as worse than death.[20]

In other words, the admonition of 1 Corinthians 6 found its first institutional embodiment in the bishop's courts.

Nonetheless, these courts were under threat of being incorporated into the imperial court system. In 318 CE, Constantine allowed one party with or without the consent of the opposing party to remove a case from the civil courts to the bishop's court at any point prior to a decision.[21] Drake argues that Constantine's motivation for this law may have had little to do with offering power to the bishops and more to do with his attempts to curb corrupt judicial practices by providing litigants a means to opt out of a corrupt civil court.[22] Regardless, the right was little invoked and short-lived. Constantine's failure to understand that bishops functioned neither as mere judges nor as mere mediators made them poor fits to his reforming purposes.[23] Julian the Apostate repealed the law, which was reenacted in 398, 408, and 452 CE, in less dramatic forms that only allowed recourse to bishop's courts upon the consent of both parties.[24]

Further, many examples of Christians participating in secular litigation can be located. Augustine writes to Pancarius to dissuade him and his followers from burning down the church of a priest who crossed Pancarius in litigation. While Pancarius's proposed response to a priest litigating ("looting and destroying" his church) is most worrisome to Augustine, the circumstances make clear that a priest was engaged in civil litigation.[25] Similarly, Harries recounts the story of Theophilos, a deacon in Lycopolis, who threatened suit against both his bishop and several priests. The matter was ultimately resolved via arbitration, but not before a Christian arbiter, but rather before Makarios, the collector of taxes, to whom the proposed litigation would have otherwise been brought.[26]

In a similar example, involving Augustine's spiritual mentor, Ambrose of Milan, a property dispute involving bishop Marcellus already begun in a Roman civil court was subsequently placed before Ambrose for arbitration.[27] Ambrose accepted Marcellus's request to intercede. He notes that he "had to take cognizance of it because of the imperial enactment and because [he] was obligated by the authority of the blessed Apostle."[28] Ambrose goes on to suggest why his was the more successful resolution of the case: he sought a compromise so as to be "sure to desire no one's defeat."[29] The case is noteworthy for its display of the complexity of the imperial church's stance. Marcellus, a Christian bishop, is in the midst of litigation within the

Roman civil courts. Imperial edict and Paul in 1 Corinthians 6 agree that Ambrose is obligated to hear the case. Which is determinative in Ambrose's mind cannot and need not be untangled. Most importantly, none of it is perceived as entirely out of the ordinary by Ambrose, who merely labels a bishop's involvement in litigation "lamentable."[30]

Returning to the broader litigation context, the character of Roman litigation remained similar to that of Corinth at the time of Paul's writing. Augustine suggests that litigation remained both rampant in the wider culture and particularly prone to abusive practices. In *City of God* Augustine asks the question, "What is the Supreme Good?" Comparing the Christian response to that of the philosophers', he argues that even friendship and society are not unequivocal goods. To prove this argument, he evidences strife in the household, city, and world, the foundational social organizations for Roman thought. In regard to the second of these social organizations, Augustine laments,

> If, then, safety is not to be found in the home, the common refuge from the evils that befall mankind, what shall we say of the city? The larger the city, the more is its forum filled with civil lawsuits and criminal trials, even if that city be at peace, free from the alarms or—what is more frequent—the bloodshed, of sedition and civil war.[31]

Litigation remained a hallmark of Roman society and the connections between litigation and the creation and maintenance of status traced in Roman Corinth in the first century remained.[32] Brown confirms this was also the case in Augustine's North Africa, where "the average African was more notorious as a lawyer" than as a writer of literature or biography.[33]

Litigation also continued to be slanted toward the rich and often a poor means of seeking justice. Our best evidence for the social conditions in the late fourth and early fifth centuries are Augustine's own writings regarding these matters. His account of the attempted bribe of his friend and later bishop, Alypius, is an example of the continuing bias in the Roman administration toward the powerful and well-connected.[34] The incident is described by Augustine as such:

> When [Alypius] was in Rome acting as assessor to the controller of Italian provincial funds, there was a very influential senator who held large numbers of people in his power, either because he had granted them favours or because they had reason to fear him. In his usual domineering way he attempted to obtain some

privilege to which he had no right in law. Alypius turned it down. Threats followed and he rebuffed them. Everyone was amazed by his extraordinary self-possession, for although this formidable man had earned widespread notoriety for his innumerable methods of patronizing or injuring others, Alypius neither desired him as a friend nor feared him as an enemy.[35]

These conditions led to efforts toward judicial reform under Constantine, Theodosius I, and Gratian.[36] These reforms included not only the incorporation of the bishop's courts into civil adjudication structures, but also the creation of the position of *defensor civitatis*. This new position was empowered to hear small claims. The forum required less expensive financial and time commitments. As such, the design was meant to offer a venue where lower-class litigants might be successful.[37] Augustine himself, frustrated with his inability to provide an adequate defense of poor Christians against corrupt imperial tax collectors, makes clear via a letter to Alypius his hopes of having imperial Rome appoint a *defensor civitatis* to Hippo.[38]

Further, in *City of God*, Augustine raises more profound issues in regard to the justice of the city of man. Augustine laments the damnable position of the civil judge, who must work with the knowledge that he is often torturing and convicting innocents while at the same time exonerating the guilty.[39] This unavoidable situation, Augustine suggests, is the human condition. It is also instructive for understanding Augustine's views on the limits of civil and criminal justice.[40] Accordingly, in answering the African judge Macedonius's question, how do the Christian bishops not participate in crime in interceding for the reduction of criminal penalties?[41]—Augustine both praises Macedonius's restraint in using only beatings while also suggesting the benefits of the Roman legal system:

> Surely, it is not without purpose that we have the institution of the power of kings, the death penalty of the judge, the barbed hooks of the executioner, the weapons of the soldier, the right of punishment of the overlord, even the severity of the good father. All those things have their methods, their causes, their reasons, their practical benefits. While these are feared, the wicked are kept within bounds and the good live more peacefully among the wicked.[42]

Nonetheless, Augustine argues that the church has an equally important role in limiting the severity of that punishment, which threatens to destroy the criminal instead of reforming him.[43] Thus, the church appropriately intercedes on behalf of criminals. This apparently leads to a happy balance: "There is good, then, in your severity which works to secure our tranquility, and there is good in our intercession which works to restrain your severity."[44] Resident aliens with "much business in this common mortal life" indeed.[45]

Augustine and 1 Corinthians 6

With the late Roman cultural context in mind, Augustine's treatment of litigation in 1 Corinthians 6 can be addressed. His use of 1 Corinthians 6 in his writings is only occasional, but, nonetheless, significant insofar as he focuses on the key structural difficulty in interpreting 1 Corinthians 6 highlighted in chapter 4: how are verses 1-6 and 7-8 related—that is, are Christians to adjudicate disputes internally or foreswear suits altogether? In what will become typical for the medieval church's approach to ethics, Augustine suggests that these apparently competing demands of 1 Corinthians 6 are lesser and greater commands, which would apply to lay versus monastic Christians respectively.[46]

Accordingly, in "The Enchiridion" Augustine argues which sins are trivial and which are heinous is a matter for God's judgment alone. As an example, he highlights sexual abstinence and Paul's apparently competing demands for celibacy and marriage in the name of weakness. Concluding this discussion, Augustine notes that regarding married persons abstaining from intercourse, Paul suggests, "But I speak this by permission, and not of commandment." Augustine surmises, "Who, then, can deny that it is a sin, when confessedly it is only by apostolic authority that permission is granted to do it."[47] Having so argued, Augustine turns to another example, litigation, which he argues works similarly:

> Now it might have been supposed in this case that it is not a sin to have a quarrel with another, that the only sin is in wishing to have it adjudicated upon outside the Church, had not the apostle immediately added: "Now therefore there is utterly a fault among you, because ye go to law with one another." And lest any one should excuse himself by saying that he had a just cause, and was suffering wrong, and that he only wished the sentence of the judges to remove his wrong, the apostle immediately anticipates such thoughts and excuses, and says: "Why do ye not rather take wrong? Why do ye not rather suffer yourselves to be defrauded?" Thus bringing us back to our Lord's saying, "If any man will sue thee at the law, and take away thy coat, let him have thy cloak

also;" and again, "Of him that taketh away thy goods, ask them not again."[48]

Augustine concludes that pursing claims regarding worldly wrongs in any forum is sinful. Nonetheless, for the sake of the weak, such suits are permitted, yet only within the context of church adjudication:

> Therefore our Lord has forbidden His followers to go to law with other men about worldly affairs. And carrying out this principle, the apostle here declares that to do so is "altogether a fault." But when, notwithstanding, he grants his permission to have such cases between brethren decided in the Church, other brethren adjudicating, and only sternly forbids them to be carried outside the Church, it is manifest that here again an indulgence is extended to the infirmities of the weak. It is in view, then, of these sins, and others of the same sort, and of others again more trifling still, which consist of offenses in words and thought (as the Apostle James confesses, "In many things we offend all"), that we need to pray every day and often to the Lord, saying, "Forgive us our debts," and to add in truth and sincerity, "as we forgive our debtors."[49]

Better not to litigate at all. If incapable of this, at least resolve the dispute before the bishop's court.[50]

Consistent with the argument of this book, for Augustine the resolution of disputes, even mere commercial disputes, is a matter related to the gospel. Augustine makes this point most explicitly in "On Christian Doctrine," when he suggests that the three modes of speech—eloquent, temperate, and majestic—and their purposes—teaching, giving pleasure, and moving—should match the importance of the occasion. He notes that legal matters that relate to pecuniary interests are of small importance and those that relate to a person's life or liberty are of great importance.[51] Yet Augustine clarifies that even disputes regarding mere pecuniary matters are important, "for justice is never unimportant" and all such things, therefore, "have reference to men's salvation."[52] Augustine then notes Paul's elevated tone in 1 Corinthians 6 as evidence of the importance of even small matters such as disputes within the body:

> Why is it, in fine, that he speaks in a tone so exalted about matters so very trifling? Did secular matters deserve so much at his hands? God forbid. No; but all this is done for the sake of justice, charity, and piety, which in the judgment of every sober mind are great, even when applied to matters the very least.[53]

It is not merely the resolution of pecuniary disputes that is at stake in litigation. Such disputes affect the working of the body of Christ. When one comes to resolve such disputes before the church, justice, piety, and charity are at stake.

With this in mind, it should not be surprising that Augustine advocates for the use of bishop's courts, his concerns regarding pursuing wrongs at all notwithstanding. In several other occasional references to 1 Corinthians 6, he argues that Christians ought to use bishop's courts to resolve their disputes. All the evidence suggests that Augustine put this advice into practice as well. In his treatise, "On the Works of Monks," he complains, "We are daily greeted by men with suppliant heads, begging us to settle their quarrels."[54] These cases, Augustine suggests, burden him with "the most annoying perplexities of other men's causes about secular matters."[55] His biographer, Possidius, noted that he often went without lunch in hearing so many cases each morning.[56] His role was more than judge, however, but also mediator and reconciler. Harries notes that "the language of healing, intercession and reconciliation" dominates Augustine's account of his work in resolving disputes.[57] Likewise, Augustine placed a clear priority on the poor in the course of his decision making.[58]

Thus, following Paul's admonition and construed through the emerging ethical construct of higher and lower commands of perfection, Augustine remains relatively close to the early church in his exegetical and practical guidance. While legal claims may be pursued, they are only appropriately pursued within church structures of dispute resolution.[59] A decision is not enough; the end of open hostilities is not enough; mediation and reconciliation is the goal. The bishop is to serve as judge only when all else has failed. What is at stake in litigation is the distinction between the church and world, the city of God and city of man. And Augustine, for all his openness to the church's participation in the city of man, in most instances sees participation in secular litigation as an impermissible blurring of that line. Nonetheless, one must not oversimplify Augustine. He took church disputes into the imperial realm and in fact turned decisions regarding doctrine over to imperial authorities.[60] Likewise, he also turned to civil authorities to seek criminal punishment of heretics and pagans on behalf of the church.[61] Post-Constantine, the boundary between church and world existed in Augustine's thought, but it was also breached, if and when needed.

6

Litigation and Reconciliation During the Reformation

The eleven-hundred-year period between Augustine's bishopric in Hippo and Luther's protest in Wittenberg defies easy summation. Nonetheless, I locate here certain key contextual changes in this period. Of most significance regarding this book are the changes in litigation and disciplinary structures within and outside the church. With the decline of the Roman Empire, the rise of the Byzantium Empire in the East and the barbarian empires in the West, and most importantly the alignment of the Roman bishop with those Western empires—embodied paradigmatically in Pope Leo III's coronation of Charlemagne in 800 CE—the line dividing church and world became yet more difficult to distinguish.[1]

Luther's Context

Even in the late medieval world, the church's juridical structures remained distinct. The bishop's courts themselves had developed into a more formal canonical court structure, with professional lawyers adjudicating suits via a systemically formulated canon law.[2] These canon law courts were well organized in contrast to the civil courts of the various Western territories. Clear lines of appeal ran within this system from the archdiaconal court to the Roman *curia* acting on behalf of the pope, with the possibility of consulting law faculties and distinguished canonists for binding or advisory opinions.[3]

In theory, the jurisdiction of canon courts was limited to "spiritual matters." Nonetheless, most medieval ecclesiastical suits were not in regard to purely ecclesiastic matters.[4] As I argue throughout this book, in fact, the line between so-called "spiritual" and temporal matters itself is problematic insofar as the "spiritual" life of the church is affected by the mode by which disputes are resolved. Regardless, in practice, the canon law courts and the secular courts engaged in various and competing turf wars over the scope of spiritual and temporal jurisdiction.[5] In this regard, the canon courts were already under attack and ceding jurisdiction to secular courts prior to the wholesale assault of Luther's Reformation.[6] Likewise, even ecclesiastical voices, such as Bernard of Clairvaux, argued that the church ought to get out of the temporal dispute resolution business and stick to the management of sin.[7]

Unfortunately, little is known of the use of these canonical courts in resolving disputes. Most modern research into both the canon and civil courts in the medieval and Reformation periods focuses on the disciplinary functions of these courts and their competing claims of jurisdiction.[8] Nonetheless, some evidence suggests that late medieval society was marked by civil litigiousness. Resort to ecclesiastical or civil law was common, and ecclesiastical courts may have received the bulk of claims in the later Middle Ages because they were better organized than the civil courts.[9]

The civil law had suffered major setbacks with the decline of the Roman Empire in the West. While the bishop's courts were transforming into more organized ecclesiastical courts, civil legal structures had been lost and were being reconstituted altogether in northern Europe. Luther called German law a "wilderness."[10] Germany was made up of 364 polities, each with its own law and fully half of which were ecclesiastical polities.[11] Imperial control of these courts was largely illusory in the period just prior to the Reformation.[12] Civil jurisdictions were often overlapped by competing sets of adjudicative bodies.[13] The clearly demarcated lines of appeal that marked the Roman imperial courts, the canon courts, and modern Western legal systems were not in place. Civil courts also continued to face problems of corruption, although some scholars focus on advocates (versus the judiciary) as the main source of corruption in medieval courts of law.[14] The development of ideas of equity and courts of equity in this period, a story that defies any univocal line of development, can be seen in part as an attempt to address inequalities in the existing systems of adjudication.[15]

The church's penitential modes of disciplining had also shifted. The "canonical penance" of the early church had been replaced by private penitential structures. Canonical penance was only for major sins, was only permitted once, and required entering into a public penitential state for a period of years, throughout which the penitent was excluded from eucharist and the Prayers of the Faithful. The penitential system that emerged in the late medieval world was private; sins were confessed to a priest, who administered absolution and a penalty on the spot; confession was to be participated in by all Christians on a yearly basis (prior to Easter eucharistic, also a yearly procedure);[16] and penance did not involve identifying oneself as separate from the community, a punishment reserved only for excommunicants. These changes were driven by the admittance to the order of penitents of spiritually motivated minor sinners, the increasingly regularized provision of canonical penance in the fifth century to those about to die, and the influence of Celtic penitential practices in the sixth and seventh centuries.[17] Nonetheless, significant continuities with the early church remained. The language of healing continued to dominate the language of penitential practice.[18]

In summary, the context of late medieval litigation and discipline was a complex web of often interrelated and at times complimentary and competing systems. Just one example, retold by G. R. Evans, helps locate the complexity of the medieval legal moment. Alicia Clement was held to be an apostate and excommunicated in the mid-1180s; her crime was leaving the convent in which she had been placed as a child, and marrying. This religious crime carried civil disabilities as well, including loss of the power to litigate in the civil courts. The Christian emperor had something at stake in supporting the church's jurisdiction and excommunication. Evans notes the difficult situation this put Alicia Clement in around 1220 in litigation involving inheritance of certain lands. Her only recourse to the courts was to accept absolution for the sin of apostasy in leaving the convent, thus restoring her civil standing to sue. However, accepting the church's absolution would have "'ratified' her profession as a nun. But if she really was a nun, she would be deemed to have surrendered her inheritance of her own free will, so she would not sue to get it back."[19]

Luther and Suits on Behalf of the Other

The scene is one of the most dramatic in the Reformation. Luther, given sixty days to recant his teachings and return to the mother church, gathers with his fellow faculty members and students on the sixtieth day, December 10, 1520, and answers the pope with an orgy of fire. In the bonfire, he burns not only the papal bull ordering him to recant, but also the entire canon law, including Gratian's "Decretum," the *corpus iuris canonici*, and a confessional manual.[20] This moment reflects the point at which critique moved to revolution. The simultaneous attack on the canon law was not merely for rhetorical flourish. Luther's church revolution would include a reformation of penitential practice, a reformation of the canon law, and the replacement of canon law courts with civil courts.[21]

Accordingly, Luther derided the use of the ban for temporal matters. Excommunication's purpose is heresy and public sin, not mere monetary disputes.[22] Luther argues that such temporal matters should be left to the civil authorities, remarkably citing 1 Corinthians 6 in support of this position.[23] Likewise, Luther strongly condemns gossiping within the church.[24] With a curious appeal to Matthew 18, he argues Christians ought to keep the sin to themselves or tell the civil magistrate.[25] To be fair, Luther does suggest in other contexts that the Matthew 18 procedure of individual admonition ought to occur before proceeding to the civil authorities,[26] but the passage is particularly striking for its relocation of ecclesiastical discipline into the civil realm. Tell it to the church has become tell it to the civil magistrate.

Litigation and canon law, Luther argues, are also properly placed in the hands of the civil authorities. In his treatise "To the Christian Nobility," Luther makes clear his preference for civil over canon law and territorial over imperial legislation.[27] Thus, the Lutheran reformers would fundamentally challenge the church's right to legislate.[28] The city ordinances drafted in response to the Reformation that flourished in the 1520s and 1530s moved many ecclesial functions into the civil sphere. As John Witte notes,

> Appeals to Rome were curbed. Removal of cases from local Church courts in the event of dispute, were voluntarily expunged from contracts and treaties, and in some polities firmly forbidden by civil law. Clerics began to lose their exemptions and immunities at civil law, and became subject to the personal jurisdiction of secular courts, in both criminal and civil cases. Urban and territorial councils and courts began to claim exclusive subject-matter jurisdiction over marriage, education, inheritance, charity, and other matters that had previously lain with the Church's jurisdiction.[29]

Luther himself aided in this project, assisting in drafting new civil laws for the cities of Wittenberg and Leisnig.[30] Into this revolutionary context, what of the bishop's courts—now become canon law courts—role in resolving disputes between Christians?

As noted already, Luther maintained a limited role for the state in the kingdom of Christ, so it would be surprising to see him taking a "spiritual" function into the secular realm. However, for Luther the two kingdoms are located within the life of each individual believer, not just in the cosmos at large. Further, Luther was left with few available options for managing his revolution. He often turned to the civil authorities to maintain the social structures, such as law and courts, that he had so effectively undercut. These twin features of Luther's thought—the internalization of the church-world divide and the ordination of the civil authorities—perhaps best explain his approach to litigation.

Foremost in Luther's mind in his occasional references to 1 Corinthians 6 is then not the use of church courts but rather the admonition to suffer wrongs patiently. In his 1524 treatise, "Trade and Usury," Luther rejects many modern financial practices, suggesting that there are three modes of dealing with temporal goods: (1) permitting others to seize one's goods by force, (2) giving freely to those who ask, and (3) lending without interest or expectation of benefit.[31] In regard to the first and in answer to Augustine and his Catholic inheritors, Luther argues that Christ's command to give to those who seek to steal from you is not merely a counsel for perfection but a command for all Christians. Accordingly, Luther goes on to say that seeking one's own via either lawsuits or the ban is in error:

> Hence it comes that lawsuits and litigations, magistrates, notaries, officials, jurists, and such fellows are as numerous as flies in summer. Hence it comes that there is so much war and bloodshed among Christians. And lawsuits must be taken on appeal to Rome, for there a lot of money is the thing most needed; and the greatest, holiest, and most common occupation in all Christendom these days is suing and being sued, which means resistance to the holy and peaceful life and doctrine of Christ. This cruel game has finally come to the point where a poor man—but a Christian, whom God has redeemed with his blood—for the sake of the trifling sum of three or four groschen is not only cited to appear many miles away, put under the ban, and driven away from wife, children, and family, but the bright boys actually look upon this as a good thing to do, and even smile about it.[32]

Luther concludes, "It is of no consequence to God that laws—be they canon or civil—permit force to be resisted with force. . . . Suing in the courts is condemned neither by pope nor emperor, but it is condemned by Christ and his teaching."[33] The kingdom of God is not the kingdom of man; litigation and self-seeking will be found in the latter but have no use in the former. As noted by David Steinmetz, for Luther, the Sermon on the Mount "is not a future kingdom of God. It provides an ethic which is applicable to the life of the Christian in the world. No Christian may seek justice for any wrong which is done against his or her own private person. Nonviolence and the renunciation of any form of vengeance lie at the heart of Christian ethics."[34]

Nonetheless, Luther must still address what will be the determinative factor in interpreting 1 Corinthians 6 for Calvin, the divine institution of civil courts. In responding to this apparent contradiction (that is, the institution of civil courts by God and the prohibition of their use by Paul), Luther provides a novel model for how litigation may proceed without the plaintiff pursuing his or her own claims:

> Now it is true that God has instituted the temporal sword and in addition the spiritual power of the church, and has commanded both those authorities to punish the wicked and rescue the oppressed. . . . This should be done in such a way, however, that no one would be the complainant in his own case, but that others, in brotherly fidelity and care for one another, would inform the rulers that this man is right and that one wrong. Thus, the authorities would proceed to punish in a just and orderly way, on proof furnished by others. Indeed, the aggrieved party ought to request and insist that his case not be brought to trial; the others in their turn, ought not to desist until the offense is punished. In this way affairs would be conducted in a friendly, Christian, and brotherly spirit, with more regard to the sin than to the injury. This is why St. Paul rebukes the Corinthians in 1 Corinthians 6[:7] for going to law with one another instead of suffering themselves to be injured and defrauded, although because of their imperfection he allowed them to appoint the least among them as judges. He did this to shame them [1 Cor 6:5] into a knowledge of their imperfection. In a like manner we must tolerate those who sue and are sued for temporal goods as weak and immature Christians; we dare not cast them off, because there is hope for their improvement. . . . We ought to tell them, however, that such conduct is neither Christian nor praiseworthy but human and earthly.[35]

Suits in the civil courts, but not by the injured party. Rather, others in the community should sue on his behalf. However, while Luther suggests that one should forgo her own claims in the manner suggested here, those who do sue are not to be excluded from the body, but merely counseled against such action.[36]

This position, which might otherwise seem bizarre, is rendered intelligible in light of Luther's two kingdoms doctrine. The kingdoms of God and man are simultaneous ruling within each Christian. In regard to self, one must obey Christ, the lord of the kingdom of God, and the dictates of the Sermon on the Mount. In regard to others, one must obey the secular magistrate, the lord of the kingdom of man. Here, participation in litigation and violence for the sake of justice on behalf of the other is not only permitted but demanded. Luther's position on war, famously taken up in this century by Reinhold Niebuhr, is the same for litigation. Just as the Christian must participate in war in defense of neighbor,[37] likewise, the Christian must litigate in defense of neighbor.

With this theological underpinning in mind, it should not be surprising to find Luther less engaged with the day-to-day resolution of disputes than Augustine. Of course, Luther was called upon on many occasions to resolve debates regarding "spiritual" matters surrounding the shape and direction of the Reformation.[38] Like Augustine, Luther complained that "each day, I am inundated with so many letters that my table, chair, footstool, desk, chests, bookshelves, and everything else are covered with letters, inquiries, disputes, complaints, pleas, and so on."[39] His role in these matters was not one he relished. Witte notes that he did not desire to become the "Protestant pope" or Wittenberg the "Protestant Rome."[40] This spiritual jurisdiction, however, did not lead to Luther's resolution of temporal disputes. As noted above, he would specifically deny the church the authority to use its spiritual sanction for what he considered temporal matters. Wrongs against oneself were to be forgiven without response; wrongs against another were to be litigated in the secular courts assigned the role of wielding the sword. The church was to exhort to both; but right preaching and teaching was its only role in the matter. Thus, in several letters in which Luther addresses whether litigants should be excluded from communion, he concludes, contrary to Calvin, that those who do not harbor personal enmity against the other disputant should be permitted to commune.[41]

Nonetheless, some contrary evidence must also be noted.[42] In several cases Luther used the threat of the ban or even recommended the ban against such worldly offenses as selling a home at an exorbitant price, taking financial advantage of one's subjects, and lending at usurious rates.[43] Likewise, Luther was supportive of the establishment of a consistory court in Wittenberg in 1542, which was "authorized to hear and adjudicate disputes that arose under prevailing religious laws." A court with chastened jurisdiction and rights, it had the powers of "censure, fines, the ban, and excommunication in extreme cases—referring cases to the civil authorities if criminal prosecutions or civil litigation was also warranted."[44] Luther's last act was the reconciliation of the counts at Mansfield. As Bainton narrates it, "He went, reconciled the counts, and died on the way home."[45]

In summary, Luther takes a strong line in denying the compatibility of secular litigation with the life of the disciple of Christ in the realm of the kingdom of God. The gap that begins to develop between Luther and the Anabaptists as well as Augustine and his Catholic canonists consists in vacating the role of the church in providing an alternative to civil litigation. Luther's broader reformation left the church a lessened role in the entire drama of salvation. His treatment of litigation is similar. For him, personal renunciation of litigation, not the formation of alternative social locations, is at the heart of Paul's message to the Corinthians.

Calvin's Geneva

Calvin is unique among those I consider in this historical survey and perhaps the voice of the three most different from the Mennonite witness that follows. Augustine was a rhetorician; Luther was headed for the magistrate's office before his lightning-bolt conversion; but Calvin alone was trained in law.[46] And it was a lawyer's mind and a lawyer's method that Calvin brought to Scripture.[47] Further, Francois Wendel, one of Calvin's biographers, attributes to him the formation of the first Protestant ecclesiastical law.[48] While discipline was still not an essential mark of the church, Calvin deemed discipline "as the sinews, through which the members of the body hold together, each in its own place."[49] Accordingly, the power to discipline was an essential right of the church over which Calvin would fight with the Genevan councils throughout his life. Further, his life was consumed in large part with the practical work of implementing his social reformation in the lives of all Genevans through the Consistory that was the cornerstone of his church.[50] It was this focus on discipline, Calvin's attempt to make the Genevan church a "fellowship of genuine and believing Christians,"[51] that led Ernst Troeltsch to suggest that Calvin was well closer to the Anabaptists he reviled than even he realized.

Unpacking Calvin's battles with the Genevan councils over the control of excommunication is illustrative of his political theology, which remains close to that of Luther yet with different emphases that produced distinctly different social forms. While Calvin retained a form of Luther's visible/invisible church distinction, for him the third use of the law, sanctification, and the progress of a public and external Reformation and church were each essential. Accordingly, despite the invisible nature of the "true" church, a sanctified church was to be emerging visibly in the lives of all Genevans.[52] Further, the church and civil magistrate work as co-ordained institutions of God for this purpose. The magistrate has been ordained by God to serve the upbuilding of the church, and the church has been ordained by God to support the work of the magistrate.[53] Yet even with this conflation of church and world, one should not overestimate the merging of church and civil authority in Calvin's work, for his life was a struggle to obtain and sustain the exclusive power of the church in its ecclesial authority.

In this regard, Calvin's relationship with the civil magistrates in Geneva can hardly be described as close. Calvin was first run out of Geneva by the civil authorities over the adoption of Bernese liturgical forms. However, the real issue was not the forms but the civil authorities' right to adopt them absent consultation with Calvin and the pastors of Geneva.[54] Upon subsequently being recalled to Geneva, Calvin immediately demanded the creation of a Consistory with spiritual jurisdiction over the lives and morals of Genevans.[55] Through a series of negotiations, Calvin obtained this right and thought he had obtained sole control of excommunication for the Consistory in his "Ecclesiastic Ordinances," promulgated in 1541. He was wrong about the latter matter. It would not be until 1554 that Calvin's Consistory would be clearly in control of excommunication.[56] All this wrestling may be properly understood as a struggle to maintain the distinction between the civil and ecclesiastical sword. The church and civil magistrate are working together for the upbuilding of the kingdom of God, but likewise, those institutions are distinct, with distinct roles and with a distinct priority on the church in Calvin's mind.

Calvin, Civil Litigation, and Discipline

The defining assumption behind Calvin's treatment of 1 Corinthians 6 is that any reading of this passage must be disciplined by the clear ordination of the civil order, and civil courts, in Romans 13.[57] Unlike Luther, Calvin begins not by setting out the radical nature of 1 Corinthians 6 but rather by presenting a series of limitations on what would appear to be the otherwise obvious suggestion that Paul is counseling forgoing suits or encouraging the use of church courts. Calvin first argues that 1 Corinthians

6 does not address believers defending themselves when they are brought before civil authorities. Second, he distinguishes public matters from private matters without much material detail as to the content of this distinction. Calvin may well have something along the lines of Luther's distinction in mind here, but this conclusion is conjecture. Regardless, Calvin suggests that 1 Corinthians 6's applicability is limited to such private matters. Public matters are outside the jurisdiction of the church altogether.[58]

Finally, Calvin limits 1 Corinthians 6 to an attitudinal admonition. He suggests that Paul is chastising the spirit in which the Corinthians are conducting themselves and the manner in which this displays a "lack of endurance" in "suffering injuries patiently."[59] Calvin concludes, "It is not out of order for Christians to pursue their rights with moderation, so long as no damage is done to love," which Calvin suggests requires no action be taken for the sake of revenge.[60] Litigation not motivated by such ill-tainted motives is permitted. While Calvin is experienced enough as a lawyer to admit "that it is a very rare thing indeed for anyone to go to law free from and innocent of every unworthy attitude of mind,"[61] he argues that resort to civil courts is not prohibited in itself. With this last limitation, Calvin has gutted the passage of any radical meaning that would require a serious break between the Christian's and the wider culture's response to disputes or means of resolving them.[62]

As noted above, Calvin's conclusions are grounded in his political theology. Civil litigation simply must be permissible to the Christian because God has ordained the political order and its various functions for the upbuilding of the kingdom. Accordingly, litigation must be permissible according to Calvin for the following reasons:

> The *first* is that the impression may not be given that God was wasting His time in establishing law-courts. The *second* reason is in order that believers may know exactly what they are allowed to do, so that they may undertake anything that would be against their conscience. . . . The *third* reason is that they may be warned that restraint must always be observed, so as not to spoil, by their own misbehavior, the remedy which God has entrusted to them. The *final* reason is that the boldness of the wicked may be checked by an unspoiled and genuine zeal; and this could only be done if we were allowed to subject them to legal punishment.[63]

In essence, Calvin sees little at stake in the apocalyptic social distance between the church and the world noted in chapter 4. Rather, for him,

Paul's instruction is merely a dispositional characteristic.[64] The reason for not emphasizing the apocalyptic distance between the church and the world for Calvin is clear: the church and civil society are moving together toward the establishment of the kingdom. To suggest a widening of the gap between church and world for Calvin would be to suggest the very failure of the kingdom's establishment.

Before turning to the practical out-workings of Calvin's views on civil litigation, I pause briefly to consider his views on discipline, for discipline was the context in which Calvin worked practically for the reconciliation of disputes. As noted above, while not concluding that discipline was a mark of the true church, Calvin fought vigorous for control of discipline in the Genevan Reformation.[65] Following Matthew 18, Calvin distinguishes between three levels of correction (private warning, warning before witnesses, and public judgment of the church) and argues that open sins against the church are immediately to be corrected via public judgment. In regard to hidden sins, if the person flatly denies the charge, the believer may proceed directly to public judgment.[66] However, warning before witnesses is appropriate when the believer acknowledges the act, but "imprudently make[s] light of their wrong and sinful action, or shamelessly excuse[s] it."[67] If these private warnings fail, excommunication is appropriate[68] and is the church's only remedy. Nonetheless, Calvin expects the civil authorities to aid the church in administering other penalties.[69] The theological purposes for these practices are to ensure (1) that those "who lead a filthy and infamous life may not be called Christians," (2) "that the good be not corrupted by the constant company of the wicked," and (3) "that those overcome by shame for their baseness begin to repent."[70] Excommunication itself, Calvin concludes, is but an announcement of the sinner's own departure from the church.[71]

The Geneva Consistory

Calvin implemented these convictions regarding discipline, reconciliation, and litigation via the Consistory, which he insisted be established at his return to Geneva in 1541. The groundwork for the Consistory is set forth in Calvin's "Ecclesiastical Ordinances" of that same year.[72] As Robert Kingdon notes, "The new institution was at once an agency of both the state and the church. Its members included both elected lay elders and the ordained pastors of the city."[73] The pastors were themselves employees of the city, and more particularly the Small Council, the most important of the civil legislative and governing bodies;[74] "the elders were elected annually in the February elections in which all municipal officials were chosen."[75] However, in most cases, the elections were merely the ratification of the slate of candidates prepared by the outgoing Small Council. Accordingly, it was a quasi-public entity, reflecting the co-working of church and city-state.[76]

Calvin served on the Consistory from its formation and, according to Wendel, "was clearly the moving spirit of the Consistory."[77] It met weekly and, as noted above, bore a contested power of excommunication. It also made regular recourse to the civil authorities, who could impose stiffer penalties "ranging from a spectacular public humiliation, to a short prison term, a small fine, or even death, executed in several brutal ways."[78] The Small Council would not only ratify sentences, however. It also served as a court of appeal with the ability to ignore the Consistory's finding of guilt or alter the Consistory's temporal sentence. Only the power to excommunicate was in the province of the Consistory alone and then only after the political battles and election successes of 1553-54 solidified that power.[79] Cases ranged from participation in rites bearing Catholic influence to blasphemy against God, that is, against the Consistory or more importantly Calvin himself, to most importantly sexual morality.[80] With this range of cases and the active participation of the whole city, William Monter has estimated that in 1569, five years after Calvin's death, one in every fifteen Genevans would have been called before the Consistory in any given year and one in twenty-five would have been excommunicated for a period in any given year.[81]

While this disciplinary work of the Consistory has received the most scholarly attention and earned Calvin a questionable reputation as autocratic, the work of the Consistory was also comprised of reconciling parties.[82] Watching Calvin at work in and petitioning to the Consistory is instructive in making sense of his theological reflections noted above. Several litigable cases out of many examples give the flavor of the Consistory's approach. A variety of disputes before the Consistory related to mere insults, but defamation was itself a significant crime. One dispute between Pernete Bochue and Anne involved alleged damage to "the chimney and the spiral staircase" in Pernete's house when Anne and her four daughters lived there. Pernete, unable to collect fifteen gros for the alleged damage, called Anne, "Witch! Witch!" The Consistory "confronted [the women] with each other," Pernete retracted her words, and the Secretary records, "They made peace together and were in accord."[83]

The facts of other cases were more difficult to clarify, or the parties proved more intractable, requiring the Consistory to send the case to "arbitration." Unfortunately no detail is given as to the forum or manner in which such arbitration would be conducted. For example, the daughters of Rolete de Pary came before the Consistory already engaged in a testamentary lawsuit "to divide their mother's goods":

> The advice of the Consistory: that they be told not to cease to love each other despite the suit, and that they make an agreement through respectable people and come here in two weeks to learn whether they have agreed together, and that they put themselves into arbitration and frequent the sermons.[84]

The case is typical insofar as many of the disputes before the Consistory involved family members in conflict over testamentary, business, or simple day-to-day matters.[85] In addition, on a few occasions the Consistory dealt with commercial matters, including usury and neighborly boundary disputes.[86] Nonetheless, the main task of the Consistory, according to the *Registers'* editors, was martial litigation, often the contractual construction of marriage promises and often with babies already on the way.[87] In such cases, business, family, and sexual morals all collide in a single dispute, making such cases ripe for the Consistory's review.[88]

The theological groundwork for the reconciling work of the Consistory is of most significance to my argument. As noted by Kingdon, the Consistory "generally agreed that people involved in violent quarrel, with 'hate in their hearts' toward others—whether family members, business partners, or neighbors—should not take communion."[89] In this, the Consistory tracks Calvin's suggestion that "unworthily partaking of the Sacrament" entails, among other concerns, communing "although they are divided and separated by hatred and ill will from their brethren, that is, from the members of Christ, and thus have no part in Charity."[90] Accordingly, the Consistory established dizainiers, who were to oversee a section of the city "to know those in their dizaines who bear ill will against each other, so that they can be reconciled before receiving the Holy Communion of Our Lord."[91] Such disputants were then reconciled by the Consistory to reestablish the communal bond; in some cases of severe disputes, the parties would even participate in a separate service of reconciliation.[92]

Despite Calvin's suggestion in commentary to 1 Corinthians that Christians ought to use the civil courts ordained by God, in practice, he was involved in the week-to-week work of reconciling Christian families, business partners, and neighbors who had come into conflicts of either a legal or a personal nature through an extrajudicial process. However, the Consistory defies easy categorization as either a civil or ecclesiastical body. It was simultaneously an instrument of the city-state and the church, although with a clear leaning to the church side of the continuum in contrast to the Small Council with which it battled for control of excommunication. Further, the Consistory worked hand-in-glove with the civil councils of Geneva, repeatedly referring offenders' cases to the councils and likewise receiving cases from the Small Council.[93] In some cases, the Consistory even suggested that the parties pursue litigation in love.[94] Reconciliation in the midst of civil litigation and civil litigation as a means to reconciliation—neither is excluded by Calvin's Consistory.

Conclusion

The purpose of these last two chapters was twofold. First, they place within critical context what I will construe as a uniquely Anabaptist witness in regard to litigation in the chapters that follow. Further, however, these chapters serve as a challenge to those outside the Anabaptist tradition to reexamine their own stance toward litigation in light of the resources within their own theological traditions. These chapters, focusing on the lives and work of critical forefathers to each of the Catholic, Lutheran, and Reformed traditions, begin this process. While each tradition has left its forefathers behind in dramatic ways, I assume each continues to see these figures as in some manner authoritative in their construal of the Christian life and, in particular, of ecclesiology.

With this purpose in mind, what has been shown is that, within each of these varying traditions, there is significant concern regard the manner in which Christians resolve disputes. Augustine and Calvin were extensively involved in the resolution of disputes between Christians; Luther was not unfamiliar to the practice. Augustine and Luther emphasized the binding nature of the Sermon on the Mount, including forgoing litigation for wrongs, as either a counsel of perfection for which all Christians must be headed ultimately or as required for all Christians within the sphere of personal wrongs. Calvin saw the reconciliation of Christians as essential to the very nature of the church; communion in the midst of disputes was to bring condemnation on oneself. Augustine, Luther, and Calvin saw some limited distinction between the Christian and world as essential to political theology.

In other words, in telling the particular Anabaptist story in the next chapters, I am telling a story that can be traced to varying degrees in the broader church. It is not a radically sectarian litigation ethic, but a radically Christian one that is offered. The hope is simply that these chapters and the broader project will spark members of these other traditions to see the necessity of examining again—in the light of the Anabaptist witness and their own history—their participation within modern Western legal systems. I cannot guarantee where that examination will lead, but the evidence that requires this going forward has been set forth.

7

Early Anabaptist Challenges to the Use of the Law

As suggested in the second chapter, the story told there can be understood only in light of the particular Mennonite context in which the actors were located. In the chapters since then I have traced the history of the treatment of litigation in the broader Christian tradition. In the next two chapters I focus explicitly on the Mennonite context. The burden of these chapters is to situate the actions and descriptions of chapter 2 as an expected outworking of broader Anabaptist life, witness, and practice in regard to reconciliation and the location of the church within the world. Therefore, in this chapter I trace traditional Mennonite reflection on the relationship of the church to civil governing structures and then explore the historical roots of Anabaptist theological reflection regarding litigation. In the chapter that follows, I explore the immediate context of chapter 2 by looking at Mennonite treatment of litigation in the last one hundred years.

Anabaptist Understandings of the State

The appropriate place to begin to explore Mennonite practice in regard to litigation is the roots of the Mennonite movement in the Reformation period. The set of related developments, now understood as foundational to the emergence of modern Anabaptists, reached a peak in Zurich, Switzerland, in January 1525, where the Reformation was already in full swing under the guidance of Ulrich Zwingli. In the eight years that Zwingli led the reformation there, Conrad Grebel, Felix Manz, and Georg Blaurock challenged Zwingli and his young reformation. These Anabaptists became notorious for "rebaptizing" those who had been baptized as children—denying the legitimacy of this first nonbeliever's baptism. The Anabaptist stance on baptism, however, was as much the outworking of a larger concern regarding the maintenance by Zwingli of a city-state church structure as it was a critique of baptismal theology. Zwingli left known sinners in the church and left authority over the church with the Zurich councils. The Anabaptists rejected both Zwingli's *Volkskirche* and the wedding of church and civil authority. They connected the adult baptismal pledge with the Christian's voluntary acknowledgment of the church's (in lieu of the city-state's) authority to discipline.[1]

An inquiry into the Anabaptist understandings of the church's relationship to litigation must, therefore, begin with an inquiry into the nature of civil authority. For the most part, the Anabaptists agreed with Luther's position, set forth in chapter 6, regarding the purpose of civil authority and its use of the sword. The disagreement between Luther and many of the Anabaptists was in regard to the proper relationship of the church to the civil authority. To summarize briefly the discussion set forth in chapter 6, Luther's two kingdoms doctrine posits simultaneously existing kingdoms: the kingdom of the world and the kingdom of Christ. The two kingdoms have two governments: the civil authority and Christ. God has ordained and established both these orders.

Only the kingdom of Christ, however, is salvific. The civil authorities, as ordained heads of the earthly kingdom, have authority only in the worldly realm, which has been created due to sin for maintaining peace and order. As violence is the only means for sustaining peace and order in a world of sin, the sword has been given to the secular authorities. Christians, according to Luther, are simultaneously members of both kingdoms. Therefore, Christians are called to forgo violence or the use of the law in regard to private wrongs, but are permitted and even required by the command of love of neighbor to defend the civil law and serve in secular government, including bearing the sword.[2]

Most early Anabaptist theological reflection on the state and the sword accepted the majority of the political theology set forth above. At the end of this chapter, I will look in detail at the problems with suggesting that there was a uniform Anabaptist "position" in regards to such abstract terms as "the state" or "civil authority." However, for now it is helpful to work with these generalizations, while keeping in mind that the necessary work of complicating this picture must still be completed. With this caveat, most early Anabaptists concurred with Luther that the state was ordained by God as a gracious response to the anarchy brought about by sin. Furthermore, they agreed that the state rightly and necessarily bore the sword, which was required to fulfill its dual purposes of punishing evildoers and safeguarding its citizens.[3] However, in sharp contrast to Luther, most Anabaptists insisted that since the sword was essential to the state, Christians must eschew participation in that work. The location of the tension between Luther and the Anabaptists was then Luther's understanding of the Christian's dual membership in the kingdom of the cross and the kingdom of the world. For Luther, the church-world dichotomy collapsed into the individual—who simultaneous acted in his private life according to the gospel and in the public realm as required to protect the neighbor. In such a construal, the church is no longer a visible alternative to the world. Anabaptists insisted to the contrary. The Anabaptists read the high ethical standard set forth in the Sermon on the Mount, not as a call to withdrawal per se, but as the ethic that must apply in every facet of the Christian's life. As the state must necessarily rely on the sword, the Christian necessarily cannot participate in at least the sword-bearing works of the state.[4]

Accordingly, the distinguishing marks of the earliest Anabaptists were (1) their commitment to a communally located church-world dichotomy, (2) their commitment to church discipline, including the ethical demands found in the Sermon on the Mount, and (3) their commitment to adult believers baptism that served to legitimate that discipline. Anabaptists' historical commitment to nonviolence grows naturally out of these commitments, confirmed by their particular experience of reactionary violence at the hands of established Catholic and Protestant governments.

Early Anabaptist Reflection on Litigation

The lives of the founders of the Anabaptist movement, beginning with Grebel, Manz, and Blaurock, were not easy. Most of the key figures in the development of the Anabaptist movement died a martyr's death after months or years of itinerant preaching, often writing while being pursued by the authorities. They did not produce the volume of writings that one finds in Lutheran or Reformed beginnings. Furthermore, there is no single dominant figure in the manner of Luther or Calvin upon which to focus exclusive attention, but rather a group of related, developing, and at times competing voices. Thus, the conclusions reached regarding litigation by the earliest Anabaptists are neither systematic nor uncontested. Nonetheless, I trace an emerging consensus in regard to Anabaptist responses to civil dispute resolution in varying social and historical contexts.

Because Conrad Grebel's sporadic writings leave the issues of nonresistance and litigation untouched,[5] the appropriate place to begin to understand

Anabaptist reflection on litigation is article 6 of the seven articles prepared in Schleitheim, Switzerland, in early 1527. The Schleitheim Confession was drafted by Michael Sattler, who stepped into a brief but momentous leadership role in the early Anabaptist movement after the death of Grebel and Manz and the retreat to Tyrol and Moravia of Blaurock and Balthasar Hubmaier respectively.[6] While not addressing litigation per se, article 6 regarding the sword is instructive in understanding Anabaptist reflection on the state and nonresistance:

> We have been united as follows concerning the sword. The sword is an ordering of God outside the perfection of Christ. It punishes and kills the wicked and guards and protects the good. In the law the sword is established over the wicked for punishment and for death and the secular rulers are established to wield the same.
>
> But within the perfection of Christ only the ban is used for the admonition and exclusion of the one who has sinned, without the death of the flesh, simply the warning and the command to sin no more.
>
> Now many, who do not understand Christ's will for us, will ask; whether a Christian may or should use the sword against the wicked for the protection and defense of the good, or for the sake of love.
>
> The answer is unanimously revealed: Christ teaches and commands us to learn from Him, for He is meek and lowly of heart and thus we shall find rest for our souls (Matt. 11:29). Now Christ says to the woman who was taken in adultery (John 8:11), not that she should be stoned according to the law of His Father (and yet He says, "What the Father commanded me, that I do") (John 8:22) but with mercy and forgiveness and the warning to sin no more, says: "Go, sin no more." Exactly thus should we also proceed, according to the rule of the ban.[7]

The article tracks closely the conclusions suggested above regarding the ordination of the state (and the sword) and Christian's nonparticipation therein. In light of these conclusions, the ban (that is, church discipline) is the only appropriate method for addressing sin and the resultant disunity it produces. Sattler's statement concerning "Congregational Order" that follows the seven articles reiterates (1) that the ban is the only appropriate means for settling disputes within the church,[8] (2) that Christians are not to judge civil disputes, and (3) that distinction between the practices of the church and those of the world must be maintained.[9] By the end of May 1527, Sattler was dead, drowned as a heretic. Consistent with the articles, in his civil heresy trial he refused a lawyer on the grounds that the issue was a religious matter not properly within the jurisdiction of the civil court.[10] His witness and the Schleitheim Confession, including an essential role for church discipline, would continue to guide the Anabaptist movement.

The connection between nonresistance and litigation was then immediately drawn within various quarters of the young Anabaptist movement. Hubmaier, who was rebaptized in 1525 and martyred just three years later on March 10, 1528, provides a particularly interesting study in regard to litigation.[11] In a treatise titled "On Fraternal Admonition," Hubmaier not only suggests that the litigious spirit is in error, he also draws the connection—essential to my argument—between forgoing litigation and reconciliation:

> Where this happens, here God will stand powerfully and wonderfully by his Word in such a way that the Christian brethren and the fellowship will be able to reconcile and conciliate such great causes and disunities, as could not have been judged in many years at great cost and with great damage.[12]

Embodying reconciliation, which is made possible only via Christ's reconciling work on the cross, is the essential reason for Christians to resolve their disputes in a more thoroughgoing manner than is offered by the civil courts.[13] Reliance on this justification leaves Hubmaier free to suggest Christians participate in the state and even serve as judges for civil disputes, while at the same time suggesting that litigating those disputes is in error.[14]

Perhaps the most thoroughly developed challenge to litigation in the earliest Anabaptist writings is found in Clemens Adler's "Das Urteil von dem Schwert," which is dated to 1529 but was not rediscovered until 1946, when it was found in the attic of a Swiss farmhouse. In a section entitled "Concerning Temporal Goods," Adler focuses exclusively on litigation:

> From this [community of goods] it follows that since members of the Christian congregation share all possessions with the poor, holding them in common because of a deep love and free, good will, how then can they go to law and quarrel with each other because of temporal goods? In the Christian congregation, no one should be deprived of his due, neither with words nor with works. . . .
>
> However, should a brother or sister be defrauded by someone

from outside, he should bear it in true patience. He should not take anyone to a worldly court or trial, for, as Christ says, If anyone wished to go to court or dispute with you concerning your coat, let him have it and the cloak also. Here no gloss is necessary; the words of Christ are plainly expressed, distinctly and clearly. They must be permitted to stand on their worth and truth without any of our additions.

In the power of the spirit, Paul, a servant of God, forbade all Christian churches to engage in such heathen litigation and practice when he wrote the Corinthians. . . .

This shows how Christians should be separated from all worldly litigation, as was described in the first part of this booklet. The world has its own laws. The law of Moses also had its own verdicts and judgments in its time, very different from worldly law, as was described in another part of this booklet. The Christian church also has its own law and order, given by Christ, not like the world and not like the Jews, for the kingdom of Christ is not physical but spiritual, also a kingdom of peace in which there is neither strife nor litigation, indeed there should be no quarreling for the Christian church is not accustomed to quarreling or going to law with anyone.[15]

Adler claims that both a church-world and a New Testament-Old Testament dichotomy are at stake in the rejection of litigation. Accordingly, more than just obedience to the texts of Matthew 5:40 and 1 Corinthians 6 are at issue for Adler; the very nature of the church as a distinct body in the world—with its alternative law of Christ—is put in question by participation in litigation.[16]

This position was repeated in other wings of the Anabaptist movement. In Peter Riedemann's *Account of our Religion, Doctrine and Faith*, the most important Hutterite confessional statement, he argues,

> Since, as is said above, all temporal things are foreign to us and naught is our own, a Christian can neither strive, quarrel nor go to law on their account; on the contrary as one whose heart is turned from the world and set upon what is divine, he should suffer wrong; as Paul saith, "Now therefore there is utterly a fault among you because you go to law one with another. Why do ye not rather take wrong? Why do ye not rather suffer yourselves to be defrauded?" Since Christians must not sue one another at law,

going to law and sitting in judgment are completely done away with among Christians.

It followeth from this that no Christian can sit upon or call a court. For Christians do not go to law in this way. Paul saith, "For what have I to do to judge them that are without?" Thus judging and bringing to law have ceased and come to an end in the Church of Christ.[17]

Riedemann not only espoused this position, but was arrested in 1539 in route to Hesse for the purpose of attempting to reconcile two brethren there.[18] In summary, as John Oyer puts it, "The Anabaptists were unalterably opposed to initiating suits at law. Although one can find an exception for almost any generalization that can be made about the Anabaptists, on this one no exception comes to mind."[19] While Oyer overstates the matter, the evidence set forth herein locates an emerging consensus on forgoing litigation within the earliest Anabaptists and a set of key theological arguments for doing so: (1) the reconciliation of Christ demands more, and (2) the identity of the church as a unique people is forsaken.[20]

Later Anabaptist Reflection on Litigation

These early Anabaptist challenges to the use of the civil courts were carried forward in key instructional literature that has informed the first Anabaptists in America.[21] Of particular importance is Thieleman J. van Braght's *The Bloody Theater*, or *The Martyrs Mirror of the Defenseless Christians*.[22] Published in final form in Dort in 1660, it was later translated into German at the request of German-speaking Mennonites in Pennsylvania in 1745 in preparation for the upcoming Revolutionary War.[23] The accounts of the Anabaptist martyrs set forth therein continue to reinforce a distinct Anabaptist response to litigation. In one description, soon-to-be Anabaptist martyrs, responding to the civil authorities in Zurich in 1639, claim that their positions on infant baptism, the state, and violence are consonant not only with those of the early church, but also with those of the early reformers, such as Luther. Included in a series of claims about Luther's early views of nonresistance is their claim that Luther once said, "Christians are forbidden to sue for their rights at law."[24]

Of equal interest is a description of the martyrdom of Christian Langedul in 1567. Van Braght includes within *Martyrs Mirror* a stirring set of letters from Langedul in the midst of his torture, trial, and ultimate execution. What is noteworthy for understanding Anabaptist views of litigation and dispute resolution is van Braght's opening line, "In the year of our

Lord, 1567, one Sunday morning, being the 10th of August, Christian Langedul went out to take a letter to his brother R. L., and then proceeded to a place called the Schelleken, whither he had been summoned to help mediate a difference between two persons."[25] Van Braght follows this brief introduction with a citation of 1 Corinthians 6:5, suggesting that this was the normal mode for Anabaptist dispute resolution to proceed.

Determining the actual practice of early Anabaptists in regard to litigation is even more difficult than answering the question of their theological claims in this regard. Yet evidence, such as Langedul's case and Riedemann's arrest in similar circumstances, suggests that at least some Anabaptists were turning to one another and church leaders to resolve disputes in lieu of using civil courts. Other cases indicate Anabaptists acting to the contrary. Yet the very fact that the cases are noteworthy testifies to the tradition's historic concerns regarding participation in litigation. Richard MacMaster relates the 1790 story of a quarrel between two Germantown, Pennsylvania, pastors, in which one party to the dispute threatened to "hand the thing over to the court."[26] The ministers of the surrounding conference gathered to ensure a nonjudicial resolution of the case.[27]

The details surrounding the fallout from a 1908 Mennonite land scheme perpetrated by Henry J. Martens are even more informative.[28] Martens sold thousands of acres in the to-be-formed "Martensdale," California, to Kansas Mennonites. Upon their arrival in California, the Kansas settlers learned that Martens did not hold legal title to the lands he had sold. A variety of suits were brought by the defrauded Mennonites against Martens, leading to Reverend Jacob Kliewer's statement to a local newspaper, "It is true we do not believe in having anything to do with actions at law, but when one has been stripped to the bone—well, it is different."[29] The cost of litigation witness, a cost too high at least for Reverend Kliewer, should not be romanticized. Yet, in the end, most of the defrauded settlers did not sue.[30]

It is apparent that as the Anabaptist tradition moved into the context of twentieth-century America, aided by certain resources (themselves contested), it had in its memory a history of alternative practices regarding dispute resolution such that it was able to envision resolving disputes apart from civil litigation structures. Equipped with that memory, Anabaptists could read 1 Corinthians 6 with radical conclusions for the church's common life together and its relationship to the state.

8
The Use of the Law

In the previous chapter I explored how Anabaptists from the sixteenth to nineteenth centuries responded to questions of the state, violence, nonresistance, and litigation. Those historical resources are the wellspring of the North American Mennonite church's discernment over the past one hundred years on what the gospel of reconciliation requires in the particular context of a quasi-democratic nation-state such as Canada or the United States. In this chapter, I outline the modern Anabaptist stance in regard to litigation by tracing its development through a series of important documents or gatherings of Mennonite leaders: (1) an article by Paul Erb in regard to litigation published in *Mennonite Quarterly Review* in 1939 and (2 and 3) papers presented at conferences held in 1956 in Laurelville, Pennsylvania, and in Goshen, Indiana, in 1961, in regard to nonresistance and litigation. These various documents and gatherings culminate in the drafting and approval of *The Use of the Law*, approved by the Mennonite Church General Assembly in 1981.

Anabaptists and Litigation in America: Early Insights

A 1939 essay by Paul Erb in the *Mennonite Quarterly Review* sets the tone for much of contemporary Mennonite reflection on litigation. "Nonresistance and Litigation" explored three essential themes from the arguments found in the last chapter in his own argument against the use of most forms of aggressive litigation practice. He argues (1) the rejection of the law is necessary to maintain the distinction between the church and the world; (2) the rejection of the law is required for faithful witness to the gospel of reconciliation; and (3) the rejection of the law is not a rule—some forms of reconciling nonadversarial litigation are permitted.

Erb begins by noting the positive purposes of law. It often serves to protect life, property, and personal well-being through its structuring role.

Nonetheless, he notes that this structuring activity is not the purpose of many lawsuits. Relying on an exposition of 1 Corinthians 6, Erb argues that the use of secular judges to decide Christian disputes must be rejected. This is necessary because the church and the world are distinct economies working under distinct rules as to the settlement of disputes.[1] According to Erb, "There is loss of Christian testimony, loss of spiritual power, defeat of the very cause of love which they're striving to build up. . . . [The church's] chief tenets are denied in the language which the world can best understand, the language of our actions." In other words, Erb suggests that the church's witness is at stake in its dispute resolution practices. Accordingly, Erb argues, "Rather than the Church should suffer such loss [of its witness], it would be much better to accept personal loss, to take wrong, to allow ourselves to be defrauded."[2]

Having developed the challenge to the use of the law, Erb emphasizes that litigation need not be rejected categorically, but only when the use of litigation will make the church's broader message of reconciliation unintelligible to the watching world. Erb's understanding of the nature of Christian ethics, which requires an ongoing process of discernment, will also be evident in later Mennonite reflection. Likewise, the distinction between uses of the law that serve or hinder reconciliation will inform the parsing between the use of lawyers for the drafting of contracts and non-adversarial litigation versus aggressive litigation in later Mennonite thought. Erb's article suggests the reasoning behind these distinctions, which are drawn by him along a line between the law's structuring functions and its aggressive or adversarial functions. In other words, the use of the law to memorialize legal relationships through contracts, deeds, and wills serves to order human relations and maintain the peace. While, on the other hand, adversarial litigation when business relations break down may only serve to further divide the parties and increase enmity.

Further, Erb suggests that even litigation, if conducted in a mode of reconciliation, is valuable. In concluding he relates the following story:

> Somewhere in the upper reaches of the great Alpine track there lies a fertile valley, occupied by the remnant of the Mennonites who early settled here. These people are nonresistance, law-abiding, and peace-loving. At the passing of the period of bitter persecution, this little group found there a place of refuge and repose, and established laws for their protection.
>
> They were farmers, tillers of the soil, and lived in the spirit of brotherly love. They were as a family of brothers living together,

each mindful not only of his own interests but equally of the interests of others.

One day a misunderstanding arose between two neighbors concerning their boundary line. They discussed the matter and tried in every way to come to a proper understanding. But they failed to agree, and rather than allow any ill-feeling among themselves, they decided to refer to the court and abide by its decision.

The day for the trial arrived and the farmer who lived farthest away, called David, came by where he found John, the other, hilling his potatoes.

"Come, John," said David, "let us go to the court."

"These potatoes will suffer if they are not hilled today," replied John; "You go to the court and tell the story. You know all about our differences and can tell them as well as I. First put your side before the court, and then mine. Stop on your way home and tell me the verdict."

So David went on alone, down the mountainside into the valley where the court held forth.

That evening at dusk David came plodding back up the mountain path. "Well, brother," he said, as John came to meet him halfway, "I went to court and put both sides before them, and the court decided in your favor."

And David continued on his way humming a little folk melody—Mary Graybill. If legal necessity requires that we go to court concerning any matter, let us go in such a spirit and in utter mutual trust.[3]

In the Shadow of Niebuhr: Litigation, the Courts, and Political Responsibility

With Erb's article as background, a significant communal engagement regarding this question was undertaken at the Conference on Nonresistance and Political Responsibility held in 1956 in Laurelville, Pennsylvania. The conference, which was part of the ongoing work of the Peace Problems Committee of the Mennonite General Conference, addressed litigation, among other issues.

However, to understand the context of the conference and the significance of its work, the influence of Reinhold Niebuhr and the challenge presented to his work at the Laurelville conference must first be understood. Niebuhr was the defining thinker in the middle of the last century in Christian ethics. His theology is driven by an account of humanity that emphasizes its fundamentally sinful nature. Niebuhr argues that Christ's ethic of love, which entails nonresistance to evil, is salutary if unachievable for individuals in their relationships with others, because of human sin. Further, for groups, an ethic of love is not only impossible, it is socially irresponsible:

> In both cases [the individual and social] the heedlessness toward the self which is implied in the *Agape* of the New Testament seems to be an embarrassment; for it contradicts the natural and justified inclination of the self to preserve and defend its own existence and it throws confusion into the nicely calculated balances and discrimination of competing interest by which society preserves a tolerable justice.[4]

Justice requires, according to Niebuhr, groups to seek their own self-interest. Therefore, in regard to such intergroup conflicts, Niebuhr counsels "politics is the art of the possible." Institutionalizing competing centers of power is the best means of achieving a tolerable limit on injustice.[5]

In the light of the requirements of justice, Niebuhr rejects any suggestion that legal rights or access to civil modes of power should be forgone by groups:

> Unwillingness or inability to put in one's claims amid the vast system of claims and counter-claims of society means that ones claims will not be considered. A saintly abnegation of interest may encourage the ruthless aggrandizement of the strong and the unscrupulous. These facts are so plain that every effort to introduce suffering love as a simple alternative to the complexities and ambiguities of social justice must degenerate into sentimentality.[6]

The ethic of agape must be adjusted to the realities of sin. This "natural law" process of reasoning suggests that equality is the appropriate stance in the interim: "Equality stands in a medial position between love and justice. If the obligation to love the neighbor as the self is to be reduced to rational calculation, the only guarantee of the fulfillment of the obligation is a grant to the neighbor which equals what the self claims for itself. Thus equality is love in terms of logic."[7]

Following Luther's account, Niebuhr then argues that Christians have an obligation to sustain civil structures, including participating in violence and the courts, in defense of the neighbor. As such, Christian ethics must accept compromises to operate within the existing civil structures and participation in activities—like war and the courts—contrary to the gospel mandate. In other words, effectiveness in the here and now is a primary requirement for any Christian ethic. In light of the necessary role that the state serves in defense of the neighbor, Christians have an obligation to maintain the status quo.

The Laurelville conference's title, which refers to "political responsibility," makes clear that Niebuhr's voice is driving the need for the conference. Mennonites' traditional commitment to nonresistance flies in the face of Niebuhr's demand that groups seek their own. Nonetheless, while the title suggests Niebuhr's influence, the conference papers themselves continued to resist the Niebuhrian approach to political theology and ethics. The opening paper of the conference set the tone for Mennonite reflection on matters of litigation and the response to arguments of Niebuhr summarized above:

> The Christian has no need for civil government. While historically Christians have always found themselves in some sort of relationship to civil government, whether under Roman imperialism, Nazi totalitarianism, Russian communistic socialism, African barbarism, or American democracy, nevertheless, they have no responsibility to erect an authority outside of the church to serve some unprovided area of life. Their heavenly citizenship is all inclusive. This is not to take a utopian view of things; rather it only stresses the totality of the Lordship of Christ in His Kingdom throughout the Church.[8]

The themes of this comment were reiterated in other papers, for example,

> Survival, however, is not the main concern of the Christian, whether we think of the preservation of the Church as an institution or maintenance of a particular political order of the state. The chief task of the church is to witness, to confront all men with the Gospel of Jesus Christ and to win them to total allegiance to Christ as Lord.[9]

In response to Niebuhr, the conference's participants argued that the church has no responsibility for sustaining one political order over another, or more particularly, the authority of the courts. Justice is God's project, not humans'. Witness is the church's task—even at the cost of its own survival or that of any particular civil government. Therefore, participation in foundational civil institutions, such as civil courts, may be questioned in a manner that most litigation ethics simply cannot.

The conference's particular reflections on litigation were then guided by three papers: (1) a summary of responses to a litigation survey sent to proprietors of various-size Mennonite businesses, (2) a short history of Mennonite reflection in regard to litigation, and (3) a short enquiry into litigation "theology" by Mennonite lawyer Samuel S. Wenger.[10] The group meeting to consider these issues then drafted a report of its findings and conclusions, which is the best guide to the conclusions reached at the conference.

The first paper, summarizing survey responses regarding Mennonite litigation practice, indicated that for the most part Mennonite businesspersons in the 1950s did avoid suits in their dealings with suppliers and customers. While noteworthy, the survey also revealed that in general Mennonite businesspersons in small, related communities did not feel that they were put at a disadvantage because of their inability to pursue claims to the point of litigation. However, this conclusion was challenged in their dealings with insurance companies, which appeared unwilling to pay claims prior to the instigation of a suit.[11]

The second paper, a brief summary regarding the history of Mennonite theological reflection, traced that reflection through Matthew 5, 1 Corinthians 6, and the Schleitheim Confession. Most significantly, the historical paper summarized "the most commonly accepted view" on litigation:

> (1) When the Christian is summoned to court charged with violation of law, he may use the services of an attorney to establish his innocence or to show that the law is in conflict with Christian conscience, as the case may be. (2) In case a civil suit is brought against a Christian by a non-Christian it is not necessarily inconsistent with the principle of nonresistance to defend his case in court by legal means, although every effort should be made in the spirit of love to make a settlement out of court even with an unjust and unchristian plaintiff. (3) It is inconsistent for the Christian to be the aggressive party to any lawsuit, even when legal justice is on his side. (4) Members of the Christian brotherhood may never settle differences among themselves by means of litigation in the civil courts. (5) Purely routine legal actions, such as suits to quiet title to real estate or to clear the records of estates or descendants, or to determine tax responsibilities, so-called friendly suits, are allowable.[12]

The summary report prepared at the end of the conference reaffirmed these five claims. Significantly, "the ministry of reconciliation"—described in 1 Corinthians 5:18-20 and highlighted above in both Hubmaier's and Erb's work—was the central argument for construing Mennonite practice in regard to litigation in the summary report. That report also set forth a series of steps to be taken and goals to be achieved in regard to litigation. These included encouraging the church to continue its stance in regard to a litigation witness and to take up various outstanding issues, such as the use of (1) various quasi-judicial procedures (that is, arbitration, administrative law hearings, etc.), (2) nonadversarial forms of civil litigation (that is, settling of estates and obtaining authoritative interpretations of law), and (3) non-Mennonite insurance programs with subrogation clauses.

Consultation on Litigation Problems (Goshen, Indiana, July 27-28, 1961)

The open issues raised at the Laurelville conference were then taken up by a committee formed to address these questions in the context of Mennonite Automobile Aid, a denominationally established mutual aid society. Mennonite Automobile Aid itself was formed in the context of concerns over litigation, in particular standard subrogation clauses in insurance policies. In light of ongoing litigation issues raised by the work of Mennonite Automobile Aid, the committee organized a conference dedicated to litigation concerns.[13] As in Laurelville, the conference was structured around a series of papers, this time with supplemental responses. Likewise, conference participants again developed a concluding report from their work.[14] It led to the promulgation of a proposed statement for adoption by the Mennonite General Conference in 1965, which was not approved. Nonetheless, the statement's failure led to the formation of the Task Force on Litigation that would draft *The Use of the Law*, addressed below.[15]

At the Goshen conference, the first paper was presented by Samuel S. Wenger, who also presented the third of the Laurelville papers. His paper addressed again the various types of litigation that the conference might consider. Issues such as quasi-judicial bodies and so-called friendly suits were at the forefront of these concerns, although Wenger also expanded on a comment from his Laurelville paper regarding distinguishing litigation involving individual Christians from that involving corporations owned in whole or in part by Christians.[16] Likewise, more detail was provided in regard to problems related to counter-claims, civil divorce proceedings, and support proceedings. A series of supplemental responses by lawyers representing Mennonites and a Mennonite-owned insurance company then raised particular concerns or related anecdotal data on actual Mennonite practice in these areas.

The second and third papers focused on scriptural concerns raised by litigation. The paper prepared by Clayton Beyler began by addressing 1 Corinthians 6, locating this passage in terms of the Old Testament system of dispute resolution and the Torah's prohibition on recourse to secular courts. However, Beyler then turned to the Sermon on the Mount and reconciliation as the key grounds for avoiding litigation: "The lesson which Jesus was trying to make was that there could be no true relations with God as long as there were unreconciled quarrels between brethren."[17] This comment was taken up again and explored in another paper presented at the conference by Carl Kreider. Kreider explicitly set reconciliation as an alternative to Niebuhr's demand for justice, writing, "The function of the Christian in society is not the attaining of justice for himself but the exercise of a 'ministry of reconciliation.'"[18]

This ministry of reconciliation was likewise essential to the argument of John Howard Yoder in his concluding paper, "Possible New Procedures for Use in Areas Where Existing Legal Procedures are not Compatible with Scriptural Principle."[19] Yoder postulated eleven presuppositions regarding litigation, largely in agreement with the Laurelville conference conclusions, the most important of which were

> A. The basic reason for rejection of litigation is nonresistant love for the neighbor, the enemy [not avoidance of scandal or reduction of conflict with government].
> B. The general emphasis of Scripture points in this direction.
> C. Litigation, resting as it does on ultimate appeal to governmental coercion, is (when used in just self-defense) morally the equivalent of the direct appeal to the services of the police. . . .[20] The rejection of self-defense by litigation is therefore a part of the general "other-cheek" attitude. . . .
> G. The Christian is not ultimately committed to any economic system. . . . The issue is not whether we accept the system; Christian [sic] accept whatever system they find in power (Romans 13). The issue is coercive self-defense.
> H. It cannot be assumed that the Christian answer to this problem will be profitable. . . . The rightness of the nonresistant position is not dependent on our finding ways for nonresistance to be made painless.
> I. The recourse to coercion is always a concession to the breakdown

of human relations.... This is the case when men resort to fists; it is also the case when they resort to the courts. Therefore Christians should be imaginatively on the lookout for more effective, prompt, personal and reconciling ways to meet such situations. This, and not making nonresistance painless, I understand to be the concern of the present conference.

J. Christians . . . are not interested only in their own moral problems; they are also inventive in developing social techniques which can be used by the world.... The time should be ripe for Christians to pioneer in procedures of mediation and adjustment which will be more rapid, less wasteful, and no less fair than the courts.

K. The New Testament . . . sees the Christian in the broader context of brotherhood. This relates to our problem in numerous ways:
   (a) The brotherhood is a source of counsel on ethical problems;
   (b) If a loss is involved in the nonresistant resolution of such a conflict the brotherhood can and should help to bear it;
   (c) It makes a difference whether the other party is a Christian. If he is, friendly mediation should always suffice. (1 Cor 6)[21]

With these guiding presuppositions, Yoder summarized the remaining open issues and then took up the imaginative task of considering new methods of addressing and resolving disputes compatible with these presuppositions.

Central to his constructive alternatives was the Mennonite commitment to mutual aid. The believer is never alone, but, like the Quintelas, always finds himself located within the community of believers and taking up the ethical challenges of witness in the context of that community. Accordingly, Yoder repeatedly turned to questions of how the burden of a nonresistant stance in regard to litigation could be borne by congregations or umbrella denominational organizations: "The assumption here is that Christians do not ultimately believe in private ownership. We conform externally to the pattern of society; but all the wealth entrusted to us belongs to God and the brethren. God and the brethren are therefore responsibly involved in how each administers that trust."[22]

In this context, several other alternative suggestions emerged, most importantly the creation of a debt adjustment agency for use by Mennonite businesses in their collection activities. Such an agency, Yoder suggested, could function simultaneously as a collection agency, a bank discount department (buying time payment contracts at a discounted rate), a means of providing mutual aid (through forbearing on collection of debts that were truly unpayable), and a loan consolidation program for those in financial difficulties. Yoder noted that something along these lines had already begun with the development of Mennonite insurance alternatives, such as Mennonite Automobile Aid, which had enabled Mennonites to avoid insurance contracts with subrogation clauses.

Yoder continued to return to this debt adjustment agency idea, despite having been told that it was impractical for Mennonites to create such an agency. In memoranda addressed to "A Few Interested Parties" in 1967 and to "Whom it may concern" in 1984, Yoder again proposed the idea. The impetus to the 1984 memorandum was a visit to a Methodist church at the request of person who headed up just such an agency. Yoder summarized his previous attempts to raise this issue, including the Goshen conference paper, and then noted,

> Last Sunday I was the guest of a Methodist church in Fort Wayne which is undertaking a series of studies on matters of Christian peace witness. The person who contacted me for this assignment turned out to be the administrator of an agency which for twenty years has been doing very successfully in Fort Wayne what Mennonite agency people had told me could not be done.... One kind of meditation that would be possible about this record is to discuss how it is that Mennonites are so embarrassed about their tradition that it is other people who are more creative in seeing how it could be modernized and made relevant than they. Both Mennonite business people and Mennonite service agency people doubt the possibility that living in the modern world is compatible with renunciation of litigation (although something of that commitment does survive elsewhere in Mennonite communities), while others find other ways.[23]

Yoder was at the forefront of the Mennonite challenge to Niebuhr's demand that Christian ethics be effective and realistic. Yet he regularly argued that similarly it ought not be surprising if the ethic of the kingdom "worked" in the here and now. His experience in Fort Wayne appeared to be such an instance.

Returning to his Goshen paper, Yoder raised two large lacunae in regard to litigation and ultimately Christians' relationship to wealth itself. First, the development of large businesses by Mennonites might mean that the stakes of the business in any one claim may reach beyond the means of the community to assist the member through mutual aid.

Likewise, the acquisition of such wealth might render the businessperson independent of need of the church and, thus, independent of the church's counsel. Second, the types of multicongregational structures proposed (which had been established in the insurance context) might lead to the development of independent businesses not wedded to local congregations and the task of witness. Such businesses would not embody faithful witness or genuine mutual aid, but rather would merely market to Mennonite church members.

The Use of the Law (Bowling Green, Ohio, August 13, 1981)

The reflections found in the documents summarized above lay the groundwork for understanding the Mennonite Church General Assembly's statement regarding the relationship of the church to litigation, *The Use of the Law*. As noted above, the failed Mennonite resolution related to the Laurelville conference led to the formation of a task force in 1976, chaired by economist and former Dean of Goshen College, Carl Kreider, to study litigation. *The Use of the Law* was drafted by the task force's secretary, Richard Yordy, and approved by the Mennonite Church's General Assembly in 1981.[24] It is the most important summary of Mennonite theological reflection and practice in regard to litigation.

The document is broken into three main sections: a resume, a summary statement, and a statement of the historical context of the document. The resume forms the summary guidance to the various Mennonite churches, and is reproduced here in full:

> 1. Mennonites understand that commitment to Christ brings them under Christ's lordship and provides resources for living in his way of discipleship, peace, and reconciliation.
> 2. The Scriptures, primarily the New Testament, are the basis for guidance to resolve disputes and questions of justice when believers use their meaning and intent to formulate a response to specific situations.
> 3. Because there is in modern society an increasing dependence on the law for resolving issues, the Christian needs discerning guidance to maintain faithfulness to Christ.
> 4. The role of law is to maintain order and to determine what justice requires in the light of society's values. Christians should uphold the intention of law and honor personal legal obligations and voluntary agreement. They are also committed by the will of God to achieve reconciliation and peacemaking.

5. The congregation, both its local and churchwide resource, should have an active role in discerning appropriate ways for resolving differences.

6. Issues involving church members as well as corporations or institutions in which Christians carry responsibility should not be brought to the courts without the counsel and support of the congregation or other church resource.

7. In seeking to achieve a settlement, the Christian is committed to going the second mile. The Christian should support various alternatives to litigation such as arbitration and meditation.

8. Are there specific occasions when the counsel of the church could be that a Christian may be involved in litigation? Approval can only be for cases that do not share those elements which New Testament examples clearly advise against.[25]

The summary statement that follows fleshes out the essential claims of this resume, in particular explicating the nature of the Christian witness to the kingdom of God, the biblical texts that have informed Mennonite reasoning regarding litigation, the historical stance of the Mennonites in regard to litigation, and the necessary role of the church in discerning with individuals, businesses, and institutions regarding involvement in litigation.

Along with the early Anabaptists and Erb, *The Use of the Law* reiterates that the law is a social good and that it should be followed and consulted in all of its positive structuring aspects.[26] Lawyers may and should be consulted and relied upon alongside the counsel of church members; however, their actions on client's behalf are moral matters and may not be taken by members or their lawyers simply because they are "accepted practices of law."[27] This latter comment is a reiteration of the underlying commitment to a church-world dichotomy first located in the Schleitheim Articles.[28] While the document seeks to open up all uses of the law that do not run afoul of the church's witness, it concludes that even foundational modern institutions, such as litigation, insurance, and the creation of corporate entities, may be outside the scope of activities permissible to Christians.[29]

The document makes clear that Christian ethics is essential to and not separate from the church's witness. Picking up on the ideas summarized in Erb's article, the summary statement suggests that the church's "litigation ethic" is grounded in the church's broader task of witness, "Those walking in the light are called to witness for Christ, often in ways that require suffering wrong. Such meekness and suffering love characterize life in the kingdom and the meaning of the cross in human relationships."[30]

The summary statement also sets forth a series of scriptural provisions and precedents, concluding, "Jesus' teachings are not cast in a legal code. They are striking illustrations of the meaning of his gospel."[31] It is in this light that *The Use of the Law* also summarizes Mennonites' historical practice regarding litigation, noting, "Mennonites have traditionally understood that bringing suit at law is a violation of Christ's call to nonresistant love, peace, and reconciliation."[32]

The most important element of *The Use of the Law* is its emphasis on the necessity of the church as the community in which the individual, business, or institution discerns the appropriateness of any particular proposed course of litigation:

> The teachings of Jesus and the apostles, the nature of Scripture, the complexity of our situation, and the conflict between selfishness and altruism within each Christian combine to create a specific need for the involvement of a Christian community or congregation to interpret and apply the Scriptures and discern the will of God in a given situation."[33]

As such, the conclusion of the document is that "counselors from the church could be involved in considering case by case whether a formal legal proceeding may be warranted or whether the case has qualities that exclude litigation generally in keeping with the New Testament examples."[34] In other words, the church—in its historical memory embodied in the Scriptures, its continued subsistence in the Holy Spirit, and its practical presence in the gathered body of believers—is the primary locus of ethical discernment.[35] Further, discernment is an ongoing task in light of the difficulties in scriptural interpretation and application of those texts in changing situations and the inherent risk of self-deception in the moral life. The church, as a communal moral actor, likewise bears the cost of discipleship collectively. Accordingly, the document returns to the themes traced by Yoder above and suggests the necessity for mutual bearing of costs in regard to forgone or undefended litigation.[36]

In light of this ongoing ethical task, the document does not categorically prohibit litigation in any situation except that of suits between believers.[37] This last conclusion is based on the decision that litigation between believers in the modern context so closely resembles that between believers in the Corinthian context that such situations are not distinguishable despite the distance in time. All other forms of litigation come with a burden of proof against them, with a commitment to going "the second mile" to seek nonlitigious resolution and with an obligation to conduct it under the discernment of the larger congregation.[38]

One area of special interest within the document is litigation on behalf of others for the sake of social justice. *The Use of the Law* permits suits in this context under the following guidance:

> A part of the church's mission of proclaiming "good news" may be to address structural and institutional evil. For some, basic inequities are rooted in economic, social, legal, and religious structures. These structures can be responsible for injustice in the way service is supplied or in the way the law and custom are construed. The poor, the illiterate, the new immigrant, and other oppressed persons are in special jeopardy, because of the difficulty of equal access to some institutions and to the structures of justice. When the church, its agencies, or groups seek justice for a third party within existing structures, or by appealing for necessary changes in law, structure or procedures, litigation may be warranted. Church persons engaged in such mission should have their proposals for litigation on behalf of others monitored by a church resource so that reconciliation and peace concerns are not overlooked.[39]

Such suits in the name of justice are at the heart of the divide, as noted above, between the Niebuhrian school and the older Anabaptist position, which was already being pressed in the 1956 Conference on Nonresistance and Political Responsibility.

This conclusion in favor of some forms of social justice litigation reflects one of the central reconfigurations that was occurring in the 1950s in Mennonite intellectual life around that divide. In the wake of the writings of Anabaptist students of the Niebuhr brothers, such as Gordon Kaufman, and the protest movements of the 1960s and 1970s, Mennonite intellectuals were rethinking traditional Anabaptist views of nonresistance as a passive or *Gelassenheit* stance and moving toward discernment of means of nonviolent resistance.[40] Such movement toward active resistance of the state ultimately reflected a role for the church in speaking to the world, articulated by Yoder in his *The Christian Witness to the State*, as the lordship of Christ in history and so-called "middle axioms."[41]

Middle axioms, according to Yoder, were the church's momentary suggestions regarding how the state might address a specific injustice. Such middle axioms are not the direct application of principles of the kingdom of Christ to the state, however, but only the setting forth of some more-limited goals. These are, nonetheless, informed by the church's knowledge of the kingdom of Christ. Some Mennonite scholars overestimate the impact of middle axioms on the church-world dichotomy, taking Yoder to imply an uncritical overlap between the church and world.[42] While still not proceeding to collapse the church-world dichotomy altogether in the manner of Niebuhr as these scholars would suggest, it is clear that Yoder's lordship language and the middle axioms represent a theological development capable of underwriting a more active engagement in the causes of social justice. In other words, the middle axioms provided the theological resources to justify the church's speaking to the world, including speaking to the world through the courts. These resources were then used in *The Use of the Law* to justify certain forms of civil litigation in pursuit of justice for the other.[43]

Conclusion

It is important to acknowledge what has been shown, what has not been shown, and what I have not attempted to show in this chapter. Throughout this book, I am conducting an imaginative experiment to see the ways in which the text of 1 Corinthians 6 might be embodied and understood in the life of the church more broadly and in its particular Mennonite instantiation. In the previous two chapters, I unearthed where within the Anabaptist and particularly Mennonite tradition the resources for the litigation questions first raised in chapter 2 might be located. A richer set of related and sometimes competing theological resources is thereby emerging: participation in a ministry of reconciliation, maintenance of church-world dualism, and self-sacrificial nonresistance, including not only nonviolence but also noncoercion via power such as the law, are all at stake in participation in litigation.

With this said, one is tempted in a chapter such as this one to suggest uniformity in the Anabaptist position from its inception to today or at least a uniform development toward its position today on these points. Here I must reiterate that this has not been shown, and I have not attempted to show it. Multiple voices with different emphases have been found. Significant gaps between theological claims and practice are also apparent. In fact, a survey of members of five prominent Anabaptist denominations conducted in 1972 and again in 1989 revealed that only a little more than one in three members of these denominations believed a Christian should not bring a suit in a court of law.[44] These findings are important insofar as they suggest both an erosion of traditional Anabaptist praxis and the influence of Niebuhrian voices within the tradition. They demonstrate ongoing and contested discernment within Anabaptist life.

These conclusions are sufficient, nonetheless, because the goal of these last two chapters is the exposition of a developing theological and practical consensus that produces the need, most significantly, to ask the questions posed in chapter 2.[45] The competing positions I located within the early Anabaptists and the diversity of positions taken toward different forms of litigation expressed within the meetings leading up to *The Use of the Law* in many ways reflect the differing social locations and accompanying modes of dispute resolution within which the church has found itself.

This should serve to highlight the difficulty of using the word *litigation* throughout this book. It cannot be assumed at any point that one knows what this word means unreflectively.[46] Further, Yoder argues that the idea that one must develop a position for once and all time in regard to the state—or litigation—itself reflects a Constantinian approach to government. In contrast, Yoder argues, "Why should it be assumed, after all, that the only respectable answers to an ethical question, especially one so complex as 'Should the Christian be a ruler?' must be an unqualified 'yes' or an unqualified 'no,' so that intermediate views are less worthy of recognition?"[47] This is why it is important to emphasize that the heart of *The Use of the Law* is not the conclusion that all litigation is prohibited, but rather the engagement of the church in an ongoing task of trying to determine in what ways do the myriad forms of dispute resolution available in modern America or Canada look analogous to the forms of dispute resolution found problematic in texts such as 1 Corinthians 6.

This acknowledgment should unsettle any idea that there is an Anabaptist "position" regarding litigation. As noted above, in the end, *The Use of the Law* is most properly seen as (1) a gathered set of texts, historical memories, and theological reflections that have been most useful and important to the tradition in discerning regarding Christians' participation in civil modes of dispute resolution and (2) some preliminary suggestions on how churches might reason about those matters that will, nonetheless, require those churches themselves to continue discerning in any particular case.

The only place that the Anabaptist witness suggests that a once-and-for-all answer regarding litigation in the secular context is appropriate is the case of church member versus church member. Here, this action directly conflicts with the gospel witness of reconciliation that Paul articulates is at stake in 1 Corinthians 6. Nonetheless, even here, discernment within churches regarding what constitutes a nonreconciling mode of dispute resolution between believers is required. The article by Erb makes clear that certain forms of what might look like contested litigation may still be appropriate.

9

The Practice of Reconciliation

The inquiry in this book has been largely historical. The project has sought to deepen the church's memory and highlight one particular tradition's insights regarding participation in litigation. In tracing an exegetical and theological history of the treatment of 1 Corinthians 6, I have hoped to bring the obscure but radical Anabaptist witness into the forefront of the church's memory. The work has been fruitful, revealing twin emphases in the church's stance toward litigation: (1) defining the critical distance between the church and the wider world and (2) naming two essential features of that distance: Christian nonresistance and the creation of the church as a reconciled body in a world of enmity. In concluding, an explicitly theological construction of these arguments is appropriate. Accordingly, in this chapter I consider again church-world dualism, nonresistance, and the role of reconciliation in the body of Christ. This work leads to an explicit treatment of discipline and discernment in the life of the church.

In arguing for the necessity for the church to be a reconciling and disciplining body, I am following John Howard Yoder's suggestion that the practices of 1 Corinthians 6 and Matthew 18 (that is, those of discipline and discernment) are essential to the church's ability to be the church. In other words, the church is incapable of witnessing to the resurrection and reign of Jesus Christ while participating in many forms of modern litigation. Accordingly, I begin this chapter, not with litigation, but with an explication of Yoder's argument regarding the nature of the church. In many ways, I have presupposed throughout this book the authority of the Anabaptist witness (as construed by Yoder), not just as to litigation but also in its broader construal of ecclesiology. In this chapter, I make evident the assumptions embodied in that choice. With that ecclesiology in place, I display the connections between this account of the church and Anabaptist practice in regard to litigation, dispute resolution, and discipline.

It is appropriate to reiterate that the deck has been stacked for the Anabaptists. Any retelling of the church's history is guided by a present set of concerns—likely, as in this case, by a sense of the proper ecclesiology toward which one is hoping to push the church. I can imagine no other kind of storyteller than one who tells a story for a purpose, however muted the presentation of one's agenda may be. The most one can do is be clear about those agendas so that dialogue around the choices made can be forthright. This chapter is most directed toward that task insofar as it makes evident my ecclesiological assumptions.[1]

Finally, it is important to remember the goal of the history-telling that has preceded these chapters. I am not suggesting that the early church or the sixteenth-century Anabaptists "got it right" and that all the church must do is return to this earlier moment. It is neither appropriate nor possible to ignore the church's changing social location or developments within church doctrine. As Yoder notes, often history is told for the purpose of mid-course correction, of looking back to inform the church's going forward.[2] A return to Corinth or Zurich could not adequately embody what the church has learned in the story I have told.

Ethics as Witness

The directive to the nascent church in the Luke-Acts narrative is simple: "You will be my witnesses in Jerusalem, in all Judea and Samaria, and to the ends of the earth" (Acts 1:8). Anticipating still the establishment of Christ's earthly kingdom, the first disciples query, "Is this the time when you will restore the kingdom to Israel?" (verse 6). Jesus ignores the question. Importantly for the post-Christendom church—which often still believes that the church is called to make history turn out right—Jesus says nothing about the church's role in establishing the kingdom. Instead he says that the timing of the kingdom is not the church's business. Working with the Spirit, the church will have one task: witness to the Christ by witnessing to the shape of the kingdom inaugurated in his life, death, and resurrection. This is the church's task in the world. Stated most succinctly: the church is the community of people both located in and called out of the world for the purpose of making known that the life, death, and resurrection of Jesus Christ is the eschatological destiny of the world.

Yoder argues that the church lives out this witness by living now in the manner of that coming eschatological kingdom itself.[3] In other words, the church makes evident that the mode of being in the world evidenced in the life of Christ is the true nature of reality by living—through the Spirit—in the radically open manner that Christ's life itself revealed. As such, the church is an eschatological forerunner (see 1 Cor 15:20-28). It lives in and under the old age, yet while already living in the manner of the new age to come.[4] The church prepares for the full instantiation of the new kingdom by living in a manner befitting that kingdom now and, in so doing, serves as a witness to the wider world of the nature of that coming kingdom.[5] In Yoder's words, "The church is . . . 'first fruits': i.e. it is or is to be in itself the beginning of what is to come. . . . The church does communicate to the world what God plans to do, because it shows that God is beginning to do it."[6]

In light of this view of witness, there is no clear line of demarcation where Christian theology ends and ethics begin.[7] Rather, Christian ethics is the ongoing practice in which the church gathers to discern in light of its memory—as embodied in Scripture and history—can it participate in a particular aspect of the wider culture (for example, litigation) and still intelligibly tell the story of Christ and his kingdom. I will have more to say about the shape of the church's ethical discernment at the end of this chapter, but for now the question for the church can be construed as something like this: can the church witness to the coming kingdom of Christ—which is marked by self-sacrificial nonresistance and reconciliation—in the midst of participation in secular litigation?[8]

Outlining the connection between ethics and theology suggests how much is at stake in the church's nonresistant stance. The church testifies to the manner in which the world works by eschewing violence and living in a reconciled manner now. Acting alone, the church would fail in this task. Yet, in the midst of a still sinful world, the church adopts the alternative politics set forth in 1 Corinthians 6 and Matthew 18—not because the church is that good but because its hope is that great. And in living in the manner of the cross now, the church declares that the cross and resurrection more truthfully narrate the world than any history of secular power and violence.[9]

Therefore, in direct challenge to the Niebuhrian ethic discussed in the previous chapter, Yoder argues that church must eschew effectiveness—at least in the short-term—as the standard for judging Christian action. Effectiveness is subordinate to eschatology:

> The key to the obedience of God's people is not their effectiveness but their patience. The triumph of the right is assured not by the might that comes to the aid of the right, which is of course the justification of the use of violence and the other kinds of

power in every human conflict; the triumph of the right, although it is assured, is sure because of the power of the resurrection and not because of any calculation of causes and effects, nor because of the inherently greater strength of the good guys. The relationship between the obedience of God's people and the triumph of God's cause is not a relationship of cause and effect but one of cross and resurrection.[10]

This connection between the logic of the cross and the church's witness has direct application to Christians in dispute. To live out the logic of cross is to see those disputes anew. As displayed in *The Use of the Law*, the proper focus for nonviolence is not the maintenance of a "passive" stance, but the active achievement of reconciliation. The manner in which disputes are resolved within and without the church is at the heart of the gospel witness. And the communal skills of discipline and discernment are the practices necessary to producing a peaceable people in a world of violence and conflict.[11]

The Reconciling Body

Because the church's praxis is its witness, we learn that much is at stake in the church's politics. In Yoder's seminal work, *The Politics of Jesus*, he patiently details the essentially political nature of Jesus' life, death, and resurrection. Jesus' life was characterized by a radically new mode of power in the world—articulated in the Sermon on the Mount and displayed in Christ's ministry and paradigmatically on the cross:

> Here at the cross is the man who loves his enemies, the man whose righteousness is greater than that of the Pharisees, who being rich became poor, who gives his robe to those who took his cloak, who prays for those who despitefully use him. The cross is not a detour or a hurdle on the way to the kingdom, nor is it even the way to the kingdom; it is the kingdom come.[12]

Yoder's conclusion is simple yet radical in light of the church's accommodation to Constantinian power structures since the fourth century: the cross is the central moment in the establishment of God's kingdom. This form of self-sacrificial power is the shape of the coming kingdom—the new reality to which the church must witness. Noting the dual meaning of martyr—to bear testimony and innocent suffering[13]—Yoder concludes, "Only at one point, only on one subject—but then consistently, universally—is Jesus our example: in his cross."[14]

Understanding the centrality of the cross to the politics of Jesus goes a long way in properly orienting the church's politics. Yet the meaning of the cross is misconstrued if it is limited to the renunciation of violence. Christ does more than simply fail to destroy his enemies. The cross is the offering of himself in lieu of all other forms of power. Thus Yoder broadens the scope of nonviolence to include noncoercion:

> What Jesus renounced is not first of all violence, but rather the compulsiveness of purpose that leads the strong to violate the dignity of others. The point is not that one can attain all of one's legitimate ends without using violent means. It is rather that our readiness to renounce our legitimate ends whenever they cannot be attained by legitimate means itself constitutes our participation in the triumphant suffering of the Lamb.[15]

Forgoing the coercion of the civil law, therefore, is but a further extension of the renunciation of violence. This claim is borne out by Christ's words (Sermon on the Mount) and Paul's guidance in 1 Corinthian 6.[16]

Yet connecting the cross to the renunciation of violence and coercion still does not tell the entire story. Christ's work on the cross is not merely an act of self-sacrifice, for many forms of self-sacrifice are wholly destructive of both the self and community. Christ's sacrifice is power-full. It is followed by resurrection. Christ's sacrifice makes possible reconciliation in a world of enmity.[17] And, despite a modern construal of Christ's work that would limit this reconciliation to the individual and God, the power of reconciliation makes possible reconciliation between humans and, beyond that, within the wider creation.

Embodying this reconciling work is what it means to be the church—a community that would break through all cultural and racial barriers.[18] The resurrection ushers in the reconciliation of "the Jew-Gentile barrier" as well as the barriers of "slavery, gender, and class."[19] One's initiation into this world is via baptism, the process by which a new society is created, "whose newness and togetherness explicitly relativize prior stratifications and classifications."[20] The church cannot witness to the life and death of Christ—and the kingdom inaugurated in that movement—if it only offers self-sacrifice without that sacrifice ushering in the power of reconciliation. In Yoder's words, "If reconciliation between peoples and cultures is not happening, the Gospel's truth is not being confirmed in that place."[21]

Whose Justice

The last section makes clear that the renunciation of self-interest and the violence and coercion necessary to sustain that interest is not passively allowing oneself to be taken advantage of, but is a call to new forms of power in the midst of deep disagreement. In Yoder's words, "Suffering creates shalom."[22] As such, the church's dispute resolution model is radically demanding because reconciliation and justice themselves are remade in light of the gospel.[23] Reconciliation as the church's form of justice is much more than the justice of law, a claim highlighted by Yoder's former colleague at the University of Notre Dame, Tom Shaffer. Shaffer (writing with Andrew McThenia) denies that "law and justice are synonymous" or that justice is "something people get from the government."[24] Instead, expositing Plato's *Republic*, he concludes, "Justice is not the will of the stronger; it is not efficiency in government; it is not the reduction of violence: Justice is what we discover—you and I, Socrates said—when we walk together, listen together, and even love one another, in our curiosity about what justice is and where justice comes from."[25] In other words, justice is a gift that one offers the other.

Thus, justice is not an "issue" for the church, but a matter of identity, which must be embodied.[26] It is offered as a gift to another via a process of mutual dialogue in which justice is discovered—instead of being handed down from government authorities or courts. As Oliver O'Donovan notes, Old Testament justice was not "a state of affairs that obtains but an activity that is duly carried out."[27] Reiterating this theme, Shaffer argues that the justice of the Jews "implies a reluctance to invoke fear—to invoke what Paul calls the power and dominion."[28] Justice understood in this light cannot be the justice of the civil courts, suggesting to Shaffer that "the reluctance to resort to fear suggests the Jewish and Christian admonitions not to go to court for the solution of disputes."[29] These accounts of Jewish understandings of justice present essential challenges to the justice of American law, which is grounded not in mutual dialogue, but in appeal to the mutual threat of the violence of the nation-state as embodied in the court.

This more demanding process of justice can ultimately be successful only insofar as the parties are able to restore a shared narrative of their lives together. In this regard, reconciliation is dependent on forgiveness, for forgiveness is necessary for truthful speech—particularly in the light of wrongs so horrific that they can never be undone.[30] Peace is therefore not simply the absence of violence. Any true peace must be a truthful one.[31] And forgiveness names the possibility that harms can be truthfully acknowledged and overcome.[32]

In contrast to this view is the shock that neophytes to American tort law face in the crass valuation of harms by the courts. The civil law, lacking the practice of forgiveness, attempts to return injured parties to the preexistent status quo. But the price of innocence lost in rape or children without parents in cases of intentional negligence cannot be given a value. The law quantifies but all involved must look away from the reality. The actuary cannot do justice to the harm suffered. Only in forgiveness, which acknowledges that there is no way to undo what has been done, is there hope that, in the power of the cross, communion may, nonetheless, be restored.[33]

The church's model for embodying justice is then the life of Christ itself, which therefore must be prior to any so-called "natural" knowledge of justice. As Chris Huebner notes, for Yoder "the only place you can start is with the life, death, and resurrection of Jesus, which you can *then* call justice."[34] Or, in Yoder's words:

> The Spirit of God . . . enables a justice of grace. We pray to be forgiven as we forgive others. That one phrase of the Lord's prayer . . . would upset the entire correctional system of our societies. God's justice, as we are told in John's first epistle, is at work in his forgiving our sins. Since the cross, "punishing" sins is revealed to be not justice but vengeance.[35]

These last comments make clear that the church's alternative forms of dispute resolution are not giving up on effectively pursuing one's interests, but rather a reconfiguration of one's understanding of their best interests in light of the new reality revealed in Christ:

> To follow Jesus does not mean renouncing effectiveness. . . . It means that in Jesus we have a clue to which kinds of causation, which kinds of community-building, which kinds of conflict management, go with the grain of the cosmos, of which we know, as Caesar does not, that Jesus is both the Word (the inner logic of things) and the Lord ("sitting at the right hand").[36]

The renunciation of litigation is not the renunciation of effectiveness measured with the grain of the universe.[37] Thus justice as remade in light of the gospel reveals that the basic modern economic models grounded in scarcity and competition are inadequate presentations of the reality.[38] In pursuing Christian justice, the either/or (that is, I win or you win) of modern justice is entirely circumvented. As Daniel Bell argues,

The sacrifice of Christ, and hence of those who would follow him, does not belong to an economy that forces one to decide between self and neighbor, with a decision for one necessarily entailing a loss of the other. On the contrary, Christ's sacrifice opens an economic space where the divine plenitude spills over with the result that that sacrifice becomes gain (Luke 9:24) and we can give ourselves as a gift of love to our neighbors without end and without loss. (Matt 22:39; Mark 12:31)[39]

In summary, the church's practices of self-sacrifice, reconciliation, and forgiveness are part and parcel of its eschatological witness. These are the practices that make possible a peaceable people capable of witnessing to the truth of the cross and resurrection.[40] Therefore, reconciliation is a prerequisite to worship.[41]

Church-World: The Dualism

If the church is to be a witness to the world, as argued above, it first must not be identical with the world. The church must live—as the Diaspora community of Israel—as both residents and aliens in the city of man.[42] As a people in but not of the world, the church must maintain unique practices, institutions, and languages in the face of the totalizing discourses of the wider public within which it finds itself. Yoder has extensively argued that this is not a "withdrawal" strategy.[43] The church's gift to the wider community is its difference by which it truthfully locates the world and offers it a salvific alternative.[44] For both the church's and the world's sake, the dualism between the church and the world must remain.[45]

What is the character of this dualism? Church and world name fundamental stances toward the lordship of Christ. The church is that part of creation that acknowledges the lordship of Christ. The world is that part of creation that remains in rebellion against the lordship of Christ.[46] The collapse of this dualism was the fundamental Constantinian error.[47] With this said, this dualism does not prevent the church from speaking to the world, which even in its rebellion, remains subject to the "already" reign of Christ.[48]

As noted in chapter 3, Paul's concern over the dissolution of the church-world dichotomy resulting from Christians' participation in civil litigation is part of the context of 1 Corinthians 6. Litigation, like violence, undermines the ability of the church to be the unique reconciled people of God. Therefore, the church must have a different set of practices to resolve disputes. As Oliver O'Donovan notes regarding the church's historical practices,

> Church judgment would be of an altogether different kind from what went on in the secular courts. The community was not in the business to divide the guilty from the innocent, taking vengeance on the one and vindicating the other. . . . The sole purpose of the church court was to make the implications of God's judgement clear, by reconciling the contending Christians in a common understanding of God's right.[49]

Yoder, along the lines of the exegesis set forth in chapter 3, concurs that 1 Corinthians 6 is at its heart a political text. In contrast to Calvin, who read 1 Corinthians 6 in light of Romans 13, Yoder reads Romans 13 in light of 1 Corinthians 6:

> The church is herself a society. . . . Paul testifies to a sort of social self-sufficiency and at the same time gives us a pointed commentary on the teaching of Romans 13, when in 1 Corinthians 6 he directs Christians to have their own judicial processes within the church, and to accept innocent suffering rather than to submit their disputes to the governmental tribunals, variously designated as "unrighteous," "those who are least esteemed by the church," and "unbelievers."[50]

First Corinthians 6 names the distance between the church and wider world. This distance is made evident by returning again to the goal of Christian dispute resolution as compared to that of modern legal practices. Modern courts in a liberal society are not places in which shared community truths are articulated and brought to bear on litigants who share commensurate accounts of the good. Rather, courts are the Enlightenment's last hedge against the chaos that might result from the destruction of those shared goods that was the result of the Enlightenment project. In Alasdair MacIntyre's influential account of that project, the goal of the Enlightenment—the production of a common ethic, absent agreement on contested and particular histories, practices, and institutions—has failed.[51] The moral congruence promised by David Hume, Immanuel Kant, or John Stuart Mill did not emerge. Instead, moral pluralism and the reduction of moral discourse to the assertion of personal preference claims has resulted.[52]

While the Enlightenment project issued in wars of the nation-state on a massive scale, insofar as it has sustained a peace, it has done so through the rise of the so-called "rule of law" in the midst of a disintegrating moral consensus. Yet justice in this context must work without resort to any substantive shared account of the good.[53] Accordingly, modern law is something very different from classical accounts of justice. Its most influential form, the discourse of "rights," is necessitated by the discontinuity of shared life forms of the people who make up any given modern nation-state.[54] According to Bell, one can trace these changes in both secular and religious accounts of justice:

> The story of the emergence of justice in the modern social teaching of the Catholic Church is the story of the adaptation of the Thomistic conception of justice to a different way of life, namely in modern liberal societies. It is the story of the gradual and subtle move away from justice as the principle of a community's solidarity and a robust sense of the common good, to justice as a fundamentally distributive force that secures rights in societies distinguished by the absence of anything but the thinnest of conceptions of the common good.[55]

Justice has been reduced, therefore, to procedure controlled by modern clergy—lawyers.[56]

Noting this fact should make clear that modern law is something different from Torah. Torah was the application of shared commitments about not only how to get along, but also the nature of God, humanity, and creation.[57] Torah was equally institution, practice, and separate language. It was community-defining and world-narrating.[58] For this reason, the application of Torah need not necessarily be coercive, because Torah is for human's freedom, that is, for the liberation of bondage to sin,[59] and because the violator of Torah freely acknowledges its authority.

MacIntyre suggests similarly that in the Aristotelian and medieval context, both law and morals were embedded within a shared narrative that was foundational for accounts of both morality and justice. It is in this context that MacIntyre understands the disagreement between Henry II and Thomas Becket, which led Henry to impose a form of penance on himself for his martyring of Becket.[60] MacIntyre notes the manner in which the discourse of forgiveness similarly relies upon the establishment of a shared narrative between the parties to a dispute:

> What is the condition of forgiveness? It requires that the offender already accepts as just the verdict of the law upon his action and behaves as one who acknowledges the justice of the appropriate punishment; hence the common root of "penance" and "punishment." The offender can then be forgiven, if the person offended against so wills. The practice of forgiveness presupposes the prac-

tices of justice, but there is this crucial difference. Justice is characteristically administered by a judge, an impersonal authority representing the whole community; but forgiveness can only be extended by the offended party.[61]

In so arguing, MacIntyre reiterates the distinctive nature of Christian justice as a gift expressed in repentance and forgiveness. Likewise, he displays why reconciliation is essentially different from modern justice, which is grounded in the incommensurability of any shared account of the good.[62]

In this regard, H. Jefferson Powell is correct in arguing that the American constitutional system has been remarkable, exactly because it has been successful in sustaining a society without any more substantial text to share than that of the Constitution.[63] As MacIntyre notes in regard to one particular piece of constitutional reasoning,

> If my argument is correct, one function of the Supreme Court must be to keep the peace between rival social groups adhering to rival and incompatible principles of justice by displaying a fairness which consists in even-handedness in its adjudications. So the Supreme Court in Bakke both forbade precise ethnic quotas for admission to colleges and university, but allowed discrimination in favor of previously deprived minority groups. Try to conjure up a set of consistent principles behind such a decision and ingenuity may or may not allow you to find the court not guilty of formal inconsistency. But even to make such an attempt is to miss the point. The Supreme Court in Bakke, as on occasion in other cases, played the role of a peacemaking or truce-keeping body by negotiating its way through an impasse of conflict, not by invoking our shared moral first principles. For our society as a whole has none. . . . Modern politics is civil war carried on by other means, and Bakke was an engagement whose antecedents were at Gettysburg and Shiloh.[64]

In the face of the incommensurability of these accounts of justice, it is constitutional law, and the American fixation on the rule of law, that protects the nation-state from degenerating into the violence into which Thomas Hobbes predicted a society without the Leviathan would collapse.[65] In this light, it should not be surprising that Christians' willingness to absent themselves from civil litigation structures—and in doing so deny that those structure are necessary to produce peace—is threatening to the society at large.

Christians acknowledge this good work of the law without feeling the necessity to participate in the project of the law or worrying about the threat they may pose to the rule of law.[66] In this regard, the Anabaptist witness appropriately suggests that Christians are not against the law and will follow it in its structuring principles,[67] yet, likewise, see that it is merely a way forward in the midst of irreconcilable differences.[68] It provides a form of closure to disputes—a real good—but often cannot provide a shared narrative substantial enough to bring the parties back into communion. Americans obey the law only because it is backed with the force of the nation-state and its violence. God's law, on the other hand, is obeyed because it is the law in which the church finds its life.

The Shape of Christian Dispute Resolution

What is the praxis that can then usher in reconciliation? Each of the practices of the church, such as baptism or eucharist, is directed toward training a people capable of being reconciled with creation, one another, and God, but in these concluding sections I focus in particular on Christian dispute resolution and decision making.[69] As argued in chapter 3, the context of 1 Corinthians 6 suggests that some form of Christian arbitration is what the Corinthian church would have understood Paul to be suggesting. The model Yoder suggests for this process is the one Christ offers in Matthew 18.[70] Going so far as to argue that the practice of discipline (that is, binding and loosing) set forth there is what it means to be the church itself, Yoder notes that Christ's use of the term ecclesia is always linked to this task.[71]

The text of Matthew 18 is much more familiar than 1 Corinthian 6, but is still worth restating here:

> "If another member of the church sins against you, go and point out the fault when the two of you are alone. If the member listens to you, you have regained that one. But if you are not listened to, take one or two others along with you, so that every word may be confirmed by the evidence of two or three witnesses. If the member refuses to listen to them, tell it to the church; and if the offender refuses to listen even to the church, let such a one be to you as a Gentile and a tax collector. Truly I tell you, whatever you bind on earth will be bound in heaven, and whatever you loose on earth will be loosed in heaven." (Matt 18:15-18)

I consider Yoder's suggestions regarding both the process and implications of Matthew 18 in this section, beginning with the radical claim that what Christians bind and loose on earth is bound and loosed in heaven.[72]

Yoder argues that binding and loosing has a two-fold meaning: (1) "Forgiveness: to 'bind' is to withhold fellowship, to 'loose' is to forgive" and (2) "Moral discernment: To 'bind' is to enjoin, to forbid or make obligatory; to 'loose' is to leave free, to permit."[73] I deal with the second meaning in the following section. I begin here with the first, which is most directly related to the resolution of disputes within the church. The critical features of binding and loosing are summarized by Yoder in the following sentence: "A transcendent moral ratification is claimed for the decisions made in the conversation of two or three or more, in a context of forgiveness and in the juridical form of listening to several witness."[74] The church, empowered by the Holy Spirit, speaks for God in the manner in which Christ himself claimed a similar authority.[75]

The goal of the Matthew 18 process is reconciliation of the brother and sister in Christ.[76] The radical challenge of the Christian dispute resolution is made material in the procedural commitment to the process set forth in Matthew 18. That process is personal. The distance of legal counselors and courts cannot achieve the goal of reconciliation. This protects against legalism in the process. The context is a "commitment to forgive."[77] In this regard, Yoder explicitly notes the connection between discipline and 1 Corinthians 6.[78]

Because of the essential connection between forgiveness and reconciliation, it is worth reiterating that forgiveness is both the ground of possibility and the goal of the process of Matthew 18. Forgiveness is the essential feature of the church's reconciliation because sin can only lead to the destruction of relationship with God and others in the absence of forgiveness. As noted already, forgiveness names the possibility of truthful speech and memory. As such, the context of forgiveness is radically beyond anything that the secular courts might offer.

With the outlines of the practice of binding and loosing in place, one caveat of most importance in light of the distinctions I have drawn between Torah and American civil law must be noted: binding and loosing is not punishment, at least as understood by Western societies.[79] It is meant literally to win the brother or sister for Christ. The process of church discipline is voluntary.[80] It is grounded in the baptized believer's own acknowledgment of the church's authority over her and is backed by only the power of exclusion from the church. Such exclusion, in a non-Constantinian context, is only meaningful insofar as the believer still voluntarily acknowledges the church's authority over her life. As such, the "discipline" of the church looks very different from the "discipline" of the state.[81]

Discipline is an evangelical act even when it leads to excommunication or the institution of the ban. As Yoder notes, "When the congregation's 'binding and loosing' is the implementation of the commonly covenanted commitment to a manner of life dictated by grace, then to leave the brother alone in his sin is not love at all but irresponsibility."[82] The most important evangelical gift that the church offers the world is the proper description that it is the world. The institution of church discipline works similarly. Baptism marks the entry of a person into the kingdom of Christ from the world. The ban marks the church's evangelical announcement that the person has forsaken the kingdom of Christ and returned to the world. The church does not exclude the member, but discerns the former member's location in relationship to the kingdom.[83] Yoder notes,

> This concentration upon the procedure of reconciliation means that ultimately no individual would be cut off from the Christian fellowship because of the specific nature of the offense he committed. . . . The real issue at stake is never the particular sinful deeds but rather the attitude of rebellion against the divine law and separation from fellowship of disciples, which is at stake.[84]

Excommunication names the reality of the situation. Discipline is an evangelical offer to return by letting the former member know that in denying the authority of the church to discipline him, he himself has made known his withdrawal from the kingdom of Christ. The church simply makes that withdrawal public and material.[85]

Dialogical Discernment

Matthew 18 offers the process for more than just the resolution of disputes, however, for it also defines the process of the church's dialogical discernment. It is the unique rationality of the church that enables it to negotiate its participation in the world while maintaining the critical distance necessary to not becoming the world. In this section, I consider how it is in Yoder's second meaning of "binding and loosing" that the church's mode of dispute resolution is also its mode of discernment. Yoder claims that Matthew 18 is the church's process for practical moral reasoning:

It is too little to see in this process an instrument of pastoral care for the individual, though it is that. It is at the same time the mode whereby the community's standards are clarified and, if need be, modified.... The ongoing rabbinic process of binding and loosing creates a deposit of precedent and principles known as halakah, the "walk" or the "way," the moral tradition.[86]

As alluded to earlier, Yoder notes that Matthew 16:19 and Matthew 18, when Christ grants Peter or the disciples respectively the power to bind and loose, "are the only places where [Jesus] used the word *ecclesia*, which we translate 'church.'"[87] More importantly, Yoder locates the church's epistemological priority over the world in the practices of community discernment.[88] The hermeneutical key to the Bible is as read in the faithful community of the church. This leads Yoder to note, "If the claim is that the words of God are most adequately understood in the listening congregation, this obliges us to make very strong and specific statements about our actual congregational activity."[89] The specific shape of this activity is the Matthew 18 process:

> The most concise statement of the Anabaptists' program of reformation, and perhaps the most radical definition of the Church ever stated in one sentence, was Conrad Grebel's appeal to Thomas Muntzer: "Go forward with the Word and establish a Christian church with the help of Christ and his rule, as we find it instituted in Matthew 18:15-18 and applied in the Epistles."[90]

Or, following Hans Denck, "No man can know Christ unless he follows after him in life."[91]

The connection between discipline and discernment demands that two further connections be articulated: (1) that between discernment and conflict and (2) that between discernment and maintenance of the distinction between the church and the world. There is a necessary link between Christians in dispute and Christian discernment, because conflict is the sign of a healthy community. Yoder notes,

> To be human is to have differences; to be human wholesomely is to process those differences, not by building up conflicting power claims but by reconciling dialogue. Conflict is socially useful; it forces us to attend to new data from new perspectives. It is useful in interpersonal process; by processing conflict, one learns skills, awareness, trust, and hope.[92]

Disputes are socially beneficial. They are the crucible in which contemporary languages and practices are assessed in light of competing readings of the church's scriptural and historical witness—as articulated by actual disputants within the church. As such, the existence of disputes, of the other, is not to be feared but welcomed as the difference without which the church cannot be the church.[93] As Romand Coles notes, for Yoder "nonviolence 'is thereby an epistemology,'"[94] which is to say it leaves the church vulnerable to a process for producing new knowledge.

It is for this reason that nonviolence is the essence of the gospel alternative. The process of dialogical discernment is the alternative to the silence of violence. Affirming this claim, Stanley Hauerwas notes that Yoder taught him and the wider Christian community that "careful argument is an alternative to violence."[95] Violence is the rejection of difficult conversation with the other in favor of the ease of silencing alternative voices. Further, Yoder contrasts this hard work of dialogue with the mere getting by that modern pluralism offers: "The lazy solution of pluralism reinforces the false view that unity is based on agreement, so that every dispute calls for division. As a matter of fact, disagreement calls not for dividing but for reconciling people."[96] But careful argument is costly, requiring a variety of dialogical virtues, most critically patience. Yet, through this time-consuming process of dialogue, the church learns to live in the midst of conflict without resort to violence and on the way toward reconciliation.

In this regard, John Paul Lederach, a Mennonite who has worked extensively in the area of mediation, argues against the use of the term "conflict resolution" as an appropriate model for Christian forms of peacemaking. Instead, he argues for "conflict transformation." In doing so, he also suggests that conflict is a social good: "[Transformation] encompasses a view that legitimizes conflict as an agent of change in relationships."[97] What this again suggests is something much more than liberalism's goal of merely maintaining the absence of violence in a world of difference, which is the goal of the courts and, according to Lederach, much of the mainstream mediation movement. The church's practice of reconciliation is grounded in a commitment to difference, without which the church fails to be itself. As I suggest below, this means that the church must therefore encourage conflict, for it is the process by which individuals and communities are remade.

Why must the church discern though? The necessity of discernment is founded in Yoder's anti-Constantinian account of history. Unlike the worst forms of Constantinianism, which locate God's work in the continuous progression of the "winners" in the movement of history, Yoder demands that the church discern the path of history. In other words, a discerning church must distinguish the work of Christ and the work of the world in the equivocal movement of history. In Yoder's words:

> Instead of asking, "What is God doing in the world?" the church should ask, "How can we distinguish, in the midst of all the things that are going on in the world, where and how God is at work?" The answer to this question will not be found by reading on the surface of daily history but by the Spirit-guided understanding of the discerning community.[98]

All that is is not of God. Yet this discerning process—like the reading of Scripture—cannot be done well alone. Rather, it is done most effectively when done practically through the presentation of competing and conflicting readings of history brought into dialogue within the body of Christ.[99]

As with discipline, the quality of this discernment is ensured by the process and the roles it calls forth—instead of through the application of moral "rules." Yoder suggests a variety of such necessary "roles" without arguing that his list is exhaustive. The roles Yoder identifies include (1) Agents of Direction (that is, prophets), whose "primary focus is neither prediction nor moral guidance," but "stat[ing] and reenforc[ing] a vision of the place of the believing community in history, which vision locates moral reasoning."[100] (2) Agents of Memory (that is, scribes), who "remember expertly, charismatically the store of memorable, identity-confirming acts of faithfulness praised and of failure repented,"[101] (3) Agents of Linguistic Self-Consciousness, who "will watch for the sophomoric temptation of verbal distinctions without substantial necessity, and of purely verbal solutions to substantial problems,"[102] and (4) Agents of Order and Due Process, who ensure "that everyone is heard, and that the conclusions reached are genuinely consensual."[103] I would add one more in light of the fact that conflict is socially productive: Agents of Dispute. Such Agents of Dispute bring competing imaginative readings of the tradition into conflict. Because conflicts produce practical non-theoretical discernment, the value of those within the community who are willing to push the boundaries and produce new and imaginative readings—alongside those who resist such readings—to the "way we have done it to now" must be affirmed. Both are agents of necessity to the church.[104]

Christian Ethics as the Task of a Disciplining and Discerning Church

In chapter 1, I argued that the project of this book reconfigures standard accounts of legal ethics insofar as it challenges the assumption that litigation ethics are for lawyers only (versus clients), may only address tactics (versus the appropriateness of suit itself), and must be written for the generic lawyer, without any further specification such as Christian, Muslim, humanist, etc. I conclude by expanding on these claims and noting the manner in which the church's ethic (set forth above) contrasts with standard assumptions regarding not only legal ethics but all of modern ethics.[105] In so doing, the goal is to display that the church's ethical practice, embodied in the Matthew 18 process, is a challenge to modern accounts of ethics and the self. The church's ethic reorients modern ethics by changing the choices and questions that ethical theories are supposed to choose by denying the following apparent dualisms: (1) consequentialism/situationalism versus deontology and (2) individualism versus communitarianism. In addition, it rejects the church's own apparent dualism of justification by faith versus works righteousness.

Weak occasionalism. The determinative question one is supposed to answer in modern ethics is that between Immanuel Kant and John Stuart Mill, between moral absolutes unfailing regardless of situation or consequences, or an ad hoc morality changing with each particular moment guided by utility in Mill's formulation or love in Joseph Fletcher's twentieth-century reformulation of situationalism.[106] Only one meaningful addition to this offering of ethical choices has been made in the past one hundred years, that of emotivism.[107] The heirs of Henry Sidgwick's and G. E. Moore's intuitionism, in light of the failure of the Enlightenment project to produce a promised common moral discourse, have argued for the radical particularity and unreasonableness of all moral claims.[108] Emotivists see only divergent preferences in moral statements—I like Pepsi, so do you. Nonetheless, emotivism produces the same ethical conclusion of Kant and Mill: autonomy is the essential moral obligation owed to the other.[109] In light of the irrationality of all such claims, individuals should be free to do as they choose.

Yet, in contrast to the entirely ad hoc and momentary nature of ethical claims as found in Mill, Fletcher, and the emotivists, or the unchanging ethical absolutes of Kant, Yoder labels the ethical practice of Matthew 18 "weak occasionalism." As Yoder describes it,

> We properly want to affirm a weak occasionalism, which insists on the insufficiency of all our memory, and on the limits to the

number of decisional constants which can be carried into one context from others, so that it is very clear that ongoing discernment of the church must be seen as God's own work and not simply our replicating or transposing what God did before.[110]

Such a weak occasionalism is grounded in the belief that God might have yet more truth to speak in and through the church.[111] The best example of this type of discernment is Acts 15, in which the church addressed a new situation guided by its historical memory and concluded, "It seemed good to us and the Holy Spirit."[112]

As noted above, the process is marked by dialogical reasoning, that is, it is an ongoing activity for addressing new situations in the light of new claims about both the meaning of the church's historical tradition and the context within which the church now finds itself. Thus, like consequentialism and situationalism, the decision is addressed to the moment. Nonetheless, the process is not open-ended assertion of preference statements. Rather, it is guided by the church's memory, as made available in the Scriptures, the liturgy, and the church's history. These resources are not undefined in the manner of Mill's utility or Fletcher's love. They bind the church. Yet the process of discernment makes clear that competing readings and accounts of the canonicity of parts of the church's memory are always open to contestation. Further, contrary to emotivism, this dialogical process produces a binding and generalizability decision for the church at large—to be obeyed by the entire church, not just those who so prefer. Yet the process does not foreclose revisiting the question to determine again if it is to be affirmed.[113]

What should become evident is—in contrast to modern ethics—no ethical "theory" is offered at all.[114] There is in fact no "Christian ethic" for lawyers or litigants, but rather a set of histories and discourses shared by Christians who find themselves lawyers or in dispute and have attempted to discern if and how one can do that faithfully in a host of different and new contexts grouped under the family resemblance, "law."[115] The processes of discipline and discernment form the guidelines of a practice through which to read the world and act. It is this feature of the church's ethic that makes it both open and binding. It commits the church, not to a closed theoretical system that can hypothetically answer every ethical dilemma abstracted from time and place, but rather to a set of practices and a group of people skilled in moving forward in their lives together.[116] This praxis is open, for it knows not the times and places in which the church must discern nor the faithfulness and skill of its participants.

Particularly in regard to the latter issue, the church relies on faith that its memory and resources will be sufficient when the time comes.

Neither individualism nor communalism. If the determinative choice of modern ethics is between Kant and Mill, the determinative commonality of modern ethics is the assumption that the individual is the level at which to construe this choice, ethics, and identity itself.[117] Individuals are to be autonomous choosers and are to grant other individuals similar rights. This mantra is the centerpiece of the Enlightenment and is reemphasized by emotivists. Yet, in the light of the failures of the Enlightenment project to produce a common ethic upon which all humans would agree, it has become clear to some communitarians that the social group is prior to the individual. In fact, the community in the strongest communitarian visions is perhaps entirely determinative of the identity of the individual. This is again a hard choice that modern ethical and political discourse offers: autonomous choice as a "free chooser"—that is, one who has no good reason for his decisions at all—or deep moral identity within closed communities—that is, the loss of the unique self.

Yet, for the church, this dualism must be rejected. As Eastern Orthodox Metropolitan John Zizioulas argues, reconciliation is itself the church's graciously being taken up into the life of God, who is one God—Father, Son, and Holy Spirit. Accordingly, Zizioulas challenges any construal of the "other" and "difference" as a threat to the possibility of unity. He argues instead, "If the church wants to be faithful to her true self, she must try to mirror the communion and otherness that exists in the Triune God."[118] Zizioulas then locates the meaning of eucharist in this reconciling event and argues that where reconciliation fails the church fails. Thus, to accept that the church faces a choice between individualism and communalism is to deny the reality of the trinitarian life of God, in whom individuality and community coexist. The church's conclusions at Nicea and Constantinople demand an alternative trinitarian logic.

The process of discipline and discernment delivers this third alternative. The process is not communalism, because it is grounded in the individual's voluntary choice to join the community of the faithful and submit to the church's discipline. It demands that the individual's voice be spoken courageously in the community and that the community engage that voice as essentially worthy to be heard. As Yoder suggests, "The alternative to arbitrary individualism is not established authority but an authority in which the individual participates and to which he or she consents."[119] With this said, the church seeks and demands a real unity, not just of abstract belief, but also of ethical praxis. The lone individual is anathema to the trinitarian and gospel vision. The body cannot be the body without unity of thought and action. Accordingly, discipline is necessary to ensure that unity.[120]

The Matthew 18 process is the practical rejection of both individualism and autonomy. Yoder notes, "None of these practices makes the individual the pivot of change. . . . No trust is placed in the individual's changed insights (as liberalism does) or on the believer's changed insides (as does pietism) to change the world. The fulcrum for change and the forum for decision is the moral independence of the believing community as social body."[121] The necessity of discipline makes clear that the action of the one affects the wider body.[122] Christians form a corporate body as a church that is together progressing toward or away from the kingdom. As noted in chapter 3, Richard Hays emphasizes that 1 Corinthians 6 must be read in light of and alongside Paul's chastisement of the Corinthian church for failing to discipline a member who was openly sinning (1 Cor 5). First Corinthians 5 and 6 are to be read together as an argument for the corporate nature of the body in Corinth.[123] Yoder argues similarly on both exegetical and theological grounds that Matthew 18 is mistranslated when the phrase "against thee" is added, suggesting that the sins of other church members are only relevant to the immediately affected. Rather, he argues that the church is to deal with sin in its midst regardless of whether that sin is particularly against any one member. Sins not committed directly "against thee," nonetheless, affect the entire body.[124]

In making ethics a communal project, the church acknowledges that sin is not only about open rebellion with God, but more subtly leads to self-deception about one's own supposed "good intentions." Fraternal admonition is required because sin persists in the church and the wider world.[125] What is perhaps most striking about Augustine's description of human identity in his *Confessions* is that even after Augustine's conversion, that conversion remains radically unstable in light of the possibility that he may still be self-deceived.[126] And by its very nature, self-deception cannot be overcome alone. One's only hope in the face of self-deception is that friends will see within one's life that which one simply cannot know alone. To reiterate the claim made throughout this chapter, the Bible and the stories of the church can only be read and retold in a diverse community, which can help one read and retell those stories with eyes other than one's own.[127]

The implications of the problem of self-deception are yet broader, however, for not only must Christian ethics be communal in light of self-deception, but rationality itself can only be enacted communally. In this regard, Alasdair MacIntyre argues that human's reasoning capabilities are always communal:

> Rational enquiry is essentially social and, like other types of social activity, it is directed towards its own specific goals, it depends for its success on the virtues of those who engage in it, and it requires relationships and evaluative commitments of a particular kind.[128]

Similarly, Christian rationality, at least since Acts 15, has been determinatively social.[129] Therefore, Christian reasoning depends on how virtuously one's friends live. This suggestion might entail that salvation itself is not an individual project, but rather turns on the faithfulness of the church.[130] My salvation cannot be separated from the lives and bodies, from the discipline and discernment, of those with whom I form the church.

Neither justification nor sanctification. The practice of church discipline makes evident that sanctification cannot be separated from justification. Having taken up Luther's justification by faith alone and Freidrich Schleiermacher's emphasis on religious experience apart from the broader context of both of these theologians work, many of the churches in America are essentially Gnostic in their approach to salvation.[131] Or, stated differently, bodies cannot be separated from belief. The best evidence of this is that salvation has been reduced to intellectual assent to proposition—and such propositions, it is suggested, are understandable apart from participation in the practices of the church. This construal of Christianity relegates religion to the private and individual sphere of belief in lieu of the public and communal life of an embodied alternative political community. This realm of private belief is the extent to which American religious liberty extends. And, thus, American religion fits nicely within the box created for it by liberal political theory.[132]

Yet the practice of discipline makes evident that intellectual assent alone is not the gospel. The church in its essence is embodied and makes demands on bodies. Discipline identifies the public nature of bodies. As William Cavenaugh notes, discipline "is essentially control over the body."[133] David Yeago concurs by noting that the failure to discipline is ultimately the failure to witness to the body's participation in salvation, both individually and corporately.[134] Accordingly, the loss of the body is intimately connected with the church's acceptance of modern accounts of freedom as disengagement and notions of identity as primarily the "inner world of the disengaged self."[135]

The admonition in James to sanctified action is not works righteousness, therefore, but points to the inseparability of sanctification from justification—and the inseparability of body from mind, soul, or spirit. Justification that does not produce an alternative ethic is misunderstood, in fact is merely the simulacrum of justification. The demand of the Zurich Anabaptists, that the church be a disciplined community, is merely the demand that the book of James be taken on its face. Justification in the New Testament is about the establishment of God's kingdom on earth.[136] If the church is to participate in this justification, then discipline must be exercised. The public and embodied nature of the church as a community with a stake in each other's bodies must be made clear.

The implications of this view are not only soteriological, however, but (or but also) epistemological. This is the essence of Hans Denck's suggestion, noted above, that "no man can know Christ unless he follows him in life."[137] Harry Huebner elaborates on this point: "[I]t is the faithful church community which makes it possible for us to understand the world around us and to do the will of God within that world. . . . Jesus meant it when he said that the key to the knowledge of God is entering into God's dramatic story in Christ."[138] What Huebner implies is that formation and action, likewise, precede knowledge. In Huebner's words, "What one knows and how one lives cannot be separated."[139] Right vision is broken by the power of sin within the body. Thus the Christian answer to sin, the virtues, cannot be limited only to spiritual, intellectual, or moral. As Joel Shuman argues through reading Aquinas, habituation in the Christian virtues "forms us 'all the way down'—at the level of the body, the will, and the intellect."[140] Lives formed in the cross and embedded within the liturgical memory and practices of the church are the ground for truthful speech about the world. Only such lives can know who it is whom they worship and the meaning of the resurrection. Whatever justification means, it must mean at least this, and accordingly the discipline of the body is essential.

10

Conclusion

The challenge throughout this book, and especially in concluding, has been resisting the desire for black-and-white answers to the problems that face Christians living in-between the times. If one agrees that it has been a grievous mistake on the part of the majority of the church to simply ignore the difficult texts in the biblical witness, like Paul's word to the Corinthians regarding litigation, then it is tempting, for both writer and reader, to lay down a categorical prohibition at every turn: Christians litigating is in error in every case. Unfortunately, as I have argued throughout this book, this approach fails to do justice to the complexity of the cosmos and the shape of Christian ethics.

Discerning the World

Christians are faced with a myriad of options for resolving disputes. Mediation has become popular enough in the private sphere to become a formal, court-ordered program in many instances. However, as a lawyer I have been involved in mediations of the court-order variety that have had no relation to the goal of reconciliation. Mediation merely served as a venue for further exacerbation of the conflict and embitterment of the parties, who had no intent to reach settlement, let alone to reconcile. Binding arbitration is now popular with corporations attempting to reduce their litigation costs. Arbitrations also have their limits; they are perceived by many to be biased toward the corporations who engage in them regularly, working with the same arbitrators in many cases. And, of course, litigation remains rampant in our culture.

However, while much more rare, litigation in the mode described by Paul Erb in chapter 8 is likewise not unheard of. Friendly suits to quiet title to unclear boundary lines do occur. Family law cases can be places in which parties seek for a common good in distributing assets and arranging for the care of children, even in the midst of the failure of divorce. In these instances, the courts serve an ordering purpose for the good. They facilitate closure to disputes that may lead to renewed or at least civil relations. As noted throughout this book, it is important to emphasize that it is better that there are courts of law than not. Even if Christians must often forgo the use of courts, it is not an indictment of the courts but the call of the church that is at stake. Particularly in a pluralist nation such as America, it is better than not to have courts and constitutions. They hold a nation together—not as a people with a shared vision, but potentially at least as a fragmented nation not at war within itself. As such, not all parties are Christians in every suit, and resolution within church structures in such instances is much harder to envision.

The complexity of the alternatives for resolving disputes is not the only reason to preclude easy answers, however. The shape of the world has also changed in regard to the basic structures through which most transactions occur. Corporations now dominate our lives. They are the mediators of most of our day-to-day interactions with other human beings. In so doing, they often shield us from accountability to those with whom we share our lives. Like the soldier following orders, the corporate employee is just following policy. And, thus local economies involve flows of funds back and forth through the great corporations and Wall Street.

As such, we are much less likely to find ourselves in dispute with our neighbor. More likely, it is the insurance company, the multimedia provider, or the cell phone company with whom we feud. When one cannot navigate through a phone system to even speak to a human being, let alone the same human being one spoke with the last time, how are Paul's words to be applied to suits against the corporate-owned hospital or the multinational polluter? Suit may be the only way to gain the corporation's attention. Of course, as noted in chapter 4, the funds involved to sue are themselves prohibitive; and thus, the suit is brought on our behalf by the law firm seeking the contingency fee as the lead firm in the class-action suit. In summary, how does the gospel apply when the notice arrives in the mail that you are a potential party to a class action you did not instigate against a corporation headquartered in another country and owned by shareholders who both claim and deny Christ? We have an idea of what counts as reconciliation between individuals. But how does one seek reconciliation with a multinational corporation? Such are the complexities of the current moment.

I provide no absolute answers to these questions—most fundamentally because words get up and walk around on us. In other words, we must seek to understand what we mean by "litigation" when Paul instructs the Corinthians that participation in litigation fails to serve the church's task in the world. As outlined throughout this book, Christians must continue to ask and answer this question in the context of the church: what does "litigation" look like today. What sorts of dispute structures serve to divide the body and destroy the church's ability to witness to the power of reconciliation in a world of enmity? Or, stated in the positive, what sorts of dispute structures serve to reestablish the communion of human with human that is made possible through the cross of Christ? Where reconciliation is happening, the church celebrates it, names it as the power of the cross, and participates in it. We cannot rule out in advance the possibility that mediation might divide or that civil-court adjudication might serve to reconcile. Likewise, suits against corporations might bring us into human communion simply by demanding that some human being take responsibility for the actions of these conglomerates on which we are both dependent and parasitic. However, these questions cannot be asked and answered in the abstract. Rather, they must be asked and answered in the practical and the particular moment of any given proposed course of action. This is the task before the church.

That task might be well served by an inquiry into the shape and character of the myriad forms of dispute resolution structures available today. However, that has not been the task of this book. While it may be disappointing to conclude without the clarity of an answer to "what I should I do in my particular case?" I presumed to start where I found the church. One need not analyze the shape of any given dispute-resolution structure until one is convinced that the manner in which Christians resolve disputes is relevant to the task of discipleship. It has been my assumption that Christians today first must be convinced that the question of dispute resolution matters.

Here I argue that the clarion call is clear—the means by which Christians resolve disputes is at the very heart of the church's witness to the gospel. The resurrection names the power of the cross to produce reconciliation in a world of violence and enmity. It marks the beginning of the restoration of the kingdom of God, in which the reconciliation of God to human, human to human, and human to creation is restored. Here the question is answered without caveat: the manner in which Christians resolve disputes is essential to the church's call to be a witness to the kingdom of God.

The Church as a Reconciling and Discerning Body

In the previous chapter, I sought an answer to the question—does dispute resolution matter to Christian discipleship? In answering that question, I offered a no to "litigation," whatever the church discerns that to mean. Likewise, I offered a yes to the church as a reconciling and discerning body. In other words, in the Matthew 18 process, the church is given a model through which to resolve disputes in a manner that will produce reconciliation. Yet further, in that process, the church discovers the practices necessary to the task of discernment made necessary by the very fact that words like *litigation* get up and walk around on us. Easy answers are not available, put the process by which Christians act as counselors to one another in discernment is found in the process through which Christians are called to resolve their disputes. Thus in the Matthew 18 process the church discovers that the process of resolving disputes—and disputes themselves—are essential to the church's life.

Perhaps surprisingly, then, conflict in churches is a good thing. It initiates the process by which the church discerns together the path of God in the wider cosmos. One of the most important reasons not to give answers is that no answer I could provide could possibly match the creative power of the community's arguments about such matters. It is precisely that power that leads John Paul Lederach to insist on speaking of conflict transformation. In contrast, it seems that often the church—failing to see the value of conflict—has damned itself to niceness. Getting along at church has been valued in lieu of the difficult and potentially transformative work of conflict. Like a marriage in which spouses no longer care enough to fight, this getting along by ignoring the differences that divide us is not the reconciliation of the cross. In fact, it is one step further removed from achieving reconciliation than Christians in open dispute, perhaps even Christians in dispute in the courts. In this regard, one conclusion that Christians should reach in light of these arguments is that healthy churches embrace conflict. Churches must engage in the messy work of discerning together—which is the work of arguing together—what is the church's call in the world.

What has been set forth in this book is a set of resources for that discernment. As suggested above, the church's discernment regarding litigation will require an understanding of the structures that the broader culture offers for resolving disputes. This work must continue and has not been the primary task of this book. Likewise, however, the church's discernment regarding litigation will require an understanding of the church's historical memory in regard to this question. In making the argument that dispute resolution matters to the gospel, I have outlined what I consider the critical histories necessary to the church's discernment going forward. Each chapter has sought to expand the church's memory by not only highlighting the concern for Christian participation in litigation—which has marked every era of the church's life up until now—but also the theological connections supporting that concern. Within these histories the church's discernment today must be grounded, as it seeks to understand any particular option to resolve disputes and then find imaginative analogies and disanalogies with these histories and theological concerns.

A Hopeful Story

In light of my resistance to offering absolute rules regarding litigation, some may be tempted to read this conclusion as tentative and therefore easing the burden of the radical nature of 1 Corinthians 6. Such readers will breathe a sigh of relief when they read that there are here no absolute prohibitions on litigation. Yet properly understood, the call to be a discerning and reconciling church is far more radical than a simple categorical avoidance of the courts. Only a history of bad habits in the church's approach to ethics and a lack of experience with churches capable of discernment lead us to think otherwise. That much should be clear from the story of the Quintelas, with which this book began. The conclusion of the dispute described there was litigation that led to settlement prior to trial. However, the point of the story was not to claim that this resolution was consistent or inconsistent with 1 Corinthians 6 or the broader biblical witness. Rather, the story displays, in the life of this family and its church, the kind of concern for the questions regarding litigation and the type of discernment within the wider church body that I have argued for throughout this book. In the Quintelas' story is found a people that understands that the resolution of disputes and the emergence of reconciliation within and without the church is at the heart of the gospel. In their story is found a church that understands that as the body of Christ, it must stand with and discern with Christians in the midst of disputes.

In the Quintelas' story is found a process that seeks after resonances of the resurrection and the reconciliation it inaugurates. The resolution of that dispute—Christians moving within a neighborhood, suing, and settling as they come to see God working elsewhere in their lives—may be less than the hope of the resurrection. Nonetheless, there was a profound witness to the watching world of the gospel's hope for reconciliation and the process through which Christians seek that reconciliation. As such, it served the church by serving its essential task to witness to the coming kingdom in the here and now.

The process displayed was remarkable. Two Christians, one a lawyer, in the face of great conflict and with ample legal claims to be pursued sought another path. In the name of the gospel of reconciliation, they persevered in seeking the peace of the city and the peace of the neighborhood block. They understood that such action was not their witness; it was the task of the church. And so, they invited—or better put, demanded—that the church be all that the Bible claims it to be. And one Mennonite church in the heart of Minneapolis began to learn to be the body of Christ. They bore the burden of the Quintelas's witness together as they prayed and stood with them in the midst of violence and conflict. They discerned with them as to the proper path for seeking peace and reconciliation. That discernment led to a lawsuit, settled short of trial. What drove a watching world to ask why was the process itself. A people called "church" lived other than "world"—in seeking reconciliation and in taking responsibility for one another's lives. In doing so, they offered a glimpse to that world of what the cross might mean.

A Realistic Ethic

In concluding, I must address a final concern: the beleaguered and broken state of the church. I rely heavily on the church as a discerning and reconciliation body. In this regard, the situation looks grim. The church has for the most part lost the ability to be an authoritative and discerning community. While gay marriage and abortion get wide condemnation in conservative churches in America, promiscuity, divorce, and greed remain the norm in most churches, virtues in some. The sins of the majority are not to be spoken of publicly, let alone disciplined. David Yeago's assessment of the situation is similar:

> The disappearance of corporate discipline is more than the abandonment of ancient custom now grown uncouth; it marks the point at which a whole array of fears and confusions and wayward cultural codes conspire to alienate us from the faith and mission of the apostolic church. This alienation is deep enough that it must seriously call into question the capacity of mainline churches, as presently constituted, to represent the reign of the crucified and risen Christ before the world. Nor is their any prospect for immediate reform.[1]

For the church to take up the tasks given it does not look realistic. I acknowledge that the church itself is both divided and broken in a host of ways. Reworking the church's litigation practice will require skills and resources I have not addressed here. Nonetheless, this concern, though relevant, is not determinative. These concerns are the life of the church. As John Howard Yoder poignantly reminds us, "If the church is not in an emergency where her life and obedience are daily fully dependent on the wonder-working grace of God, she is no longer the church. . . . Since Adam and Eve left the garden human existence has been by definition an emergency."[2] My suggestion is that the church is in such an emergency, but as Faith Mennonite Church of Minneapolis shows, not a hopeless one. In forgotten and unreported corners, the grace of God continues to sustain a people willing to be called out of the world into a resurrection community.

A people capable of witnessing to the power of the resurrection must offer the world an alternative it rarely sees: reconciliation in the midst of difference and violence. In so doing, the church rejects that the courts are the best that people can do in resolving disputes. More than an end to open hostilities is demanded, and the church claims within its body and the practices of Matthew 18 the resources to heal broken relationships. That reconciliation is sometimes unrealistic in the world in which the church lives—broken and shattered by sin that divides—is true. But if it is the God of Nicea and Constantinople that the church rightly worships, unity can emerge even in the midst of difference. If Christ's body has been resurrected, it is not unrealistic to hope that the body of the church could be a reconciled one.

The church must look to this emergency (as with others) with the vision that Yoder offered to the drafters of *The Use of the Law*:

> When we move to recognizing the increasing complexity of our society it should be with confidence that also in this new society we can be faithful, rather than selling out to the mood of many of our younger urbanized people which is that complexity is ground for unfaithfulness. It is this difference in tone which I find it hard to express. Do we look at the greater complexity as a challenge, in the confidence that we can meet it and be faithful? Or do we look at is as self-evident refutation of the applicability of the old ways?[3]

What has been offered here is an attempt to make new those old ways of resolving disputes even in the light of the complexity of the present moment.

Notes

Chapter 1
Litigation as Theological and Ethical Topic

1. John Howard Yoder, "Possible New Procedures for Use in Areas Where Existing Legal Procedures are not Compatible with Scriptural Principle" (paper presented at Mennonite General Conference, Peace Problems Committee Consultation on Litigation Problems, Goshen, Ind., 27-28 July 1961), Harold and Wilma Good Library, Goshen College, Goshen, Ind., 37.

2. John Howard Yoder, *The Politics of Jesus: Vicit Agnus Noster*, 2d ed. (Grand Rapids: Eerdmans, 1994), 237.

3. See generally Richard Hays, *First Corinthians* (Louisville, Ky.: John Knox Press, 1997).

4. Ephesians 2 suggests that the reconciliation of Jew and Gentile is possible in the blood of Christ and that that reconciliation is the building of the new temple itself. See Ephesians 2:11-22.

5. Lynn Buzzard and Laurence Eck cite a representative study that concluded that in one "medium-size metropolitan area" an estimated eight thousand lawsuits per year involved persons on both sides who claimed Christianity. See *Tell It to the Church* (Elgin, Ill.: David C. Cook, 1982), 25.

6. See "Archbishop warns of bankruptcy," *Associated Press State and Local Wire*, 18 June 2003.

7. See Calvin Sims, "Boston Archdiocese is Sued by San Bernardino Diocese," *New York Times*, 3 April 2003, Late ed., National Desk, A14 (reporting on cross-claim filed by the Archdiocese of San Bernardino against the Archdiocese of Boston regarding the actions of Rev. Paul R. Shanley, who was transferred from Boston to San Bernadino with a letter of good standing from Boston officials); "Indiana Franciscan order sues LA archdiocese," *Associated Press State and Local Wire*, 7 April 2003 (reporting on cross-claim filed by the Province of Our Lady of Consolation Covenantual Franciscan Friars (Mt. St. Francis, Ind.) against the Archdiocese of Los Angeles regarding the actions of a friar on loan to the archdiocese during the period in which alleged abuse against an altar boy occurred). The Archdiocese of San Bernardino dropped its suit in light of the appointment of

a new Archbishop in Boston. See Eric Convey, "California diocese will drop lawsuit over Shanley," *Boston Herald*, 5 July 2003, News 9.

8. Michael Fisher, "Decision to sue troubles bishop," *Press Enterprise* (Riverside, Calif.), 7 May 2003, B1. Likewise, Patrick Shiltz, dean of the St. Thomas Law School and a former attorney for various Catholic dioceses, said, "The bishop of San Bernardino has a duty to the people of San Bernardino to shift the burden to the other diocese." Wendy Davis, "Diocese's suit seen as first of trend," *Boston Globe*, 3 April 2003, B3.

9. By *catholic* I mean all churches that claim Christ as Lord and the Scriptures as in some manner the authoritative reference point for understanding that lordship. For an introduction to the "church" and the "world" as those concepts are used in my argument, as well as the possibilities and limits of catholic theology, see Michael G. Cartwright, "Radical Reform, Radical Catholicity: John Howard Yoder's Vision of the Faithful Church," in John Howard Yoder, *The Royal Priesthood: Essays Ecclesiological and Ecumenical*, ed. Michael G. Cartwright (Scottdale, Pa.: Herald Press, 1998).

10. Canon 1395 provides as follows: "Section 1. Outside the case mentioned in can. 1394, a cleric who lives in concubinage or a cleric who remains in another external sin against the sixth commandment of the Decalogue which produces scandal is to be punished with suspension; and if such a cleric persists in such an offense after having been admonished, other penalties can be added gradually including dismissal from the clerical state. Section 2. If the cleric has otherwise committed an offense against the sixth commandment of the Decalogue with force or threats or publicly or with a minor below the age of sixteen, the cleric is to be punished with just penalties, including dismissal from the clerical state if the case warrants it." Catholic Church, *Code of Canon Law*, Latin-English ed., trans. Canon Law Society of America (Washington, D.C.: Canon Law Society of America, 1983), canon 1395. The Catholic Church has generally seen the sixth commandment as entailing not just adultery but all sexual sins.

11. See, for example, Thomas Shaffer, with Mary Shaffer, *American Lawyers and Their Communities: Ethics in the Legal Profession* (Notre Dame, Ind.: University of Notre Dame Press, 1991); *American Legal Ethics: Texts, Readings, and Discussion Topics* (New York: M. Bender, 1985); *On Being a Christian and a Lawyer: Law for the Innocent* (Provo, Utah: Brigham Young University Press, 1981).

12. See generally such journals as *Mediation Quarterly*, *Arbitration Journal*, and a host of others.

13. See generally Alasdair MacIntyre, *Whose Justice, Which Rationality* (Notre Dame, Ind.: University of Notre Dame Press, 1988) and *After Virtue: A Study in Moral Theory*, 2d ed. (Notre Dame, Ind.: University of Notre Dame Press, 1984).

14. Thomas Shaffer's work is an important exception to this argument. Shaffer sought a common ground for a general legal ethic, but argued that even if a common legal ethic could be sustained in the practices and institutions of the law, as it perhaps was in the Gentleman's Ethic of Atticus Finch, for Christians legal practices and institutions cannot be more determinative of their identity than the practices of the church. See generally Shaffer, *On Being a Christian and a Lawyer* (Provo, Utah: Brigham Young University Press, 1981).

15. Each of these assumptions could be located in a variety of a standard legal ethics. For example, in Charles Fried's "The Lawyer as Friend," *Yale Law Journal* 85 (1976): 1060-89, Fried responds to challenges from utilitarians (1) as to why the one client's good should be valued by the lawyer over the wider society's good and (2) as to the means by which this particular client's good should be sought. See ibid., 1062-63. Fried argues along Kantian and Rawlsian lines that everyone would agree that all should be permitted to pursue their own interests and that of particular others they have selected. See ibid., 1070. In so arguing, he reiterates the absolute priority of the individual and his autonomy in the moral life. The lawyer, as "special-purpose friend" to the individual, "adopts your interests as his own." Ibid., 1071. Accordingly, Fried suggests that the lawyer must take up the client's interests as her own in an almost entirely uncritical manner, drawing limits on the lawyer's advocacy only at the line of the lawyer's autonomy, the autonomy of other clients, illegal activity, or activity that thwarts the autonomy of the client's adversary.

These assumptions can likewise be seen in the dominant practical legal ethics, the American Bar Association's *Model Rules of Professional Conduct*, which serves as the model for most of the state bars' rules of professional conduct. Like Fried, the *Model Rules* assume that lawyers are the primary moral actors in litigation. While the *Model Rules* do prohibit the filing of "frivolous suits," the bulk of rule 3, dealing with litigation, addresses the conduct of that litigation, not the appropriateness of litigation in the first place. Finally, the Model Rules assume any more particular description of their ethic, such as Christian, Muslim, or feminist, is not necessary. See American Bar Association, *Model Rules of Professional Conduct*, 1983 as modified, http://www.abanet.org/cpr/mrpc/mrpc_toc.html, 1 February 2005.

16. See, e.g., Stanley Hauerwas and Charles Pinches, "Practicing Patient: How Christians Should Be Sick," in *The Hauerwas Reader*, ed. John Berkman and Michael Cartwright (Durham, N.C.: Duke University Press, 2001), 348-66.

17. See John Howard Yoder, "To Serve Our God and To Rule the World," in *The Royal Priesthood, Essays Ecclesiological and Ecumenical*, ed. Michael G. Cartwright (Scottdale, Pa.: Herald Press, 1998), 139-40.

18. In these chapters, I attempt to work along the lines of those set

forth in John Howard Yoder's *The Politics of Jesus*, reporting on the state of scholarship regarding 1 Corinthians in the service of a broader theological argument. See Yoder, *The Politics of Jesus*, vii.

19. See, e.g. Matthew 5 (discussed below); Matthew 7 (judge not lest you be judged); Matthew 18 (steps for confronting the brother or sister/forgive seventy-seven times); Matthew 26–27 (the trial of Jesus); Acts 15 (the Council at Jerusalem); Romans 12-15 (marks of the new life in Christ/submission to authorities); 1 Corinthians 1, 3, and 5 (division/sin in the Corinthian church); 2 Corinthians 5 (discussed above); Galatians 6 (restore the transgressor with gentleness); Philippians 4 (exhortation to Euodia and Syntyche to reconcile their differences); Colossians 3 (bear with one another and forgive each other's complaints); 1 Timothy 5 (procedure for disciplining elders); James 4 (do not judge others); and Jude (judgment on sinners in the midst). This list is developed along the lines of that suggested by Raymond W. Beaver and Ronald S. Kraybill in their short book *Resolving Conflicts in the Churches* (Madras, India: Christian Literature Society, 1983).

20. Matthew 5:21-26, 38-42 ("You have heard that it was said to those of ancient times, 'You shall not murder'; and 'whoever murders shall be liable to judgment.' But I say to you that if you are angry with a brother or sister, you will be liable to judgment; and if you insult a brother or sister, you will be liable to the council; and if you say, 'You fool.' you will be liable to the hell of fire. So when you are offering your gift at the altar, if you remember that your brother or sister has something against you, leave your gift there before the altar and go; first be reconciled to your brother or sister, and then come and offer your gift. Come to terms quickly with your accuser while you are on the way to court with him, or your accuser may hand you over to the judge, and the judge to the guard, and you will be thrown into prison. Truly I tell you, you will never get out until you have paid the last penny. . . . 'You have heard that it was said, 'An eye for an eye and a tooth for a tooth.' But I say to you, Do not resist an evildoer. But if anyone strikes you on the right cheek, turn the other also; and if anyone wants to sue you and take your coat, give your cloak as well; and if anyone forces you to go one mile, go also the second mile. Give to everyone who begs from you, and do not refuse anyone who wants to borrow from you").

21. See discussion above.

22. As will be set forth in detail in chapter 3, the "state," like "litigation," is too abstract to do meaningful theological work. Accordingly, there is not one appropriate stance toward the "state," but a variety of stances that the church must consider in light of the particular outworking of civil authority with which it is attempting to negotiate a faithful relationship.

23. See generally Mennonite General Assembly, *The Use of the Law: Resume, Summary Statement and Context of this Statement* (1981),

http://www.mhsc.ca/index.asp?content=http://www.mhsc.ca/encylclopedia/contents/U78.html, 7 February 2005.

24. David Yeago notes, "One could write a full-fledged history of the modern transmutation of Christianity from the perspective of this theme, as the story of how the very idea of public discipline of common life gradually became unthinkable in those western churches that most fully exposed themselves to modernity." David S. Yeago, "The Office of the Keys: On the Disappearance of Discipline in Protestant Modernity," in *Marks of the Body of Christ*, ed. Carl E. Bratten and Robert W. Jenson (Grand Rapids: Eerdmans, 1999), 106.

25. Of course, this claim itself is ultimately contested as well. While an important project, it is not the project of this book to defend the possibility of discourse across denominations and even religions.

26. Joel Shuman has written on this topic in the context of medical ethics. Relying on the work of John Zizioulas, "Communion and Otherness," *Sobornost: The Journal of the Fellowship of St. Alban and St. Sergius* 16 (1994): 7-19, Shuman argues in regard to the church's practical moral reasoning, "Hence the body's diversity is crucial to its morality, which requires for its sustenance voices of prophecy, memory, and practical wisdom, as well as particularly strong examples of faithfulness to the community's ideal." Joel James Shuman, *The Body of Compassion: Ethics, Medicine, and the Church* (Boulder, Colo.: Westview Press, 1999), 111. My suggestion is that the Mennonite witness in regard to litigation is such a particularly strong example of faithfulness to the community's ideal.

27. Yoder's own response to the suggestion in *The Use of the Law* that Mennonites share their decisions regarding litigating with others in the church is telling: "I welcome very much sections VI-VIII with the strong attention to the resources of the church. This may very well be unrealistic for the present but that is simply because we have not kept the vision alive." John Howard Yoder, Elkhart, Indiana, to Richard Yordy, St. Jacobs, Ontario, 6 August 1980, Carl J. Kreider Collection, Hist. Mss. 2/5, entitled "Litigation, 1976-81," Mennonite Church USA Archives, Goshen, Indiana.

Chapter 2
A Hopeful Story

1. Robert Kreider and Rachel Waltner Goossen, *When Good People Quarrel: Studies in Conflict Resolution* (Scottdale, Pa.: Herald Press, 1989), 15.

2. Ron Kraybill writes in the foreword, "This book is significant because it begins with the assumption that conflict is a part of life. . . . The starting point of effectiveness in conflict is accepting that it is normal." See ibid., 11.

3. Ibid.

4. Ibid., 12.

5. See generally Stanley Hauerwas, "Vision, Stories, and Character" and "A Story Formed Community: Reflections on Watership Down," in *The Hauerwas Reader*, ed. John Berkman and Michael Cartwright (Durham, N.C.: Duke University Press, 2001), 165-70, 171-99.

6. Kreider and Goossen, *When Good People Quarrel*, 12-13. One would assume that Kraybill has Yoder's important essay, "The Original Revolution," in mind here. See John Howard Yoder, "The Original Revolution," in *The Original Revolution: Essays on Christian Pacifism* (Scottdale, Pa.: Herald Press, 1977), 13-33.

7. One might similarly tell the story of how majors like "peace studies" and institutions such as Mennonite Conciliation Service emerge in displaying the manner in which 1 Corinthians 6 is embodied by a people. Mennonite Conciliation Service, a project of Mennonite Central Committee, was formed around the time of the drafting of *The Use of the Law*, discussed in chapter 8. Its work is the practical exemplification of the hopes embodied in the document. The same Mennonite general assembly that approved *The Use of the Law* noted, "The Task Force on Litigation has recommended the increased use of mediation, arbitration, and other less adversarial ways to resolve disputes. In addition, the report of the Joint Study Committee on Justice and the Christian Witness has urged the church to develop skills in conflict resolution and suggests that the extent to which the church models methods of reconciliation will be one test of our witness in the world. One vehicle for implementing this concern has been initiated by the Mennonite Central Committee through the establishment of the Mennonite Conciliation Service for the promotion and training of conflict resolution skills." Mennonite Church General Assembly, *Proceedings: Sixth Mennonite Church General Assembly, August 11-16, 1981, Bowling Green State University, Bowling Green, Ohio* (Lombard, Ill.: Mennonite Church General Assembly, 1981), 9. Accordingly, Action 12 of the delegates concluded, "We hereby . . . commend MCC for sponsoring this program [Mennonite Conciliation Service] and urge MCC to provide resources for enlarging this ministry throughout its entire constituency." Ibid.

Perhaps the most important of the institutional responses to litigation, however, was the formation of Mennonite Automobile Aid. It was formed in the context of concerns over subrogation clauses in standard insurance contracts. Founding board member Harold Swartzendruber relates the following incident in his unpublished autobiography as a foundational example behind the necessity for Mennonite Automobile Aid: "It seems a Mennonite was driving down the road in his automobile with children in the back seat of the car. As he attempted to stop his children from their misbehaving he lost control of the car and veered into the ditch, hitting a sign advertising fresh produce in front of a farm. There was damage to the car. His insurance company paid promptly and he thought all was well. But soon after, he saw in the newspaper that there was a court case whereby he was suing the farm owner for damages. This could not be, because he was the deacon, and the farm owner was the Bishop of the local Mennonite Congregation." Harold Leon Swartzendruber, "An Autobiography by Harold Leon Swartzendruber," September 2003, Mennonite Mutual Aid, 1945-, Central Correspondence Office Files, 1945-1968 Collection, Mss. 12-6, box 3, entitled "Hochstetler, Ray V., 1959-62, MCC Mutual Aid Conference, 1954-55," Mennonite Church USA Archives, Goshen, Indiana, 129.

8. Richard Hays, *First Corinthians* (Louisville, Ky.: John Knox Press, 1997), 1-2.

9. See Ibid., 42-43.

10. See Helen Wells Quintela, *Out of Ashes* (Scottdale, Pa.: Herald Press, 1991).

11. Helen Quintela's account places their actions explicitly in the context of Matthew 18, noting Mennonites' traditional commitment to resolution of disputes via this procedure. See ibid., 112.

12. See Kreider and Goossen, *When Good People Quarrel*, 44-45.

13. See Quintela, *Out of Ashes*, 66-69.

14. Kreider and Goossen, *When Good People Quarrel*, 47.

15. Ibid., 48.

16. John Howard Yoder, *Nevertheless: A Meditation on The Varieties and Shortcomings of Religious Pacifism* (Scottdale, Pa.: Herald Press, 1971), 124, quoted in Quintela, *Out of Ashes*, 81.

17. Kreider and Goossen, *When Good People Quarrel*, 49.

18. Ibid., 50.

19. Ibid.

20. Quintela, *Out of Ashes*, 107. Helen Quintela locates the need to shift away from Mennonite's historical commitment to not litigating in their movement from closed rural communities to urban mixed communities. Ibid., 112-13. In Yoder's various conversations on litigation witness, while open to the need for discernment in changing contexts, he almost always notes this argument and rejects it. See, e.g., John Howard Yoder, Elkhart, Indiana, to Richard Yordy, St. Jacobs, Ontario, 6 August 1980, Carl J. Kreider Collection, Hist. Mss. 2/5, entitled "Litigation, 1976-81," Mennonite Church USA Archives, Goshen, Indiana ("Many Mennonites see this problem as a left-over vestige of a specifically rural life-style which has to be sacrificed when we become urban. This connection of things biblical with things Mennonite and then of Mennonite with rural, so that in the modern world we should become unbiblical, is a typical defense pattern for people who have not seen some point in the biblical witness as being relevant").

21. Ibid., 109-10.

22. Ibid., 112-13.

23. Ibid., 108. A related case in chapter 20 of Kreider and Goossen's book addresses the challenges in Newton, Kansas, to Jim Crow laws in the 1960s. One man, A. W. Robertson, was instrumental in the removal of the laws. Robertson, a railway postal clerk, came to Newton in 1944 and established a branch of the National Association for the Advancement of Colored People. His activism was also deeply embedded within his roots in the African-American church. Robertson began his assault on Jim Crow laws by unsuccessfully lobbying local businesses for open lunch counters. After three years, with a new state law prohibiting lunch-counter discrimination in hand, Robertson was successful with the threat of litigation looming behind his activism. He next turned to African-American use of the city pool. He raised money for a legal challenge; the city board capitulated. Robertson also broke through color barriers in theater seating and in high-school athletic programs. See Kreider and Goossen, *When Good People Quarrel*, 142-47. Much of Robertson's work, though seeking reconciliation and conciliation, preceded with the threat of litigation as an available option. In this regard, it is important to reiterate that all litigation in every context need not necessarily be avoided. It will be in exactly this area, litigation on behalf of the other, that recent Mennonite reflection will be most sympathetic to litigating.

24. Kreider and Goossen, *When Good People Quarrel*, 51.

25. Ibid.

26. Quintela, *Out of Ashes*, 146.

Chapter 3
The Corinthian Context

1. See Richard Hays, *First Corinthians* (Louisville, Ky.: John Knox Press, 1997), 99.

2. To put it this way oversimplifies the complexity of Constantine's "conversion." I take up this issue in much greater detail in chapter 5, while exploring Augustine's treatment of litigation.

3. Bruce Winter, "Civil Litigation in Secular Corinth and the Church: The Forensic Background to 1 Corinthians 6:1-8," *New Testament Studies* 37 (1991): 559-60. Winter concludes that the two texts may be reconciled by distinguishing obedience to the Roman civil authorities in regard to the criminal law from the actions of corrupt local magistrates and juries that would have controlled civil litigation in Corinth. See ibid., 572. Wayne Meeks concurs: "The exousiai to which Christians are urged here [in Romans 13] to be submissive are without doubt the functionaries of the imperial government rather than the municipal magistracies." Wayne Meeks, "'Since Then You Would Need to Go Out of the World': Group Boundaries in Pauline Christianity," in *Critical History and Biblical Faith: New Testament Perspectives*, ed. Thomas J. Ryan (Villanova, Pa.: College

Theology Society, 1979), 21. Yet Winter concludes in his book-length treatment of 1 Corinthians that the Roman officials who adjudicated criminal cases, which were prosecuted by private citizens, were also biased toward the upper classes. In fact, Winter argues that it is exactly the church's unwillingness, along the lines of the corrupt Roman governors, to discipline an upper-class member of the body in 1 Corinthians 5 for criminal incestuous conduct that Paul is challenging immediately prior to 1 Corinthians 6. See Bruce Winter, *After Paul Left Corinth: The Influence of Secular Ethics and Social Change* (Grand Rapids, Mich.: Eerdmans, 2001), 44-57. This conclusion regarding criminal cases would suggest that the distinction between criminal and civil litigation and government officials is not compelling. In contrast to Winter and Meeks, Markus Barth suggests, "To the Romans who were witnesses of slowly increasing attempts to deify the Roman emperor, Paul wrote that all authority, even political authority, is from God, i.e., under God, and that it should be treated accordingly." Markus Barth, "Christ and Law," *Oklahoma Law Review* 12 (1959): 81.

4. Here I am roughly following Martin's suggestion: "Throughout my interpretation of this passage, as throughout this book, I want to insist that ascertaining Paul's authorial intention is not an adequate goal for interpretation, even if it were possible. What I am attempting here is a reconstruction not of Paul's conscious intentions but of the ideological matrix in which the veiling of women could be thought necessary during the act of prophecy." Dale Martin, *The Corinthian Body* (New Haven, Conn.: Yale University Press, 1995), 244-45. I might substitute "in which the forgoing of litigation or the use of alternative means of dispute resolution would be necessary" for the issue of veiling during prophecy.

5. Hays suggests, "To discern how the word comes to us through this ancient letter, we must be alert to discovering imaginative analogies between the world of the letter and the world we inhabit. While recognizing that 1 Corinthians is not written to us, we learn to read it as though it were. We project ourselves imaginatively into the faraway life of the Corinthian congregation and thereby learn to see our own lives in strange and challenging new ways.... Interpretation, then, always involves a dialectical process of distancing ourselves from the text enough to see its foreignness and then allowing the text to draw near again and claim us." Hays, *First Corinthians*, 1-2.

6. See Martin, *The Corinthian Body*, xvii-xviii. T. W. Manson, while drawing the lines of division along Jew and Gentile, helpfully suggests that these two issues both concern Paul's attempts to resist either overly exclusive or overly inclusive views of the Christian body in Corinth. See T. W. Manson, *Studies in the Gospels and Epistles*, ed. Matthew Black (Philadelphia: Westminster Press, 1962), 193. Martin is careful to distinguish one remaining hierarchy in Paul's thought, that between men and women. Martin suggests

that both hierarchy and pollution are relevant to the role of women in the Corinthian body, and Paul, following ancient commonplaces, assumes that women's bodies are more susceptible to pollution. As such, the bodies of women remain biologically below those of men. According to Martin, this hierarchy remains in Paul's thought despite his suggestion that men and women will be equal in the eschatological kingdom. Martin argues that this is because the unified eschatological body that Paul envisions will be male; that is, women's bodies will not be equal to men's bodies but will in the end become male bodies. See Martin, *The Corinthian Body*, 248-49.

7. See ibid., 69-76. Martin argues that class division is the more appropriate distinction than many scholars' suggestion that the Strong were Gnostics or proto-Gnostics. Martin demonstrates that many of the "Gnostic" views of the Strong were held widely even prior to the Gnostic movement. The Strong's apparent deprecation of the body is not in lieu of an insubstantial spiritual world, but rather in lieu of a spiritual substance. Accordingly, the Platonic, Gnostic, and Cartesian dualisms through which it is tempting to read 1 Corinthians are in error. See generally Martin, *The Corinthian Body*, 104-36.

John Chow concurs, having set forth what he considers the three main scholarly alternatives for the nature of the Strong at Corinth: (1) Gnostics, (2) Hellenized Gentiles with an overly realized eschatology (that is, all things are permissible to me . . .), and (3) Judizers arguing for strict adherence to Jewish law by the Gentile converts at Corinth. See John Chow, *Patronage and Power: A Study of Social Networks in Corinth*, Supplement Series 75, *Journal for the Study of the New Testament* (Sheffield: Sheffield Academic Press, 1992), 114-20. As will become evident, I follow Martin and Chow in rejecting the Gnostic/proto-Gnostic reading and will find informative content in both of the latter two constructions.

The use of the term the "Strong" is particularly important in light of recent sociological work that has made clear that social status is not tied in a lock-step manner to wealth, but is a more multifaceted category. For a helpful introduction to these matters in the Corinthian context, see Anthony Thiselton, *The First Epistle to the Corinthians: A Commentary on the Greek Text* (Grand Rapids, Mich.: Eerdmans, 2000), 12. Thiselton also provides a helpful introduction to the historical debates surrounding the social status of the Corinthian Christians in Pauline scholarship, which has passed through various consensus positions, beginning with the claim that the church was all lower-class Corinthians, to predominately wealthy Christians, to the current scholarly consensus that the church was predominately made up of lower-class Corinthians but included a significant number of upper-class members as well. See generally ibid., 25-26.

8. See Wayne Meeks, *The First Urban Christians: The Social World of the Apostle Paul* (New Haven, Conn.: Yale University Press, 1983), 68; see

also Alan Mitchell, "Rich and Poor in the Courts of Corinth: Litigiousness and Status in 1 Corinthians 6.1-11," New Testament Studies 39 (1993): 575.

9. Thiselton, *The First Epistle to the Corinthians*, 28.

10. Margaret Mitchell challenges this conclusion on several fronts, suggesting that Paul was following rhetorical convention, not subverting it, in raising up the value of the lesser members of the body. Accordingly, in detailing the common use of the "body" metaphor for the polis, Mitchell argues that Plutarch similarly extols the importance of the lesser, but necessary, parts of the body. See Margaret Mitchell, *Paul and the Rhetoric of Reconciliation: An Exegetical Investigation of the Language and Composition of 1 Corinthians* (Louisville, Ky.: John Knox Press, 1992), 159, n. 570. Similarly, in regard to the valuing of individual gifts for the benefit of the community, she suggests that Paul is following rhetorical convention. See ibid., 268. Furthermore, she is more skeptical regarding Paul's subversion of existing hierarchies. Mitchell suggests that Paul is affirming the necessity of hierarchy in the body in 1 Corinthians 12:28: "And God has appointed in the church first apostles, second prophets, third teachers; then deeds of power, then gifts of healing, forms of assistance, forms of leadership, various kinds of tongues." See ibid., 164.

11. Martin, *The Corinthian Body*, 16.

12. Ibid., 21.

13. Ibid., 40.

14. Martin suggests, "Homonoia has as its aim not equality or strength for all members but the preservation of the 'natural' relation of strength to weak." Ibid., 41. This account of the polis is a reiteration of the Greek assessment that oligarchy is the best form of government. See ibid., 42.

15. Ibid., 96.

16. Martin notes, "Paul's appropriation of the rhetoric of unity is surprising and quite at odds with the dominant goal of homonoia speeches, which is to solidify the social hierarchy by averting lower-class challenges to the so-called natural status structures that prevail in society. Paul was well acquainted with the rhetoric of concord, but in 1 Corinthians he turns it against its usual role as a prop for upper-class ideology." Ibid., 47. The suggestion that what is natural for Christians will be different from what is natural for the world alludes to Paul's second issue, taken up in more detail below, the maintenance of boundaries between the church and the world.

17. Martin, *The Corinthian Body*, 76; see also Alan Mitchell, "Rich and Poor in the Courts of Corinth," 572, 575-81.

18. Martin, *The Corinthian Body*, 78. Alan Mitchell argues that the goal of 1 Corinthians 6 may have been to move dispute resolution into a nonlitigation setting, such as the church, where such class bias would be irrelevant and in fact where the majority of members who might be called

on to discern in such a case would be from the lower classes. See generally Alan Mitchell, *First Corinthians 6:1-11: Group Boundaries and the Courts of Corinth* (Ann Arbor, Mich.: U.M.I., 1986), 75-131.

19. Winter concurs that boundary issues are at the heart of Paul's first letter to the Corinthian Christians. See Winter, *After Paul Left Corinth*, 27.

20. See generally Martin, *The Corinthian Body*, 140-59. These alternative constructions of the body, likewise, relate back to the proper understanding of the polis as a body and the Strong's understanding that disease/disunity is caused by imbalance within the body or a rising up of the lower class. Ibid., 159.

21. Martin locates this theme in Paul's treatment of a man having sexual relations with his stepmother (1 Cor 5), consorting with prostitutes (1 Cor 6:12-20), eating meat sacrificed to idols (1 Cor 8–10), and improperly eating of the Lord's Supper (1 Cor 11:17-34). See ibid., 163-97.

22. Martin, *The Corinthian Body*, 177. Martin notes that 1 Corinthians also subverts the dominant understandings of sexual relations insofar as it suggests that a man, who was in the dominant position of penetration, nonetheless, "sins into his own body," that is, is penetrated or corrupted by the woman. Ibid.

23. Victor Paul Furnish argues that the establishment of boundaries between the church and cosmos, that is, a reorientation of the wisdom of the world toward the wisdom of the cross, is likewise the heart of the first four chapters. See generally Victor Paul Furnish, *The Theology of the First Letter to the Corinthians* (New York: Cambridge University Press, 1999), 28-48. Nonetheless, Furnish suggests that Paul is willing to allow these boundaries to blur at times. Furnish notes, among other examples, Paul's own work converting unbelievers (9:19-23) and his openness to marriage with unbelievers, which may lead to conversion (7:16), as evidence that Paul is willing to allow these boundaries to be breached when necessary. Ibid., 53.

24. Thiselton, *The First Epistle to the Corinthians*, 421. Furnish concurs in attempting to reconcile Paul's competing concerns for litigation before unbelievers or the use of litigation to resolve disputes at all. He concludes, "Paul's remarks in 6:1-11 point to another sense in which boundaries can be blurred. His initial counsel (vv. 1-6) is that 'the saints' should not be taking their legal disputes before pagan magistrates, who are of the 'the unrighteous' (*hoi adikoi*). His greater concern, however, is that wrongdoing (*adikein*) is present at all within the church, and along with it the corresponding impulse to seek legal remedies (vv. 7-8). In these respects believers are already beginning to resemble unbelievers, even if in other ways the boundaries between the church and the world appear to remain intact." Furnish, *The Theology of the First Letter to the Corinthians*, 53-54.

25. Martin, *The Corinthian Body*, 170. See, e.g., 1 Corinthians 5:9-12 ("I

wrote to you in my letter not to associate with sexually immoral persons—not at all meaning the immoral of this world, or the greedy and robbers, or idolaters, since you would then need to go out of the world. But now I am writing to you not to associate with anyone who bears the name of brother or sister who is sexually immoral or greedy, or is an idolater, reviler, drunkard, or robber. Do not even eat with such a one. For what have I to do with judging those outside? Is it not those who are inside that you are to judge?").

26. Furnish, *The Theology of the First Letter to the Corinthians*, 49. This conception of the church's participation with the world is found in the work of Karl Barth and Yoder, among others. I consider Yoder in detail on this question in chapter 9. For now, it is worth noting that Barth suggests that church law serves this purpose of making clear the distinction between the church and the world: "The decisive contribution which the Christian community can make to the upbuilding and work and maintenance of the civil consists in the witness which it has to give to it and to all human societies in the form of the order of its own upbuilding and constitution. . . . It is itself only a human society moving like all other to His manifestation. But in the form which it exists among them it can and must be to the world of men around it a reminder of the law of the kingdom of God already set up on earth in Jesus Christ, and a promise of its future manifestation." Karl Barth, *Church Dogmatics*, vol. 4, pt. 2, *The Doctrine of Reconciliation*, trans. G. W. Bromiley (Edinburgh: T&T Clark, 1958), 721.

Chapter 4
Reading 1 Corinthians 6

1. Jean Hering, for example, suggests that Paul is not indicting the quality of the Roman courts, merely their use. See Jean Hering, *The First Epistle of Saint Paul to the Corinthians*, trans. A. W. Heathcote and P. J. Allcock (London: Epworth, 1962), 39.

2. Bruce Winter notes, "Corinth differs little from elsewhere. Dio Chrysostom records c. AD 100 that there were 'lawyers innumerable perverting justice.' A decade later Favorinus refers to the unjust treatment which he has received at the hands of the leading Corinthian citizens. . . . Later in the second century Apuleius inveighs against the Corinthians alleging 'nowadays all juries sell their judgments for money.'" Bruce Winter, "Civil Litigation in Secular Corinth and the Church: The Forensic Background to 1 Corinthians 6:1-8," *New Testament Studies* 37 (1991): 564. Andrew Clarke disagrees with Winter that juries would have been used in these cases. He argues that civil cases would have been heard by the magistrates and appointed judges. See Andrew D. Clarke, *Secular and Christian Leadership in Corinth: A Socio-Historical and Exegetical Study of I Corinthians 6-8* (New York: E. J. Brill, 1993), 60. Despite this disagreement, both agree on

the potential problems of bias toward the upper classes in litigation by either juries or judges.

3. Winter argues, "The right to prosecute was not granted to everyone. If the defendant was a parent, a patron, a magistrate, or a person of high rank, charges could not be brought by children, freedmen, private citizens, and men of low rank respectively. Generally, lawsuits were conduced between social equals who were from the powerful of the city, or by a plaintiff of superior social status and power against an inferior." Bruce Winter, *After Paul Left Corinth: The Influence of Secular Ethics and Social Change* (Grand Rapids, Mich.: Eerdmans, 2001), 60.

4. Winter, "Civil Litigation in Secular Corinth and the Church," 565.

5. See ibid., 565-66. Clarke argues that the following characteristics of Corinthian litigation made it particularly troublesome: "First, the Graeco-Roman world of legal suits was a world where the socially inferior were severely disadvantaged. They were prejudiced against both in legal procedure and legal privilege. Secondly, the law courts provided a forum where the successful litigant could greatly enhance his own reputation, whilst at the same time injuring that of his opponent. Thirdly, the aspiration to support friends and denigrate enemies was in many cases more important than to speak the truth or see justice done. Fourthly, it may be assumed that plaintiffs were almost entirely people of high social status. The requirements of reputation and influence in order to be successful in litigation precluded many of those from the lower classes ever initiating legal proceedings." Clarke, *Secular and Christian Leadership in Corinth*, 67-68.

6. T. W. Manson, for example, notes, "In protesting against this practice Paul is at one with Jewish sentiment and custom. . . . As to the [rabbinical rulings], it was laid down by R. Tarphon and R. Eleazar b. Azariah (both c. A.D. 100) that Jews must not sue one another before pagan courts. The proof text was found in Exod. xxi. 1, and it is clear that the Rabbis were only declaring what had long been the rule. . . . In the Diaspora it seems clear that Jews went to their own courts, which had competence to deal with civil cases where both parties were Jews." T. W. Manson, *Studies in the Gospels and Epistles*, ed. Matthew Black (Philadelphia: Westminster Press, 1962), 197-98; see also Anthony Thiselton, *The First Epistle to the Corinthians: A Commentary on the Greek Text* (Grand Rapids, Mich.: Eerdmans, 2000), 425. Brian Rosner argues that the process may also parallel Moses's establishment of adjudicative bodies in the desert at Jethro's advice in Exodus 18. Tracing a variety of connections between that passage and 1 Corinthians 6, Rosner concludes, "Just as Moses appointed wise and righteous laymen to decide lesser civil cases (including fraud) between their brothers, so also Paul rejected unrighteous judges and told the Corinthians to appoint wise laymen to decide such cases between their brothers. Paul is, despite the absence of explicit indication, in

effect, depending upon and obeying Torah as he understands its application to his new situation." Brian Rosner, "Moses Appointing Judges: An Antecedent to 1 Cor 1-6?" *Zeitschrift fur die neutestamentliche Wissenschaft und die Kunde der alteren Kirche* 82 (1990): 278.

Peter Richardson points out that this issue may have been of particular interest to Paul, who was taken to the secular court of Gallio by the Corinthians as described in Acts 18:12-17. See Peter Richardson, "Judgment in Sexual Matters in 1 Corinthians 6:1-11," *Novum testamentum* 25 (1983): 37. Interestingly, it is Gallio who refuses to hear the Corinthians' case. See Acts 18:12-17 ("But when Gallio was proconsul of Achaia, the Jews made a united attack on Paul and brought him before the tribunal. They said, 'This man is persuading people to worship God in ways that are contrary to the law.' Just as Paul was about to speak, Gallio said to the Jews, 'If it were a matter of crime or serious villainy, I would be justified in accepting the complaint of you Jews; but since it is a matter of questions about words and names and your own law, see to it yourselves; I do not wish to be a judge of these matters.' And he dismissed them from the tribunal. Then all of them seized Sosthenes, the official of the synagogue, and beat him in front of the tribunal. But Gallio paid no attention to any of these things").

7. See Manson, *Studies in the Gospels and Epistles*, 197-98.

8. Markus Bockmuehl, *Jewish Law in Gentile Churches: Halakhah and the Beginning of Christian Public Ethics* (Edinburgh: T&T Clark, 2000), 146, 168.

9. Ibid., 151. The most important of these laws are those prohibiting fornication, bloodshed, and idolatry, according to Bockmuehl. Ibid., 161.

10. Along these lines, Manson locates the divisions within the Corinthian body between followers of competing leaders (Paul and Peter) with competing understandings of the necessity of Jewish practices for the Corinthian Gentiles. See Manson, *Studies in the Gospels and Epistles*, 193.

11. Martin suggests that women's bodies were seen to be even less stable and, thus, more open to corruption than men's bodies. This fact accounts for the heighten concerns regarding women and veiling, concerns Paul does not undercut but shares. See, e.g., Martin, *The Corinthian Body*, 199.

12. Ibid., 57.

13. Winter cites J. M. Kelly's work in this regard. See Winter, "Civil Litigation in Secular Corinth and the Church," 567. Kelly notes, "What the Romans called *reprehensio vitae* or *vituperatio*—a personal attack on the character of one's opponent—was taken as absolutely normal; and rhetorical manuals dealt in great detail with the most effective ways to construct a *vituperatio*. . . . [It] was the rule also in ordinary civil cases as well." J. M. Kelly, *Studies in the Civil Judicature of the Roman Republic* (Oxford: Clarendon, 1976), 98-99. Winter concludes, "Litigation caused personal enmity and liti-

gation was used to aggravate personal enmity. The proceedings were not conducted dispassionately by the parties but with great acrimony." Winter, "Civil Litigation in Secular Corinth and the Church," 566. Winter also suggests that litigation would have entailed the likelihood of larger damage awards, including "punitive" damages that would not have been available in arbitration. See Winter, *After Paul Left Corinth*, 67. Large damage awards would obviously further divide the disputants. Clarke concurs that enmity would have been one of the markers of secular Corinthian leadership that was being evidenced in the Corinthian church through litigation. See Clarke, *Secular and Christian Leadership in Corinth*, 66. For a general introduction to the role of enmity in Roman society and the role of litigation in either creating relationships of enmity or working out enmity, see David Epstein's *Personal Enmity in Roman Politics, 218-43 BC* (New York: Croom Helm, 1987), chap. 5, "Inimicitiae and the Courts."

14. Winter, *After Paul Left Corinth*, 71. Winter relies heavily on the work of Epstein in this regard. See Epstein, *Personal Enmity in Roman Politics*, 27-28.

15. Winter concludes, relying on evidence that Roman litigation was constitutively grounded in class distinctions, that the initiation of suit necessarily relied upon the assertion of class distinctions. He argues, "The initiation of legal proceedings against a brother was thus seen as a sign of defeat in relationships long before the verdict was pronounced in court." Winter, "Civil Litigation in Secular Corinth and the Church," 571; see also Winter, *After Paul Left Corinth*, 194.

16. Hays, *First Corinthians*, 93, quoting Gordon Fee, *The First Epistle to the Corinthians* (Grand Rapids: Eerdmans, 1987), 230. He notes that Paul's essential concern in allowing the *adikoi* to judge disputes is more than merely unjust judges, but the use of secular judges altogether. Hays notes all of the evidence set forth above for injustice in the Roman courts, but, nonetheless, concludes, "The judges in such courts are 'unrighteous' (*adikoi*) in the sense that they do not belong to God's covenant community." Richard Hays, *First Corinthians* (Louisville, Ky.: John Knox Press, 1997), 93. Hays argues that this boundary concern explains the continuity of chapters 5 and 6: "Just as they have failed to discipline the incestuous man, so they are failing to take responsibility for settling their own disputes." Ibid. Alan Mitchell also concludes that one of the key concerns of 1 Corinthians 6 is to establish the church as an alternative community: "When the values of the outside world have too much influence over the internal relations and operations of the community, an unacceptable boundary breach has occurred and must be remedied. The measure of boundary permeability has to be delicately maintained, since the Corinthian Christians cannot be out of the world. Too much permeability gives way to a betrayal of their baptism, to the extent that, when they appropriate the behavior of those outside, the offending individuals forget who they are." Alan

Mitchell, "Rich and Poor in the Courts of Corinth: Litigiousness and Status in 1 Corinthians 6.1-11," *New Testament Studies* 39 (1993): 564. In light of the church's inability to establish full-fledge Jewish "courts" in Corinth, Mitchell concludes that Paul must have internal arbitration of disputes in mind. See ibid., 568, 585. In this regard, Boaz Cohen notes, "Arbitration is of singular significance to students of legal history and comparative law, for it constitutes one important method whereby foreign rules of law could be admitted into another system, especially in proceedings involving civil cases." Boaz Cohen, "Arbitration in Jewish and Roman Law," *Revue internationale des droits de l'antiquite*, 3e Serie, 5 (1958): 181. Put differently, arbitration is the method by which the "law" of the kingdom of Christ can be admitted into the varying legal contexts within which Christians may find themselves.

17. Wayne Meeks credits recovering an apocalyptic view of the early church to Ernst Käsemann's 1960 article, "The Beginnings of Christian Theology," in *New Testament Questions of Today*, trans. W. J. Montague (Philadelphia: Fortress Press, 1969), 82-107. See Wayne Meeks, *The First Urban Christians: The Social World of the Apostle Paul* (New Haven, Conn.: Yale University Press, 1983), 171.

18. Meeks locates an eschatological and/or apocalyptic thrust in 1 Corinthians 1:7; 2:7-10; 3:13, 17; 4:5; 5:5; 6:2-3, 9, 13-14; 7:26-31; 11:26, 32; 15:24, 51-54; and 16:22. See ibid., 177-78.

19. See 1 Corinthians. 1:18-25 ("For the message about the cross is foolishness to those who are perishing, but to us who are being saved it is the power of God. For it is written, 'I will destroy the wisdom of the wise, and the discernment of the discerning I will thwart.' Where is the one who is wise? Where is the scribe? Where is the debater of this age? Has not God made foolish the wisdom of the world? For since, in the wisdom of God, the world did not know God through wisdom, God decided, through the foolishness of our proclamation, to save those who believe. For Jews demand signs and Greeks desire wisdom, but we proclaim Christ crucified, a stumbling-block to Jews and foolishness to Gentiles, but to those who are the called, both Jews and Greeks, Christ the power of God and the wisdom of God. For God's foolishness is wiser than human wisdom, and God's weakness is stronger than human strength"). For a general introduction to the apocalyptic context of the first two chapters of 1 Corinthians, see Alexandra Brown, *The Cross and Human Transformation: Paul's Apocalyptic Word in 1 Corinthians* (Minneapolis: Fortress Press, 1995).

20. Hays, *First Corinthians*, 94. Hays notes that it is a rather surprising and unprecedented claim, however, to go on to suggest that the church will judge angels. Ibid.

21. Ibid., 93.

22. Ibid. Additionally, these verses make clear that the character of the

disputes themselves is troubling. They are mere "matters pertaining to this life." It is not only the adjudication of theological questions by the Corinthian courts that is of concern. If Paul's experience in Corinth is any indication, it is likely that the Corinthian courts would not have heard such cases. See Acts 18:12-17. Rather these were everyday matters that the Corinthians were taking to the civil courts.

23. C. K. Barrett suggests the following translation might be rendered: "If it is absolutely necessary to have suits dealing with everyday affairs, show your contempt for them by singling out the meanest and most despised members of the church and appointing them as judges." He concludes, however, that the interrogative construction is to be preferred. C. K. Barrett, *A Commentary on the First Epistle to the Corinthians* (London: A. & C. Black, 1968), 137.

24. See Hays, *First Corinthians*, 94.

25. As Winter notes, "The question [in v. 4] is to be taken as a reflection of Paul's concept of status in the Christian ἐκκλησία, as against the city's ἐκκλησία. For him, those who had status by reason of their birth, wealth and position in the latter context did not thereby have any special status in the Christian ἐκκλησία." Bruce Winter, "Civil Litigation in Secular Corinth and the Church," 570.

26. For the opposing view on the "least esteemed," see Brent Kinman, "'Appoint the Despised as Judges!' (1 Cor 6:4)," *Tyndale Bulletin* 48 (1997), 345-54.

27. Paul's use of this method in 1 Corinthians 6:1-11 lends credence to the claim that the litigation troubling the Corinthian church was being initiated by the Strong. Along these lines, Hays translates this verse, "If you people are so 'wise,' why can't you even settle your differences among yourselves rather than going to outside authorities?" Hays, *First Corinthians*, 95.

28. For example, Hering argues that Paul is setting forth the prototype of ecclesiastical courts. Hering, *The First Epistle of Saint Paul to the Corinthians*, 38-39. It is Josephus who records, for example, a decree granting the right to adjudicate suits within the Jewish community in Sardis. See Meeks, *The First Urban Christians*, 34.

29. Alan Mitchell notes that the Diaspora communities that did have such an option were designated as a πολίτευα, which would have required Roman approval and significant standing within the Roman political context. Alan Mitchell, *First Corinthians 6:1-11: Group Boundaries and the Courts of Corinth* (Ann Arbor, Mich.: U.M.I., 1986), 200. Mitchell believes the Jews in Corinth did not have the political significance to obtain this designation, and certainly the young Christian movement in Corinth in 54 CE would have lacked this political clout. Another option to the rabbinical courts, explored by Mathias Delcor, is the creation of courts along the lines of those set up in the

Qumran community of the Essenes. See Mathias Delcor, "The Courts of the Church of Corinth and the Courts of Qumran," in *Paul and Qumran: Studies in New Testament Exegesis*, ed. Jerome Murphy-O'Connor (Chicago: Priory Press, 1968), 69-84. Delcor notes that while the texts left by the Essenes do not indicate a prohibition on outside litigation, such a prohibition must have existed as the Qumran community clearly made use of its own courts. Ibid., 73. However, Delcor concludes that the analogies between Corinth and Qumran should not be too closely drawn. The Essenes did set up full-fledged courts along the lines of the rabbinical courts. Delcor believes that Paul is suggesting in Corinth the use of internal arbitration in lieu of the creation of Christian courts. Ibid., 75. Delcor suggests that relying on the Qumran structure in which the whole church would gather to decide on spiritual matters would plausibly explain why Paul calls the whole church to gather to discipline the incestuous son in chapter 5 of 1 Corinthians, while relying on individual arbitrators regarding temporal matters in chapter 6. Ibid., 78-79.

30. See generally Alan Mitchell, *First Corinthians 6:1-11: Group Boundaries and the Courts of Corinth*, 198-205. This alternative form of dispute resolution then opens up the possibility for an alternative set of values to be expressed in the resolution of conflicts. The ancient writer, Seneca suggests that arbitration need not follow the dictates of law, but "mercy has the freedom in decision; it sentences not by the letter of the law but in accord with what is fair and good; it may acquit and it may assess at any value it pleases." Ibid., 115, n. 70. In other words, arbitration allows for something more akin to equity in modern courts. I consider the question of "justice" in detail in chapter 7. For now, I would follow Mitchell in suggesting that informal methods of resolving disputes should be considered the model for Paul's approach to the Corinthian's resolving disputes.

31. Mitchell suggests "the baptized person lives in the state of transformed existence, in which the real effects of baptism are made concrete in the self sacrificing denial of the need for justice as the world knows it." Ibid., 17.

32. Ibid., 4-5.

33. Rudolf Bultmann, "The New Testament and Mythology," in *New Testament and Mythology and Other Basic Writings*, ed. and trans. Schubert M. Ogden (Philadelphia: Fortress Press, 1984), 9.

34. Ibid., 30. It is instructive to compare Bultmann's reading of this passage to that of John Howard Yoder, "'If anyone is in Christ, new is creation,' or more smoothly, 'there is a whole new world' (NEB)." Yoder, *The Politics of Jesus: Vicit Agnus Noster*, 2d ed. (Grand Rapid, Mich.: Eerdmans, 1994), 222-23.

35. Meeks notes, "Paul began to understand that these notions were not descriptions of what was to happen in the objective world, but symbols expressing an 'existential self-understanding.' The end of the world really

meant that the Christian in his inner life was free from everything in the world, to face the future afresh in every moment, naked of every 'self-contrived security.'" Meeks, *The First Urban Christians*, 171.

36. Brown, *The Cross and Human Transformation*, 5.

37. Alan Mitchell, *First Corinthians 6:1-11: Group Boundaries and the Courts of Corinth*, 45. Mitchell supports this argument through a variety of means, including locating linguistic and structural parallels between verses 4-6 and 7-8.

38. Ibid., 179.

39. Meeks, *The First Urban Christians*, 179. Citing 1 Corinthians 6:12 ("'All things are lawful for me,' but not all things are beneficial. 'All things are lawful for me,' but I will not be dominated by anything") and 10:23 ("'All things are lawful,' but not all things are beneficial. 'All things are lawful,' but not all things build up"), Victor Paul Furnish suggests, "Some, or perhaps even most, of the congregation believed that in reigning with Christ they were delivered from needing to worry with questions of right and wrong, and with distinguishing moral from immoral actions." Victor Paul Furnish, *The Theology of the First Letter to the Corinthians* (New York: Cambridge University Press, 1999), 11.

40. Meeks, *The First Urban Christians*, 179. Along these lines, G. W. H. Lampe concludes, "The primitive Church clearly understands that moral perfection is an object of eschatological hope; that the Spirit enables the believer to possess the assurance and first-fruits of the age to come, but that he still lives in the flesh and stands within the present order; that in this life the implications of his baptismal enlightenment have to be worked out in the daily following of Christ and in dying and rising with him." G. W. H. Lampe, "Church Discipline and the Interpretation of the Epistles to the Corinthians," in *Christian History and Interpretation*, ed. W. R. Farmer, C. F. D. Moule and R. R. Niebuhr (Cambridge: Cambridge University Press, 1967), 341.

41. See generally Meeks, *The First Urban Christians*, 100, 104.

42. Gordon Fee, *The First Epistle to the Corinthians* (Grand Rapids, Mich.: Eerdmans, 1987), 17.

43. The deutero-Pauline author of Ephesians describes the church becoming God's temple in fulfilling this reconciling project. See Ephesians. 2:13-22 ("But now in Christ Jesus you who once were far off have been brought near by the blood of Christ. For he is our peace; in his flesh he has made both groups into one and has broken down the dividing wall, that is, the hostility between us. He has abolished the law with its commandments and ordinances, that he might create in himself one new humanity in place of the two, thus making peace, and might reconcile both groups to God in one body through the cross, thus putting to death that hostility through it. So he came and proclaimed peace to you who were far off and peace to those who were near; for through him both of us have access in one Spirit to the Father.

So then you are no longer strangers and aliens, but you are citizens with the saints and also members of the household of God, built upon the foundation of the apostles and prophets, with Christ Jesus himself as the cornerstone. In him the whole structure is joined together and grows into a holy temple in the Lord; in whom you also are built together spiritually into a dwelling place for God"). This suggestion refers back to 1 Corinthians, where Paul first employs this image for the church in 3:16-17: ("Do you not know that you are God's temple and that God's Spirit dwells in you? If anyone destroys God's temple, God will destroy that person. For God's temple is holy, and you are that temple"). Modern individualist readings aside, Paul, using the plural form of *you* and having already described the church as a building, specifies the nature of the building as the temple itself.

44. See 1 Corinthians 12:12-14 ("For just as the body is one and has many members, and all the members of the body, though many, are one body, so it is with Christ. For in the one Spirit we were all baptized into one body—Jews or Greeks, slaves or free—and we were all made to drink of one Spirit. Indeed, the body does not consist of one member but of many").

45. As Meeks notes, "To be sure, to sue one another in pagan courts is an appalling transgression of the boundaries, but what is really polluting is that their suits imply a desire to cheat one's 'brother,' which is behavior typical of what they were, as outsiders, before 'you were washed, you were made holy, you were justified . . .' (6:1-11). That allusion to baptism, as we saw, led Paul's argument back to concern with sexual matters, now in terms of the purity of the individual body." Meeks, *The First Urban Christians*, 153-54. Meeks argues that baptism is a boundary marker between converts leaving the world and entering the church. One of the markers of the believer's emergence into the church is the unity of Jew and Greek, slave and free, male and female. See ibid., 155. Hays suggests similarly that "it is possible, though not certain, that verse eleven echoes the actual language of the baptismal ceremony (note the implicit Trinitarian structure of the formula: 'in the name of *the Lord Jesus Christ* and in *the Spirit of our God*')." Hays, *First Corinthians*, 100.

46. Meeks suggests, "Furthermore, if we array these opposites according to the temporal stages of the ritual, the result is two nearly symmetrical movements. The first, characterized by descending action, climaxes with the 'burial' in the water; it signifies the separation of the baptizand from the outside world. The second, a rising action, marks the integration of the baptized into another world, the second on one plane, the heavenly reality on another." Meeks, *The First Urban Christians*, 156.

47. A variety of other important connections between verses 1-8 and verses 9-11 might also be located. Richardson notes, for example, the repetition of the phrase "Do you not know" in verses 2 and 3, and again in 9. See Richardson, "Judgment in Sexual Matters in 1 Corinthians 6:1-11," 42.

48. Margaret Mitchell, *Paul and the Rhetoric of Reconciliation: An Exegetical Investigation of the Language and Composition of 1 Corinthians* (Louisville, Ky.: John Knox Press, 1992), 231.

49. Furnish, *The Theology of the First Letter to the Corinthians*, 18.

50. Ibid., 142-43.

51. For example, Stanley Hauerwas argues, "Christian ethics is not what one does after one gets clear on everything else, or after one has established a starting point or basis of theology; rather it is at the heart of the theological task. For theology is a practical activity concerned to display how Christian convictions construe the self and world. Therefore theological claims concerning the relationship of creation and redemption are already ethical claims." Stanley Hauerwas, *The Peaceable Kingdom: A Primer in Christian Ethics* (Notre Dame, Ind.: University of Notre Dame Press, 1983), 55.

52. Here Hays's suggestion should be remembered: "To discern how the word comes to us through this ancient letter, we must be alert to discovering imaginative analogies between the world of the letter and the world we inhabit. While recognizing that 1 Corinthians is not written to us, we learn to read it as though it were. We project ourselves imaginatively into the faraway life of the Corinthian congregation and thereby learn to see our own lives in strange and challenging new ways. . . . Interpretation, then, always involves a dialectical process of distancing ourselves from the text enough to see its foreignness and then allowing the text to draw near again and claim us." Hays, *First Corinthians*, 1-2.

53. See generally Lucy S. McGough, "Starting Over: The Heuristics of Family Relocation Decision Making," *St. John's Law Review* 77 (2003): 291-343. McGough suggests that the most destructive force within divorce is the enmity between parents produced by litigation. Based on this conclusion, she argues for the resolution of relocation claims in custody battles via mediation. McGough cites one recent Nevada case, in which the court lamented in a footnote, "This appeal is the culmination of protracted litigation between Laura and Christopher. The district court judge, counting some thirty-five different court appearances in the instant case, expressed dismay that the parents were 'ambushing' each other through the courts 'without really beginning to realize the detrimental effect on the children.'" *Schwartz v. Schwartz*, 812 P.2d 1268, 1273, n. 8 (Nev. 1991). These concerns are also relevant to business litigation, however. The Chicago law and economics school now takes account of the "costs" of enmity produced by litigation. See generally Ward Farnsworth, "The Economics of Enmity," *The University of Chicago Law Review* 69 (2002): 211-62.

54. Furthermore, it is not at all clear that litigation in America, like litigation in Corinth, is not also weighted toward the wealthiest and best lawyered parties, often used to seek injustice, and, in the end a means by which those of superior status are able to oppress the weak. Insofar as Roman litigation con-

tinued to be biased toward the powerful and wealthy, J. M. Kelly argues that Roman litigation was a stepping-stone between self-help, which relied solely on the individual plaintiff's power, and the modern Western rule of law or judicial process, in which the weak and poor have just as good an opportunity to prevail in court as the well connected and wealthy. See J. M. Kelly, *Roman Litigation* (Oxford: Claredon Press, 1966), 173-74. Kelly's argument appears to be naïve to the realities of current forms of adjudication that offer poor litigants not much more hope than the Weak in Corinth. Without discounting real improvements in the reduction of judicial fraud and bias or the development of legal aid programs, contingency fee arrangements, and class action arrangements, the average poor American has little chance of adequately defending or prosecuting a civil claim with his or her landlord, credit card company, or health insurer. As such, many forms of litigation within the body, and perhaps litigation outside the body, as much today as in Corinth, threaten the unity of the body of Christ that Paul argues is essential to the church.

55. Several companies now invest in litigation. See, e.g., the press release from the publicly traded LitFunding Corp., touting itself as "one of the nation's largest public companies specializing in the funding of litigation primarily through plaintiff's attorneys." "Press Release: Correcting and Replacing LitFunding Investor Confidence Continues—Successfully Attracts Third Round of Financing," http://biz.yahoo.com/bw/041209/95720_1.htm, 9 Dec. 2004. The myriad legal TV dramas need not be cataloged. For a general introduction, see Robert M. Jarvis and Paul R. Joseph, eds., *Prime Time Law: Fictional Television as Legal Narrative* (Durham, N.C.: Carolina Academic Press, 1998). Further, long before *Survivor* started the rush to "reality" TV, Judge Wapner was dispensing reality law on *People's Court*. See generally Ryan Brett Bell and Paula Odysseos, "Sex, Drugs, and Court TV? How America's Increasing Interest in Trial Publicity Impacts Our Lawyers and the Legal System," *Georgetown Journal of Legal Ethics* 15 (2002): 653 ("America is fascinated with reality television.... On any given day, network television also airs a multitude of courtroom-based reality television, including *Divorce Court, Judge Hatchett, Judge Joe Brown, Power of Attorney, Judge Mathis, People's Court*, and *Judge Judy*. Cable television offers us a twenty-four hour network, Court TV, dedicated to bringing viewers a full range of legal entertainment; from live trial coverage to television dramas. Court TV's website even enables Internet users to voice their opinions on current issues in the courts by participating in a daily interactive survey called 'The Thirteenth Juror'").

56. See generally Connie J. A. Beck, Bruce D. Sales, and G. Andrew H. Benjamin, "Lawyer Distress: Alcohol-Related Problems and Other Psychological Concerns Among a Sample of Practicing Lawyers," *Cleveland State University Journal of Law and Health* 10 (1995/1996): 1-60. For a

more general introduction to the psychological costs of litigation on lawyers, see Wayne D. Brazil's "The Attorney as Victim: Toward More Candor About the Psychological Price Tag of Litigation Practice," *The Journal of the Legal Profession* 3 (1978): 107-18. Brazil notes the culture of manipulation and suspicion that pervades the litigator's life, leading to objectification of adversaries and alienation from the larger community.

57. See Paul Brace and Melinda Gann Hall, "'Haves' Versus 'Have Nots' in State Supreme Courts: Allocating Docket Space and Wins in Power Asymmetric Cases," *Law and Society Review* 35 (2001), 393-416 (documenting differences in access to court dockets and win rates); Donald J. Farole Jr., "Reexamining Litigant Success in State Supreme Courts," *Law and Society Review* 33 (1999), 1043-58 (documenting differences in win rates in the state supreme courts of Alabama, Kansas, New Jersey, South Dakota, and West Virginia between 1975-1990); Donald Songer, Reginald S. Sheehan, and Susan Brodie Haire, "Do the 'Haves' Come Out Ahead Over Time? Applying Galanter's Framework to Decisions of the U.S. Court of Appeals, 1925-1988," *Law and Society Review* 33 (1999), 811-32 (documenting differences in win rates in the U.S. Courts of Appeals and noting similar research that the federal government is more likely to prevail in decisions of the Canadian Supreme Court). Countervailing research related to lay jury bias against large corporate interests also exists. See Honorable Kimberly A. Moore, "Populism and Patents," *New York University Law Review* 82 (2007), 69-111 (documenting jury bias against corporate patent holders for individual inventors and noting similar research regarding tort jury awards against large corporations).

58. See, e.g., Tali Schaefer, "Disposable Mothers: Paid In-Home Caretaking and the Regulation of Parenthood," *Yale Journal of Law and Feminism* 19 (2008), 305-51.

59. See Justin D. Levinson, "Forgotten Racial Equality Implicit Bias, Decisionmaking, and Misremembering," *Duke Law Journal* 57 (2007), 345-424 (documenting research on memory of legally relevant facts that suggests potential jurors more likely to remember or misremember salient facts based on the race of the alleged perpetrator); Myra C. Selby, "Examining Race and Gender Bias in the Courts: A Legacy of Indifference or Opportunity?" *Indiana Law Review* 32 (1999), 1167-82 (noting the creation of various task forces to address racial and gender bias and citing various anecdotal and statistical research regarding the same).

60. See generally David M. Zlotnick, "The Future of Federal Sentencing Policy: Learning Lessons from Republican Judicial Appointees in the Guidelines Era," *University of Colorado Law Review* 79 (Winter 2008), 1-76.

Chapter 5
Litigation and Reconciliation in the Early Church

1. For a general introduction to the history of interpretation of 1 Corinthians 6, see Lukas Vischer, *Die Auslegungsgeschichte von I. Kor. 6, 1-11: Rechtsverzicht und Schlichtung* (Tübingen, Germany: Mohr, 1955).

2. See H. A. Drake, *Constantine and the Bishops: The Politics of Intolerance* (Baltimore: John Hopkins University Press, 2000), 90.

3. Drake notes, "A successful mass organization . . . creates an atmosphere favorable to the heterogeneity that follows from a relatively low threshold for members, and it also creates mechanism to resolve amicably the differences that inevitably come with such heterogeneity." Ibid., 77.

4. Traditionally inquiry into the appropriate forms of church discipline begins with Jesus' admonition in Matthew 18:15-18: "If another member of the church sins against you, go and point out the fault when the two of you are alone. If the member listens to you, you have regained that one. But if you are not listened to, take one or two others along with you, so that every word may be confirmed by the evidence of two or three witnesses. If the member refuses to listen to them, tell it to the church; and if the offender refuses to listen even to the church, let such a one be to you as a Gentile and a tax collector. Truly I tell you, whatever you bind on earth will be bound in heaven, and whatever you loose on earth will be loosed in heaven." This text is taken up in detail in chapter 9.

5. Drake argues that Constantine's "conversion" was a political revelation that he could unite the Christian and pagan monotheists in the empire as a formidable political alliance. Drake suggests that this project was not entirely successful. The church was deeply divided within itself. And Constantine's story, as told by Christians, obscured his commitment to a nondescript monotheistic God in favor of the God of Abraham, Isaac, and Jacob. See generally Drake, *Constantine and the Bishops*.

6. "The So-Called Letter to Diognetus," in *The Library of Christian Classics*, vol. 1, *Early Christian Fathers*, ed. and trans. C. C. Richardson (Philadelphia: Westminster Press, 1953), 217, quoted in Drake, *Constantine and the Bishops*, 78.

7. Drake notes that the first Christian historian, Eusebius of Caesarea, describes Constantine "not only as God's 'friend' . . . but also as his counterpart on earth. In fact, Eusebius asserts that death would not stop Constantine from ruling." Drake, *Constantine and the Bishops*, 185. Drake ultimately attributes this wedding of divine pleasure to political security as the cause of Christian coercion. See ibid., 479.

8. Gerald Schlabach argues that it would perhaps be better to suggest that Augustine set the terms for the question of Christian political theology insofar as he suggested that the city of God must determine how to seek the peace of

the city of man as resident aliens (à la Jeremiah 29). Schlabach argues that Augustine does not answer this question. See Gerald Schlabach, "The Christian Witness in the Earthly City: John H. Yoder as Augustinian Interlocutor," in *A Mind Patient and Untamed: Assessing John Howard Yoder's Contributions to Theology and Peacemaking*, ed. Ben C. Ollenburger and Gayle Gerber Koontz (Telford, Pa.: Cascadia Publishing House, 2003), 221-22. According to Schlabach, what has been taken as his answer is Augustine's description of the dilemma Christians face in general and Christian rulers face in particular. Ibid., 225. Schlabach argues that Yoder and Niebuhr offer competing alternatives for how to answer this question. Ibid., 228-31.

9. Jean Bethke Elshtain, *Augustine and the Limits of Politics* (Notre Dame, Ind.: University of Notre Dame Press, 1995), 105.

10. See Drake, *Constantine and the Bishops*, 91.

11. Elshtain, *Augustine and the Limits of Politics*, 26. Peter Brown concurs in Elshtain's assessment of *City of God*: "In the *City of God* . . . Augustine will judge the Empire on its merits as a purely human institution: he will reduce it to the level of any other state, in order to beat out the gods from its history; and he will discuss its contribution to the life of a Christian in terms so general, as to assume that the Empire's function might be taken over by any other state." Peter Brown, *Augustine of Hippo: A Biography* (Berkeley: University of California Press, 1967), 266.

12. Augustine writes, "God's city lives in this world's city, as far as its human element is concerned; but it lives there as an alien sojourner." Augustine, *Concerning the City of God Against the Pagans*, trans. Henry Bettenson (New York: Penguin, 1972), 18.1, 761.

13. Elshtain, *Augustine and the Limits of Politics*, 91.

14. Brown, *Augustine of Hippo*, 239.

15. Ibid., 291. Augustine's appreciation of Theodosius should be carefully understood, however. Rowan Williams argues that Augustine praises Theodosius because he is a ruler who is willing to accept limitations on imperial power and because his coercive activity is motivated by love (not glory). While acknowledging one may quibble with Augustine's assessment of Theodosius, Williams distinguishes Augustine's treatment of Theodosius from Eusebius's treatment of Constantine. See Rowan Williams, "Politics and the Soul: A Reading of the *City of God*," *Milltown Studies* 19/20 (1987): 64-65.

16. According to Brown, "[The temporary resident] must accept an intimate dependence on the life around him. . . . So the *City of God*, far from being a book about flight from the world, is a book whose recurrent theme is 'our business within this common mortal life'; it is a book about being otherworldly in the world." Brown, *Augustine of Hippo*, 324, quoting Augustine, *Concerning the City of God Against the Pagans*, 15.21, 634-35.

17. Roman law was also changing in this period as various rules undertook massive efforts at systemization. Diocletian's reforms and the codes of Theodosius II (438 CE) and Justinian (533-34 CE) set the high-water mark for Roman law prior to the decline of the empire. See generally Jill Harries, *Law and Empire in Late Antiquity* (Cambridge: Cambridge University Press, 1999), 9.

18. Jerome argues, "The laws of Caesar are different, it is true from the laws of Christ: Papinianus commands one thing; our own Paul another. Earthly laws give a free reign to the unchastity of men merely condemning seduction and adultery; while lust is allowed to range unrestricted among brothels and slave girls." Jerome, "Letter LXXVII: To Oceanus," in *A Select Library of the Nicene and Post-Nicene Fathers*, ser. 2, vol. 6, *St. Jerome: Letters and Selected Works* (Grand Rapids, Mich.: Eerdmans, 1979), para. 3, 158. Similarly, Gregory of Nazianus suggests to Verianus, who desired his daughter's divorce, "I should most willingly have given my opinion to my son Verianus that he should pass over much of what is in question, with a view not to confirm the divorce, which is entirely contrary to our law, although the Roman law may determine otherwise. "Epistle CXLIV," in *A Select Library of the Nicene and Post-Nicene Fathers*, ser. 2, vol. 7, *S. Cyril of Jerusalem, S. Gregory of Nazianzen* (Grand Rapids, Mich.: Eerdmans, 1978), 480. In Gregory's follow-up letter, he chastises Verianus: "If the worse and more cruel course is to be taken, seek for some one more suitable to your purpose," noting "[our Admirable Governor] proposed me not as Judge, but as Bishop." "Epistle CXLV: To Verianus," in *A Select Library of the Nicene and Post-Nicene Fathers*, ser. 2, vol. 7, *S. Cyril of Jerusalem, S. Gregory of Nazianzen*, 481; see also Harries, *Law and Empire in Late Antiquity*, 150, 206.

19. See Harries, *Law and Empire in Late Antiquity*, 192-93.

20. Ibid., 192. In its early form, only the clergy were granted jurisdiction to resolve such disputes. Ibid. *The Didascalia Apostolorum* purports to have been written at the Council of Jerusalem described in Acts 15, but is now dated by scholars to the third century. The *Constitutiones Apostolorum* partially overlaps the content of the *Didascalia Apostolorum* and is dated to the fourth century. See ibid.

21. See Drake, *Constantine and the Bishops*, 323, 486-87.

22. See ibid., 331-33.

23. See Harries, *Law and Empire in Late Antiquity*, 196.

24. See ibid., 199-201; see also Serge Lancel, *Saint Augustine*, trans. Antonia Nevell (London: SCM Press, 2002), 259.

25. Augustine, "251. Augustine gives greeting in the Lord to Pancarius, his beloved lord and deservedly honored son," in *Saint Augustine: Letters*, vol. 5, (204-70), trans. Sister Wilfrid Parsons, SND (New York: Fathers of the Church, 1956), 243-44; see also Brown, *Augustine of Hippo*, 192.

26. See Harries, *Law and Empire in Late Antiquity*, 182.

27. See ibid., 208-10.

28. See Ambrose, "Ambrose to Marcellus," in *Saint Ambrose: Letters*, trans. Sister Mary Melchoir Beyenka, OP (New York: Fathers of the Church, 1954), 121.

29. Ibid., 121.

30. Ibid., 123. This conclusion is not surprising as the empire became Christian, for there is no reason to assume that the civil officials hearing the cases above in their civil capacity were not also Christians. While the church had traditionally seen magistrate as a suspect profession, the church council at Elvira early in the fourth century permitted Christians to serve as civil magistrates, only prohibiting their attendance at church during their year of service. See Drake, *Constantine and the Bishops*, 223-24; E. Glenn Hinson, "The Quest for Integrity in Early Christianity: Third- and Fourth-Century Baptismal and Catechical Procedures in the Shaping of Human Motives and Goals," *Perspectives in Religious Studies* 24 (1997): 54. Similarly, the Council of Arles went on to sanction Christians in public office and the military. See Drake, *Constantine and the Bishops*, 230-31. Augustine himself assumes that Christians may serve as judges; in so doing, he praises a judge who used restraint in merely beating in lieu of using hooks to torture in a trial. See Harries, *Law and Empire in Late Antiquity*, 148-49.

31. Augustine, *Concerning the City of God against the Pagans*, 14.5, 859.

32. See, e.g., Brown, *Augustine of Hippo*, 32.

33. Ibid., 23.

34. See Drake, *Constantine and the Bishops*, 333. According to Drake, Constantine may well have seen in the Christian courts an opportunity to try to give more valuable appeal rights to the poor and weak in the empire. Drake notes that this was Constantine's own justification of this provision and that allowing the testimony of a single bishop (in lieu of the standard two witnesses) did nothing to honor bishops, but rather limited "the wicked seeds of litigation, so that wretched men, entangled in the long and nearly endless snares of legal procedure, may have a timely release from mischievous pleadings or absurd love of disputation." Drake, *Constantine and the Bishops*, 326.

35. Saint Augustine, *Confessions*, trans. R. S. Pine-Coffin (New York: Penguin, 1961), 6.10, 124-25. Augustine also discusses "when verdicts and testimony are sold" in great detail in his letter to Macedonius, discussed in detail below. See Augustine, "Augustine, bishop, servant of Christ and of his household, gives greeting in the Lord to his beloved son, Macedonius (414)," in *Saint Augustine: Letters*, vol. 3, (131-64), trans. Sister Wilfrid Parsons, SND (New York: Fathers of the Church, 1953), 300. Alypius would remain the lawyer after becoming a bishop, in Brown's words, becoming "the profes-

sional lawyer of the Catholic episcopate" and "the searching judge of the Christian community." Brown, *Augustine of Hippo*, 162.

36. See Harries, *Law and Empire in Late Antiquity*, 153-71.

37. Harries notes that when Valentinian I made official these already existing local legal structures, he "laid heavy emphasis on the duty of his new-style defensor to act in the interests of the 'innocent and peaceful country folk' against the corruption of the courts and the abuses of the powerful." Ibid., 54; see generally *The Theodosian Code and Novels and the Sirmondian Constitutions*, ed. Th. Mommsen, trans. C. Pharr (Princeton: Princeton University Press, 1952), 1.29.5, 32-34; see also A. H. M. Jones, *The Later Roman Empire 284-602: A Social, Economic, and Administrative Survey*, vol. 1 (Baltimore: Johns Hopkins University Press, 1986), 479-80, 499.

38. See Augustine, "Letter 22*," in *Saint Augustine: Letters*, vol. 6, (1*-29*), trans. Robert B. Eno (Washington, D.C.: Catholic University of America Press, 1989), para. 4, 157; Lancel, *Saint Augustine*, 261. For an example of Augustine's difficulties with corrupt tax collectors, see Augustine, "247. Augustine gives greeting in the Lord to the beloved lord, his son, Romulus," in *Saint Augustine: Letters*, vol. 5, (204-70), 232-36, in which Augustine unbraids a Christian tax collector: "If I am unfair in making this demand of you that wretched, needy men should not have to pay twice what they owe, when farm workers have paid their overseers, subject in their turn to their overlord and doing his bidding—and he cannot say that he did not receive it—if, then, I am unfair because it seems unjust to me that men who are hard put to pay once should have the tax extorted from them twice over, do what you like; but if you see that it is unjust, do what befits you, do what God commands and I ask." Ibid., 233.

39. See St. Augustine, *Concerning the City of God Against the Pagans*, 14.6, 860. Harries argues that Augustine's critique of corporeal judicial methods never touches the use of those methods themselves, but rather only the necessity that they are sometimes unjustly inflicted on the innocent. See Harries, *Law and Empire in Late Antiquity*, 132. She suggests that the necessity of pain to the judicial process was such a commonplace for Roman thinkers, to question its use itself was beyond any imperial Roman critique. Nonetheless, she argues that Christians focused attention on particular abuses of punishment, relocating the purpose of punishment from retribution to reform. See generally ibid., 135-52. Thus, according to Lancel, "charity, or love, implied the correction of the sinner, but not his excessive suffering, and must rule out his death." Lancel, *Saint Augustine*, 264.

40. In the first Sirmondian Constitution, Constantine himself acknowledges the limits of civil justice: "Whoever, therefore, having a suit, whether defendant or plaintiff, either during the start of the suit or after the allotted time has run out, when closing arguments are being made or when sentence

is about to be pronounced, should choose the court of the high priest of the sacrosanct law, instantly, without any hesitation, even if the other party is opposed, let the parties to the suit be directed to the bishop. For many thing which in a court of law the captious bonds of legal objection do not allow to be brought forth, the esteem of the sacrosanct religion finds out and makes known." "First Sirmondian Constitution," translated and appended to Drake, *Constantine and the Bishops*, 486-87; see also *The Theodosian Code and Novels and the Sirmondian Constitutions*, 477.

41. Lancel notes that Augustine was a vigorous defender of the rights of the church to intercede for criminals and offer asylum within the church's walls. See Lancel, *Saint Augustine*, 265-67.

42. Augustine, "To his beloved son, Macedonius (414)," 293. Augustine goes on to ground this defense of the state and its violence in Romans 13: "These words of the Apostle show the usefulness of your severity." Ibid., 296.

43. See ibid., 294.

44. Ibid., 295. According to Harries, "the interaction of the *severitas* of the state with the intercession of the Church produced the ideal compromise, of benefit to society as a whole." Harries, *Law and Empire in Late Antiquity*, 148.

45. Brown, *Augustine of Hippo*, 324, quoting Augustine, *Concerning the City of God Against the Pagans*, 15.21, 634-35.

46. See Brown, *Augustine of Hippo*, 248. Augustine's acceptance of this "moral specialization" makes evident one of the central distinctions that emerged between Augustine and Pelagius. Augustine was willing to tolerate a measure of sin in a mixed church of true believers and unbelievers. According to Brown, Augustine's good Christian layperson could merely be someone "with a few good works to his name, who slept with his wife, *faute de mieux*, and often just for the pleasure of it; touchy on points of honour, given to vendettas; not a landgrabber, but *capable of fighting to keep hold of his property, though only in the bishops' court*." Ibid. (emphasis added), citing Augustine, "A Treatise Against Two Letters of the Pelagians," in *A Select Library of the Nicene and Post-Nicene Fathers, First Series*, vol. 5, *St. Augustin: Anti-Pelagian Writings* (Grand Rapids, Mich.: Eerdmans, 1971), bk. 3, chap. 14, 408-09; see also, e.g., Augustine, "157. Augustine, bishop, servant of Christ and of his Church, gives greeting in the Lord to his beloved son, Hilarius (414)," in *Saint Augustine: Letters*, vol. 3, (319-54), in which Augustine counsels Christ's command to the rich young man to sell all he has is read by Augustine as a counsel of perfection. Ibid., 342, 347.

47. Augustine, "The Enchiridion," in *A Select Library of the Nicene and Post-Nicene Fathers*, ser. 1, vol. 3, *St. Augustin: On the Holy Trinity, Doctrinal Treatises, Moral Treatises* (Grand Rapids, Mich.: Eerdmans, 1978), chap. 78, 263.

48. Ibid.

49. Ibid.

50. Augustine provides a similar argument in "Reply to Faustus the Manichaean." In responding to Faustus's claim that the Manichaeans live more holy lives than Christians, Augustine argues that many Christians refrain from sexual intercourse and practice continence. Nonetheless, he cites Paul's permission/command distinction regarding abstaining from sexual intercourse and then follows up with 1 Corinthians 6 as another example of permitted versus commanded activity. Augustine notes generally regarding Paul's nonbinding admonitions: "For in the kingdom of heaven there are not only those who, that they may be perfect, sell or leave all they have and follow the Lord; but others in the partnership of charity are joined like a mercenary force to the Christian army, to whom it will be said at last, 'I was hungry, and ye gave me meat,' and so on. Otherwise, there would be no salvation for those to whom the apostle gives so many anxious and particular directions about their families, telling the wives to be obedient to their husbands, and husbands to love their wives; children to obey their parents, and parents to bring up their children in the instruction and admonition of the Lord; servants to obey with fear their masters according to the flesh, and masters to render to their servants what is just and equal. The apostle is far from condemning such people as regardless of gospel precepts, or unworthy of eternal life. For where the Lord exhorts the strong to attain perfection, saying, 'If any man take not up his cross and follow me, he cannot be my disciple,' He immediately adds, for the consolation of the weak, 'Whoso receiveth a just man in the name of a just man shall receive a just man's reward; and whoso receiveth a prophet in the name of a prophet, shall receive a prophet's reward.' So that not only he who gives Timothy a little wine for his stomach's sake, and his frequent infirmities, but he who gives to a strong man a cup of cold water only in the name of a disciple, shall not lose his reward." Augustine, "Reply to Faustus the Manichean," in *A Select Library of the Nicene and Post-Nicene Fathers*, ser. 1, vol. 4, *St. Augustin: The Writings Against the Manichaeans and Against the Donatists* (Grand Rapids, Mich.: Eerdmans, 1979), bk. 5, para. 9, 166.

In construing Psalm 81, Augustine provides a similar but slightly different reading of 1 Corinthians 6, suggesting the two commands are higher and lower levels of purification. In his exegesis of Psalm 81:15 ("Those who hate the Lord would cringe before him, and their doom would last forever") he introduces the concept of the purifying fire and explains the phrase "How those that build with wood, hay, stubble, on the foundation do not perish, but 'are saved, yet so as by fire,'" found in 1 Corinthians 3. Augustine, "Psalm 81," in *A Select Library of the Nicene and Post-Nicene Fathers*, ser. 1, vol. 8, *St. Augustin: Expositions on the Book of Psalms* (Grand Rapids, Mich.: Eerdmans, 1979), 394. In doing so, he distinguishes the person who despises all things of the world from the person who "robs not another of his estate, but so loves his own, that if he loses it he will be disturbed. He does not covet another's wife, but so clings to his own, so cohabits with his own, as not therein to keep the measure prescribed in the laws, for the sake of begetting children. He does not take away other men's things, but reclaims his own, and has a lawsuit with his brother." Ibid. These characteristics, including lawsuits, Augustine calls a fault, but, nonetheless, he notes that suits in defense of such worldly goods are permitted. See ibid., 394-95. In this slightly more nuanced reading, Augustine suggests that suing in church courts, meeting the highest standards for conducting litigation, and renouncing suits are steps in the way of sanctification, the lower step of which must be overcome at some point before achieving the kingdom.

51. However, he goes on, "Of course, if we were giving men advice as to how they ought to conduct secular cases, either for themselves or for their connections, before the church courts, we would rightly advise them to conduct them quietly as matters of little moment." Augustine, "On Christian Doctrine," in *A Select Library of the Nicene and Post-Nicene Fathers*, ser. 1, vol. 2, *St. Augustin: The City of God, Christian Doctrine* (Grand Rapids, Mich.: Eerdmans, 1979), bk. 4, chaps. 17-18, 558-87.

52. Ibid., chap. 18, 586.

53. Ibid.

54. Augustine, "33. Augustine to the honorable and well-beloved Proculeianus," in *Saint Augustine: Letters*, vol. 1, (1-82), trans. Sister Wilfrid Parsons, SND (New York: Fathers of the Church, 1951), 130.

55. In his treatise, "On the Work of Monks," Augustine suggests that he is not placing a burden on monks he himself has not undergone insofar as he is burdened with these suits. Augustine, "Of the Works of Monks," in *A Select Library of the Nicene and Post-Nicene Fathers*, ser. 1, vol. 3, *St. Augustin: On the Holy Trinity, Doctrinal Treatises, Moral Treatises* (Grand Rapids, Mich.: Eerdmans, 1978), para. 37, 521.

56. See Possidius, "The Life of Saint Augustine," translated by F. R. Hoare in *Soldiers of Christ: Saints and Saints Lives from Late Antiquity and the Early Middle Ages*, ed. Thomas Noble and Thomas Head (University Park, Pa.: Pennsylvania State University Press, 1995), 51-52. In this regard, Possidius suggests that Augustine "followed the teaching of the Apostle," in 1 Corinthians 6. Ibid. Brown, while tracing his apparent resentment to this burden, concludes, "Augustine thought of himself as the successor of the upright judges of Israel. And, in delivering judgement, he would always look forward, with terror to the Last Judgment." Brown, *Augustine of Hippo*, 196.

57. In disciplining one unjust Christian tax collector, Augustine notes, "Truth is both sweet and bitter. When it is sweet it spares us; when bitter it cures us. If you do not refuse the draught which I offer in this letter, you will prove the truth of what I say." Augustine, "247. Augustine gives greeting in the Lord to the beloved lord, his son, Romulus," 232.

58. Lancel notes both Augustine's exculpatory comments regarding the crimes of the poor and his attempts to have a *defensor civitas* appointed to Hippo for the sake of defending the poor against unscrupulous tax collectors. See Lancel, *Saint Augustine*, 260-61. Brown takes a much less sympathetic view of Augustine and the poor, noting that his desire to maintain the unity of the church in the midst of schism led him to gloss over inequalities between poor and rich. See Brown, *Augustine of Hippo*, 250-51.

59. This distinction has to do with differences in Catholic and Anabaptist ecclesiology, which differently locate the church within the hierarchy and gathered community. There is agreement that the dispute is to be decided by the church; the disagreement is over what is the church.

60. See generally Brown's discussion of the Donatist and Pelagian controversies, both of which relied on appeals to imperial authorities for the adjudication and suppression of heretical doctrine. See Brown, *Augustine of Hippo*, 332-36, 360-64.

61. For example, after an uprising of pagan violence directed toward the Christian community in Calama in 408 CE, Augustine sent the bishop of Calama with personal letters of appeal to Honorius and one of his officials, Olympus, to seek imperial redress. Honorius responded with a new law threatening, among other provisions, capital punishment to pagans that attacked churches or clerics. See Harries, *Law and Empire in Late Antiquity*, 88-91.

Chapter 6
Litigation and Reconciliation During the Reformation

1. See Walter J. Woods, *Walking with Faith: New Perspectives on the Sources and Shaping of Catholic Moral Theology* (Collegeville, Minn.: The Liturgical Press, 1998), 189-95.

2. See G. R. Evans, *Law and Theology in the Middle Ages* (London: Routledge, 2002), 42-43. The publication of Gratian's "Decretum" in 1148 is typically used to mark the beginning of the formulization and systemization of the canon law. Gratian approached the canon law topically. All previous compilations of the canon law were chronological. Gratian's "Decretum," it should be noted, was not a compilation per se, but a treatise with extensive full citations of supporting legal texts, which enabled it to serve practically as a compilation.

3. As described by John Witte, "Most cases were heard first in the consistory court, presided over by the archdeacon or a provisory judge. Major disputes, however, involving annulment, heresy, or clerical felonies, were generally heard by the consistory court of the bishop, presided over by the bishop himself or by his principal official. Periodically, the pope or a strong bishop would deploy itinerant ecclesiastical judges, called inquisitores, with original jurisdiction over discrete questions that would normally lie within

the competence of the consistory courts." John Witte, *Law and Protestantism: The Legal Teachings of the Lutheran Reformation* (Cambridge: Cambridge University Press, 2002), 37.

4. See Evans, *Law and Theology in the Middle Ages*, 92.

5. See Witte, *Law and Protestantism*, 48.

6. See Harold J. Berman, "Conscience and Law: The Lutheran Reformation and the Western Legal Tradition," *Journal of Law and Religion* 5 (1987): 184; see also Quentin Skinner, *The Foundations of Modern Political Thought*, vol. 2, *The Age of Reformation* (Cambridge: Cambridge University Press, 1978), 54-61.

7. See Evans, *Law and Theology in the Middle Ages*, 108.

8. Beat Kümin's article, "Parishioners in court: litigation and the local community, 1350-1650," in *Belief and Practice in Reformation England: A Tribute to Patrick Collinson from his Students*, ed. Susan Wabuda and Caroline Litzenberger (Brookfield: Ashgate, 1998), 20-39, is a helpful exception.

9. Kümin notes, "Early modern people . . . were a litigious lot, whose daily life should not be idealized. The plentiful evidence for conflict in the English parish seems to substantiate this point." Ibid., 21.

10. Martin Luther, "To the Christian Nobility of the German Nation Concerning the Reform of the Christian Estate," in *Luther's Works*, vol. 44, *The Christian in Society I* (Philadelphia: Fortress Press, 1966), 204.

11. Witte, *Law and Protestantism*, 33.

12. See ibid., 42; Berman, "Conscience and Law," 183.

13. See Evans, *Law and Theology in the Middle Ages*, 108.

14. Ibid., 65. The existence of continuing denunciations of bribes suggests the judiciary continued to face charges of corruption as well, however. See ibid., 111.

15. See ibid., 85. Evans notes several competing and unresolved descriptions of equity as (1) seeking fairness unobtainable through the law or offering mercy that the law might rightly demand and (2) providing equality (treating all the same regardless of class, wealth, and other distinctions) or providing particularity (addressing the uniqueness of the situation). See ibid.

16. A provision of the Fourth Lateran Council passed in 1215 CE; see Woods, *Walking by Faith*, 268-69.

17. See generally ibid., 195-219. Woods argues that the failure of the Carolingian reformers in the ninth century to return the church to the canonical penance model marked the triumph of the private penitential system. See ibid., 215-16. For a detailed introduction to the Celtic penitentials, see Hugh Connolly, *The Irish Penitentials and Their Significance for the Sacrament of Penance Today* (Dublin: Four Courts Press, 1995).

18. This marks perhaps the most enduring distinction between either dispute resolution or discipline in the ecclesiastical or civil setting. Secular juris-

diction was grounded in a retributive/punishment model; ecclesiastical jurisdiction was essentially grounded in a corrective/medicinal/restorative model. See Evans, *Law and Theology in the Middle Ages*, 162. While Evans notes a retributive function to penitential practices also noted by Connolly, see ibid., 18, 172-74, Connolly argues that such juridical language as used and as transferred to mainland Europe was a corruption of the penitentials' theological underpinnings. See Connolly, *The Irish Penitentials*, 157. Evans notes, "In a Christian context this discharging of the penalty is surely above all an act of reconciliation, and here it is most signally distinct from the judicial punishment. . . . An aspect of penitential restoration and reconciliation is the strong mediaeval 'medical' theme of the healing of the individual." Evans, *Law and Theology in the Middle Ages*, 173-74.

19. Ibid., 26. Witte concurs that cooperation and tension were both evident in the ecclesiastical and civil workings of the late Middle Ages. He notes, "When Church courts or inquisitors condemned heretics, civil authorities were to torture and execute them. When Church courts encountered contumacious defendants or witnesses, civil authorities were to punish them. When the clergy or property of the Church needed protection, civil authorities were to supply the troops. When the Church's goods were stolen or misplaced, the civil authorities were to retrieve them. Church officials, in turn, were to support and protect the civil authorities. When civil authorities sought to execute a felon, a ranking ecclesiastic was required to give his acquiesce. When a prince sought to discipline or depose a lower official, the bishop was expected to lend his suasion and sanction." Witte, *Law and Protestantism*, 46-47.

20. See ibid., 53.

21. See generally ibid. and Berman, "Conscience and Law," covering similar material and providing complimentary accounts. Witte notes the simultaneous movement of charitable and educational projects from the church to the civil authorities in the Lutheran territories as Luther attempted to stabilize his own revolutionary work into a structured society. See generally Witte, *Law and Protestantism*, 15-23. Much of this must be attributed to necessity as well as theology. Just as Constantine turned to the bishop's courts as an alternative to corrupt magistrates because they were there, Luther turned to civil structures because they were there.

22. Luther argues, "The ban should not only be used against those who oppose faith, but also against those who sin in public, as was indicated above by St. Paul, who calls for the ban against slanderers, usurers, fornicators, drunkards, etc. But in our time one leaves such sinners alone, especially when they are big shots, and—to the disgrace of this noble power—one puts someone under the ban because of a financial debt sometimes so small that correspondence and costs amount to much more than the original debt." Martin Luther, "A Sermon on the Ban," in *Luther's Works*, vol. 39, *Church and*

Ministry I (Philadelphia: Fortress Press, 1970), 9); see also Martin Luther, "Exhortation to All Clergy Assembled at Augsburg," in *Luther's Works*, vol. 34, *Career of the Reformer IV* (Philadelphia: Fortress Press, 1960), 33.

23. Luther suggests, "What are rulers and counselors for if in their city, community, and among their own subjects, they do not deal with and judge such temporal matters and debts? Spiritual authorities should deal with the word of God, with sins, and with the devil; they should lead souls to God, leave temporal goods alone, and judge the world, as Paul writes in 1 Corinthians 6[:2-3]." Luther, "A Sermon on the Ban," 22.

24. See, e.g., Martin Luther, "An Exposition of the Lord's Prayer for Simple Laymen," in *Luther's Works*, vol. 42, *Devotional Writings* (Philadelphia: Fortress Press, 1969), 68-69.

25. Luther writes, "Thus nobody is permitted to speak evil of a neighbor except those to whom this has been committed, as a judge and his assessor are obliged to examine and call witnesses in order to correct faults. Therefore God has ordained the government to do this: it is its office to speak of the sins of others . . . Therefore, if your neighbor does evil, tell it to the burgomaster or the judge [Christ speaks of this in] Matthew 18[:15-17]. Nobody should say: I will punish no one. But if you are not willing to declare your neighbor's evil publicly to the government, then keep it to yourself, for if you carry it into all the houses with your scandalous, poisonous tongue, you do not improve it, but only make it worse. Therefore, declare it where you should declare it." Martin Luther, "Ten Sermons on the Catechism," in *Luther's Works*, vol. 51, *Sermons I* (Philadelphia: Fortress Press, 1959), 159-60.

26. In expositing the Sermon on the Mount's command to be peacemakers, Luther writes, "But if you will or must talk about an evil deed, do as Christ has taught you. . . . You should discuss it between yourself and your neighbor alone (Matthew 18:15). If you must tell it to others, however, when the first method does not work, then tell it to those who have the job of punishing, father and mother, master and mistress, burgomaster and judge." Martin Luther, "The Sermon on the Mount," in *Luther's Works*, vol. 21, *The Sermon on the Mount (Sermons) and the Magnifcat* (Philadelphia: Fortress Press, 1956), 43.

27. Luther supports this political offering to the territorial princes with the text of 1 Corinthians 6: "The secular law—God help us—has become a wilderness! Though it is much better, wiser, and more honest than the spiritual law, which has nothing good about it except its name, nevertheless, there is far too much of it. Surely, wise rulers, side by side with Holy Scripture, would be law enough. As St. Paul says in 1 Corinthians 6[:5-6], 'Is there no one among you who can judge his neighbor's cause, that you must go to law before heathen courts?' It seems just to me that territorial laws and customs should take precedence over general imperial laws, and the imperial laws be

used only in case of necessity. Would to God that every land were ruled by its own brief laws suitable to its gifts and peculiar character." Luther, "To the Christian Nobility," 204-05; see also Witte, *Law and Protestantism*, 33.

28. Witte notes, "In Luther's view, God vested His legal authority in the prince, not the pope. The prince and other civil magistrates were for Luther God's vice-regents called to appropriate and apply God's law in governing human society.... By promulgating and enforcing canon law, the pope and his bishops had usurped the prince's authority and 'obscured the Gospel, faith, grace, and true divine service.' 'Neither pope nor bishop nor any other [clerical] man has the right to impose a single syllable of law upon a Christian....'" Ibid., 57; see also David Steinmetz, *Luther in Context* (Bloomington, Ind.: Indiana University Press, 1986), 12.

29. Witte, *Law and Protestantism*, 64.

30. See Witte, *Law and Protestantism*, 189.

31. Luther suggests that (1) value should not be tied to demand and ideally would be state regulated and (2) that serving as a surety for another or lending at interest are sins. See Martin Luther, "Trade and Usury," in *Luther's Works*, vol. 45, *The Christian in Society II* (Philadelphia: Fortress Press, 1962), 261-73.

32. Ibid., 276-77. Luther argues similarly in other occasional references. In another interesting engagement with 1 Corinthians 6, he addresses whether evil ought not be restrained. He first draws a distinction between public individuals, placed in responsible office by God, whose function it is to judge, and private individuals. The latter may take three procedures in regard to their own cases: seeking vengeance and judgment on their own behalf, not seeking vengeance and judgment, and seeking judgment, not on their own behalf but for the betterment of the offender. In regard to this first group of private individuals that would seek vengeance and judgment in their own case, Luther following Augustine indicates that Paul's counsel in 1 Corinthians 6 is an accommodation to the greater command to suffer wrong. See Martin Luther, "Two Kinds of Righteousness," in *Luther's Works*, vol. 31, *Career of the Reformer I* (Philadelphia: Fortress Press, 1957), 305. Similarly, in expositing Psalm 70:1, which Luther translates, "Be pleased, O God, to deliver me!" he notes that the Corinthians were "sternly charge[d] that they no longer suffered wrong but brought lawsuits for the sake of food and provisions"; Luther suggests "who knows whether it was lawful? But it is evident that it was not expedient." Martin Luther, "Psalm Seventy," in *Luther's Works*, vol. 10, *First Lectures on the Psalms I, Psalms 1-75* (Philadelphia: Fortress Press, 1974), 385.

33. Luther, "Trade and Usury," 277-78. Likewise, Luther argues that there are four Christian ways of exchanging external goods in trade: (1) allowing the other to rob or steal, (2) giving freely to any who has need, (3) lending without interest or demanding return, and (4) buying and selling for cash or

payment in kind. Ibid., 256-60. In responding to the argument that all property will be taken or borrowed and unreturned in light of the first three modes of exchange, Luther suggests, "This is why the world needs a strict, harsh temporal government which will compel and constrain the wicked to refrain from theft and robbery, and to return what they borrow (although a Christian ought neither to demand nor expect it). . . . Let no one think that the world can be ruled without bloodshed; the temporal sword must and shall be red and bloody, for the world will and must be evil, and the sword is God's rod and vengeance upon it. . . . But where men are not Christians, the temporal authorities ought to compel them to repay what they have borrowed. If the temporal authorities are negligent and do no compel repayment, the Christian ought to tolerate the robbery, as Paul says in 1 Corinthians 6[:7], 'Why not rather suffer wrong?' But you may exhort, insist, and do what you will to the man who is not a Christian; he pays no attention because he is not a Christian and has no regard for Christ's doctrine." Ibid., 258-59. Luther's apparently contradictory advice (do not pursue civil litigation against believers/let the civil authorities act to defend your rights) is reconciled by his novel model of litigation by the other on one's behalf, noted below.

34. Steinmetz, *Luther in Context*, 122.

35. Luther, "Trade and Usury," 278-79.

36. Ibid. Luther's approach to litigation is similar to his approach to Christian participation in violence, and, accordingly, helps make sense of how to reconcile the nearly Anabaptist Luther counseling peasants to submit to wrongs and the Luther challenging and undercutting ecclesial structures, moving ecclesial functions into the civil realm, and ultimately counseling Christian participation in state-sanctioned violence. See generally Eric W. Gritsch, "Martin Luther and Violence: A Reappraisal of a Neuraligic Theme," *Sixteenth Century Journal* 3 (1972): 37-55. The former advice to the peasants is striking for the strength of Luther's challenge to violence and litigation. Accordingly, in 1525 Luther again dealt with 1 Corinthians 6 in his "Admonition to Peace," written in response to the peasant revolt in Swabia and "The Twelve Articles," the manifesto of that movement. In "Admonition to Peace" Luther agrees that many of the abuses and wrongs that the peasants allege are legitimate. However, he denies the name "Christian" to the peasants' movement and "The Twelve Articles" because the peasants were unwilling to suffer wrongs in lieu of armed rebellion. Luther argues that this is in contradiction to the gospel: "In Romans 12[:19] Paul says, 'Beloved, never avenge yourselves, but leave it to the wrath of God.' In this same sense he praises the Corinthians for gladly suffering if someone hits or robs them, 2 Corinthians 11[:20]. And in 1 Corinthians 6[:1-2] he condemns them for going to court for the sake of property rather than suffering injustice. Indeed, our leader, Jesus Christ, says in Matthew 7 [5:44] that we should bless those

who insult us, pray for our persecutors, love our enemies, and do good to those who do evil to us. These, dear friends, are our Christian laws. On the basis of these passages even a child can understand that the Christian law tells us not to strive against injustice, not to grasp the sword, not to protect ourselves, not to avenge ourselves, but to give up life and property, and let whoever takes it have it." Martin Luther, "Admonition to Peace," in *Luther's Works*, vol. 46, *The Christian in Society III* (Philadelphia: Fortress Press, 1967), 29. Luther then concludes with an argument that has surprising resonances with the Anabaptist position: "Christians do not fight for themselves with sword and musket, but with the cross and suffering, just as Christ, our leader, does not bear a sword, but hangs on a cross. Your victory, therefore, does not consist in conquering and reigning, or in the use of force, but in defeat and weakness." Ibid., 32. Nonetheless, having read carefully the political message of nonviolence, Luther proceeds in addressing the individual articles to take an entirely nonpolitical tact.

37. Steinmetz notes, "Christians must allow personal wrongs to pass unavenged, but they cannot allow injustices perpetrated against the poor and weak of this world to remain unopposed. The state is a vehicle for the expression of responsibility for the neighbor and for the pursuit of justice for the oppressed. Therefore, Christians may assume public office not only because the state is God's government . . . but also because it provides a legitimate outlet for that love of neighbor which is awakened in everyone who is justified by faith alone." See Steinmetz, *Luther in Context*, 122-23.

38. Witte suggests that Luther was also engaged in resolving temporal disputes, but provides no evidence for this claim. Witte, *Law and Protestantism*, 69.

39. D. *Martin Luthers Werke: Briefwechsel*, vol. 5 (Weimar: Hermann Bohlaus Nachfolger, 1930-83), no. 100, translated in Witte, *Law and Protestantism*, 69.

40. Witte, *Law and Protestantism*, 69.

41. See Ruth Götze, *Wie Luther Kirchenzucht übte: eine kritische Untersuchung von Luthers Bannsprüchen und ihrer exegetischen Grundlegung aus der Sicht unserer Zeit* (Göttingen, Germany: Vandenhoeck and Ruprecht, 1958), 27-28. Nonetheless, Götze considers two cases in which Luther recommended either the ban or exclusion from communion for disputants who persisted in an irreconcilable attitude. See ibid., 26-27.

42. One should note that Luther's first disheartening trip to Rome as an Augustinian monk was as a representative of his order in a dispute among the Augustinians being resolved by the papal authorities. See Roland Bainton, *Here I Stand: A Life of Martin Luther* (New York: Abingdon-Cokesbury Press, 1950), 48. Likewise, the peasants appealed to Luther to act as an arbiter in the Peasants War of 1525. As noted by Bainton, "No formal court was ever established, and no legal judgment was ever ren-

dered. But Luther did pronounce a verdict on the demands of the peasants." Ibid., 273.

43. See Götze, *Wie Luther Kirchenzucht übte*, 9-13, 15-16, 33-34. In addition, Luther threatened or recommended the ban for several marital-related offenses that sit closer to the temporal/ecclesiastic line. See ibid, 16-19, 28-33 (regarding the validity of secret engagements and an unfaithful woman).

44. Witte, *Law and Protestantism*, 185.

45. Bainton, *Here I Stand*, 383.

46. See generally Francois Wendel, *Calvin: Origins and Development of His Religious Thought*, trans. Philip Mairet (Grand Rapids, Mich.: Baker Books 1997), 15-45.

47. See David Steinmetz, *Calvin in Context* (New York: Oxford University Press, 1995), 7. Alister McGrath concludes similarly in *A Life of John Calvin: A Study in the Shaping of Western Culture* (Oxford: Basil Blackwell, 1990), 59. Wendel gives a much less flattering account of Calvin's use of legal hermeneutics at *Calvin*, 359.

48. Wendel, *Calvin*, 307.

49. John Calvin, *The Library of Christian Classics*, vol. 21, *Calvin: Institutes of the Christian Religion*, ed. John T. McNeill, trans. Ford Lewis Battles (Philadelphia: Westminster Press, 1960), 4.12.1, 1230.

50. See Wendel, *Calvin*, 71. Calvin was also called upon by Genevan civil authorities to aid in the drafting of civil statutes. See McGrath, *A Life of John Calvin*, 59.

51. Ernst Troeltsch, *The Social Teachings of the Christian Churches*, vol. 2, trans. Olive Wyon (New York: Macmillian, 1931), 593. Troeltsch argues that Calvin adopted a strong view of sanctification and a legalistic ethic. Troeltsch associates this view with his sect type churches, but he notes that the "'Old Testament' character of Calvinism" is its practical concern for the "life of the nation." Troeltsch argues that this led Calvin to simply assume such an ethic could not entail all of society living out the Sermon on the Mount. Ibid., 601. Rather, Troeltsch suggests for Calvin such admonitions "must be solely designed to serve the spirit of holiness and brotherly love." Ibid., 599. Calvin says exactly as much in regard to 1 Corinthians 6 and litigation.

52. As noted by Wendel, Calvin's Consistory was charged with the control of Geneva's morals, not merely those within the church. The reason for this is clear: Calvin believed, and attempted to ensure in his required Confession of Faith for all Genevans, that all Geneva was the church. See Wendel, *Calvin*, 50-51; see also William Mueller, *Church and State in Luther and Calvin: A Comparative Study* (Nashville: Broadman Press, 1954),106.

53. According to Wendel, "each of these autonomous powers, State and Church, was conceived as issuing from the Divine will, and for that reason responsible for inspiring, each in its own manner, respect for the Two Tables

of the Law.... The fact that the Magistracy is a Christian Magistracy means that Church and State owe one another mutual aid and collaboration." Ibid., 79. Mueller catalogs Calvin's duties under the following categories: (1) to maintain the honor of God and preserve public worship, (2) to protect the church of Jesus Christ, (3) to preserve public law and order, and (4) to remember their accountability to God. See Mueller, *Church and State in Luther and Calvin*, 138-47. While being careful to emphasize Calvin had no Zwinglian theocracy in mind, Wendel notes, "[Calvin] did recommend, and tried to put into practice, a system of close collaboration between the two powers, which committed them to reciprocal aid. The ministers of the Church were obliged by their function to contribute to the moral education of the citizens, and to explain to the members of the Magistracy the requirements of the Word of God, to which the civil legislation had to conform itself. The Magistrates, on their side, were in duty bound to protect the Church and promote respect for the open preaching of the Gospel." Wendel, *Calvin*, 309-10.

54. See ibid., 55-56.

55. See ibid., 71. In addition, a ministerial association was formed for the disciplining of pastors. See Michael Girolimon, "John Calvin and Menno Simons on Religious Discipline: A Difference in Degree and Kind," *Fides et Historia* 27 (1995): 9-10.

56. See generally Wendel, *Calvin*, 72-75, 99-100, 106. Geneva was a city controlled by the episcopal authorities and under the protection of the Duke of Savoy. Geneva's pre-Reformation court system was controlled by the Duke, who had been ceded this jurisdiction by the city's ruling bishop at some point. These powers were in turn ceded to the city's ruling syndics in 1527. See generally Robert Kingdon, "Was the Protestant Reformation a Revolution? The Case of Geneva," reprinted in Robert Kingdon, *Church and Society in Reformation Europe* (London: Variorium Reprints, 1985), 202-22. In light of the short time in which the city's legal and disciplinary structures had been out of the hands of the ecclesial authorities and in the hands of the city's civil officials, it is not surprising they resisted any perceived attempt to reinvest these powers in the ecclesiastical sphere. In this regard, Kingdon notes that while Calvin is often portrayed as attempting to develop a theocracy in Geneva, at no time did he possess the powers of the ruling pre-Reformation bishop. See ibid., 216.

57. See John Calvin, *Calvin's Commentaries: The First Epistle of Paul the Apostle to the Corinthians*, ed. David W. Torrance and Thomas F. Torrance, trans. John W. Fraser (Grand Rapids, Mich.: Eerdmans, 1960), 122; Calvin, *Institutes of the Christian Religion*, 4.20.4, 4.20.17, 1489-90, 1506.

58. Calvin, *The First Epistle of Paul the Apostle to the Corinthians*, 119-20. Similarly, in the *Institutes*, Calvin makes explicit the necessary distinction

and interaction implicit in the ecclesiastical and civil jurisdictions. See Calvin, *Institutes of the Christian Religion*, 4.11.3-4, 8-10, 4.20, 1215-17, 1219-23, 1485-1521. Calvin argues that while the civil and ecclesiastical spheres are to aid one another, the Roman church had erred in vesting civil powers, including the sword, with the bishops. In so arguing, Calvin further limits the importance of 1 Corinthians 6: "In the past, if any conflict arose, the pious, to avoid the necessity of a law suit, committed the judgment to the bishop, because they had no doubt about his integrity. The ancient bishops were often involved in such decisions, to their great annoyance (as Augustine somewhere attests), but they reluctantly took this trouble, that the parties might not rush before a contentious court. The Romanists have made of voluntary arbitration—something wholly unlike the noise of the law courts—an ordinary jurisdiction." Ibid., 4.11.10, 1222. Likewise, he argues that clergy and bishops should be subject to civil courts. See ibid., 4.11.15-16, 1227-29.

59. Calvin, *The First Epistle of Paul the Apostle to the Corinthians*, 121.

60. Ibid., 122; see also Calvin, *Institutes of the Christian Religion*, 4.20.18-21, 1506-09.

61. Calvin, *The First Epistle of Paul the Apostle to the Corinthians*, 123; see also Calvin, *Institutes of the Christian Religion*, 4.20.18, 1506-07.

62. Interestingly, however, in defending the saint's judgment of the world, also located in 1 Corinthians 6, Calvin distinguishes the art of judging disputes from other human sciences of which he argues the church is incapable. See Calvin, *The First Epistle of Paul the Apostle to the Corinthians*, 118-19. Accordingly, while focusing on the permissibility of litigation, Calvin leaves open some space for church adjudication. He suggests that such adjudication does not necessarily require technical knowledge in all cases. Nonetheless, he does suggest that certain questions of law may require specific knowledge only held by the lawyer through legal education.

63. Ibid., 123.

64. Calvin's conclusion in regard to 1 Corinthians 6 implies that "the subjects should provide their obedience toward [their rulers], when by obeying their proclamations, or by paying taxes, or by undertaking public offices and burdens which pertain to the common defense." Calvin, *Institutes*, 4.20.23, 1510. Nonetheless, having argued that believers ought to obey even wicked rulers, he finishes by noting, "We are always to make this exception, indeed to observe it as primary, that such obedience is never to lead us away from obedience to him, to whose will the desire of all kings ought to be subject, to whose decrees all their commands ought to yield, to whose majesty their scepters ought to be submitted." Ibid., 4.20.32, 1520.

65. Elsie Anne McKee distinguishes Calvin from Zwingli on this point. Calvin, in exegeting Matthew 18, insists that the church, not the magistrate, is the proper location for church discipline. Elsie Anne McKee, "Calvin,

Discipline, and Exegesis: The Interpretation of Mt. 18, 17 and 1 Cor. 5, 1ff. in the Sixteenth Century," in *Théorie et pratique de l'exégèse: actes du troisième colloque international sur l'historie de l' exégèse biblique au XVIe siècle* (Genève 31 août-2 septembre 1988) (Genève: Droz, 1990), 319-27.

66. Calvin, *Institutes*, 4.12.3, 6, 1231, 1234-35. According to Calvin, "the phrase 'against thee' does not indicate an injury done to a person, but is a distinction between hidden and open sins." John Calvin, *Calvin's Commentaries: A Harmony of the Gospels Matthew, Mark and Luke*, vol. 2, ed. David W. Torrance and Thomas F. Torrance, trans. T. H. L. Parker, (Grand Rapids, Mich.: Eerdmans, 1972), 227.

67. Ibid., 228.

68. In his *Institutes*, Calvin further distinguishes between faults versus crimes and shameful acts: the former only merit admonition, while the latter require excommunication. Calvin, *Institutes*, 4.12.4, 6, 1231-32, 1234-35.

69. See ibid., 4.11.5, 1216-17. However, Calvin still intends that the civil authorities aid the church in disciplining through its coercive power. See ibid., 4.11.4, 1216. Discipline is to be undertaken by the elders (in lieu of a single bishop), as was the Jewish practice. Calvin notes that Christ must have in fact been referring to the Jewish practice of binding and loosing since he spoke the words in Matthew 18 prior to the founding of the church. Calvin, *A Harmony of the Gospels Matthew, Mark and Luke*, 229; see also Calvin, *Institutes of the Christian Religion*, 4.11.6, 1217-18; McKee, "Calvin, Discipline, and Exegesis," 324. However, Calvin like Luther is alert to not overstate the power of excommunication, in light of his own battles with the Roman church. Accordingly, he emphasizes in an exegesis of 1 Corinthians 5:1-5 (regarding fornicators in the Corinthians' midst) that the power to excommunicate should never reside in one but "that this particular discipline must be exercised by the elders, and with the consent of the people." Calvin, *The First Epistle of Paul the Apostle to the Corinthians*, 107.

70. Calvin, *Institutes*, 4.12.5, 1232-33.

71. Calvin argues, "The Lord testifies that such judgment by believers is nothing but the proclamation of his own sentence." Ibid., 4.11.2, 1214. He goes on to suggest that "although excommunication punishes the man, it does so in such a way that, by forewarning him of his future condemnation, it may call him back to salvation." Ibid., 4.12.10, 1238.

72. See Wendel, *Calvin*, 69. The relevant provisions of the Ordinances are available as an appendix in *Registers of the Consistory of Geneva in the Time of Calvin*, vol. 1, 1542-44, ed. Thomas A. Lambert and Isabella M. Watt, trans. M. Wallace McDonald (Grand Rapids, Mich.: Eerdmanns, 2000), 419-21.

73. Robert Kingdon, "The Control of Morals in Calvin's Geneva," in *The Social History of the Reformation*, ed. L. P. Buck and J. W. Zophy (Columbus: Ohio State University Press, 1972), 6.

74. See ibid., 8.

75. Ibid., 6.

76. Calvin's "Ecclesiastical Ordinances" did carve out a niche for the city's pastors though, requiring that "the small council consult the city's pastors on the nominations it made annually both of the elders and of the deacons." Ibid., 7.

77. Wendel, *Calvin*, 85.

78. Kingdon, "The Control of Morals in Calvin's Geneva," 10. The most celebrated case of discipline in Calvin's Geneva was the burning of Michael Servetus for heresy. Though Calvin through a pupil initiated the action against Servetus and was clearly supportive of the outcome, while counseling a less severe method of execution, Servetus was tried by Genevan civil institutions not the Consistory. See ibid.; Wendel, *Calvin*, 95-96.

79. See Wendel, *Calvin*, 99-100. In 1553, a citizen of Geneva appealed to the Small Council for reinstatement to communion. The Council granted the request, suggesting it retained the power to overturn the Consistory's judgment of excommunication. This action was followed by a decision of the Council of Two Hundred that the Consistory "should not go further than simple admonitions." Ibid., 99. Elections in 1554 overwhelming supported pro-Calvin/Consistory candidates, reversed the above decisions, and solidified the Consistory's exclusive control over excommunication.

80. See Kingdon, "The Control of Morals in Calvin's Geneva," 9-10; Wendel, *Calvin*, 84.

81. E. William Monter, "The Consistory of Geneva, 1559-1569," in *Renaissance, Reformation, Resurgence: Papers and responses presented at the Colloquium on Calvin & Calvin Studies, held at Calvin Theological Seminary Grand Rapids, Michigan on April 22 and 23, 1976*, ed. Peter De Klerk (Grand Rapids, Mich.: Calvin Theological Seminary, 1976), 77.

82. As described by Kingdon, "If the case involved several people, for example some sort of public quarrel within a family, among business partners, or between neighbors, the scolding [that was the typical disciplinary punishment of the Consistory] might be followed by a formal reconciliation. In serious cases this reconciliation would itself become a kind of public ceremony." Robert Kingdon, "A New View of Calvin in the Light of the Registers of the Geneva Consistory," in *Calvinus Sincerioris Religionis Vindex: Calvin as Protector of the Purer Religion*, ed. Wilhelm H. Neuser and Brian G. Armstrong (Kirksville, Mo.: Sixteenth Century Journal, 1997), 23.

83. Ibid., 126.

84. Ibid., 240.

85. See, e.g., ibid., 205, 282-84.

86. See, e.g., ibid., 192-93, 364-65.

87. See ibid., xix.

88. See, e.g., ibid., 262-633, 342-43. As noted above, Calvin was clearly

the driving force on the Consistory, delivering many of the admonitions that concluded cases. Calvin also sought the services of the Consistory, twice on behalf of his brother seeking to divorce his wife, Anne Le Fert, based on claims of adultery. The first case ended with a finding of imprudence but not adultery and a process of reconciliation between Anne, Calvin's brother, and Calvin. The second case was concluded with the charge of adultery sustained, divorce approved, and Anne banished from Geneva. See generally Kingdon, "A New View of Calvin," 28.

    89. Ibid., 30.

    90. Calvin, *Institutes*, 4.17.40, 1417-18; see also 1 Corinthians 11:27-30.

    91. *Registers of the Consistory of Geneva*, 115. Not only did the Consistory take this view but the *Registers* suggests that the average layperson held a similar understanding, for many disputants brought before the Consistory testify that they are already abstaining from communion on account of their quarrel and ill will toward another. See, e.g., ibid., 415-16; see also ibid, xxii. This understanding of communion was not unique to Geneva. David Warren Sabean traces similar sentiments in the visitation records for the duchy of Württemberg in the period from 1580-1820. See David Warren Sabean, *Power in the Blood: Popular culture and village discourse in early modern Germany* (Cambridge: Cambridge University Press, 1984), 37-60 ("Communion and community: The refusal to attend the Lord's Supper in the sixteenth century").

    92. See Kingdon, "A New View of Calvin," 23.

    93. See, e.g., *Registers of the Consistory of Geneva*, 156-57, 228, 271-73.

    94. While often counseling arbitration, the Consistory also counsels the continuation or even instigation of litigation to resolve a dispute. For example, in the dispute between the Noble Pierre Mercier and Humbert Exerton over the payment of four hundred florins, the Consistory extorted the two men "to live in peace and to receive Communion. The said Mercier says that if he is [f. 184v] paid what is due to him first he will be a friend afterwards. The said Exerton says that the matter will be tried tomorrow. They are remanded to agree between now and Tuesday. The said Mercier wants only his money, and meanwhile they will agree." Ibid., 370-71. In another remarkable case, the Consistory orders irreconcilable parties to civil suit before the Small Council. The cause of the dispute between Petremand Pellouz and Noble Claude Phillipe remains obscure in the Consistory's records. The secretary only records Pellouz's claim that "it would have been better . . . if his enemy had killed him rather than done as he did." Both men had been abstaining from communion on account of the matter; one attempt at reconciliation had already failed. The Consistory faired no better, offering that "they can make a compromise and pursue the case at law or that they can be brought to peace in order to receive Communion." Pellouz responded that he "would not know

how to pardon" Phillipe. Accordingly, the Consistory remanded them to the Small Council "since they do not want to agree." See ibid., 415-16.

Chapter 7
Early Anabaptist Challenges to the Use of the Law

1. See generally, e.g., William R. Estep, *The Anabaptist Story: An Introduction to Sixteenth Century Anabaptism*, 3d ed. (Grand Rapids Mich.: Eerdmans, 1996), 19-21. For example, Balthasar Hubmaier's "Form for Baptism" includes a question and answer acknowledging the church's right to discipline: "Now if you sin in the future and your brother knows it, will you let him discipline you once, again, and a third time before the church, and willingly and obediently accept brotherly discipline, then say: I WILL." Balthasar Hubmaier, "Eine Form zu Taufen," in Balthasar Hubmaier, *Schriften*, ed. Gennar Westin and Torsten Bergsten (Gutersloh, Germany: Verlagshaus Gerd Mohn, 1962), 350, translation from Jean Runzo, *Communal Discipline in the Early Anabaptist Communities of Switzerland, South and Central Germany, Austria, and Moravia, 1525-1550* (Ann Arbor, Mich.: U.M.I., 1978), 170.

2. For two helpful introductory essays on Luther and the Anabaptists regarding the state, see David Smolin, "A House Divided? Anabaptist and Lutheran Perspectives on the Sword," in *Christian Perspectives on Legal Thought*, ed. Michael McConnell, Robert Cochran Jr., and Angel Carmella (New Haven, Conn.: Yale University Press, 2001), 370-85; Marie A. Failinger and Patrick R. Keifert, "Making Our Home in the Works of God: Lutherans on the Civil Use of the Law," in *Christian Perspectives on Legal Thought*, 386-405.

3. See generally Hans J. Hillerbrand, "The Anabaptist View of the State," *Mennonite Quarterly Review* 32 (1958): 84-88.

4. See, e.g., Pilgram Marpeck's "Men in Judgment and the Peasant Aristocracy," in *The Writings of Pilgram Marpeck*, ed. and trans. Walter Klaassen and William Klassen (Scottdale, Pa.: Herald Press, 1978), 470. Marpeck suggests that those who continue in sin have not yet entered the kingdom of Christ.

The conclusion that the state is God-ordained to bear the sword, but the church is necessarily to avoid participation in the state because of this task is awkward in some ways. In attempting to address this tension, Walter Klaassen notes that several Anabaptists accepted participation in civil authority hesitantly. See Walter Klaassen, "Government," in *Anabaptism in Outline: Selected Primary Sources* (Scottdale, Pa.: Herald Press, 1981), 245. According to Hans Hillerbrand, many other Anabaptists simply left the tension unresolved. See Hillerbrand, "The Anabaptist View of the State," 98. The uneasy conclusions reached by the Anabaptists should not suggest that Luther's view of a simultaneous dual citizenship in the two kingdoms was not without its own difficulties. Further, Luther leaves the individual to discern when he is properly acting in the name of the other versus in the name or defense of self. In this regard, Luther fails to account for the myriad ways one might be self-deceived in his pursuit of violence or litigation in the name of the other, which in the end is self-serving.

5. See generally Leland Herder, ed., *The Sources of Swiss Anabaptism: The Grebel Letters and Related Documents* (Scottdale, Pa.: Herald Press, 1985).

6. See Estep, *The Anabaptist Story*, 64.

7. John Howard Yoder, ed. and trans., "Brotherly Union of a Number of Children of God Concerning Seven Articles," in *The Legacy of Michael Sattler* (Scottdale, Pa.: Herald Press, 1973), 39-40.

8. The "Congregational Order" notes, "When a brother sees his brother erring, he shall warn him according to the command of Christ (Matt 18:15) and shall admonish him in a Christian and brotherly way, as everyone is bound and obliged to do out of love." Ibid., 44.

9. Article 5 continues: "Second, is asked concerning the sword: whether a Christian shall pass sentence in disputes and strife about worldly matters, such as the unbelievers have with one another. The answer: Christ did not wish to decide or pass judgment between brother and brother concerning inheritance, but refused to do so (Luke 12:13). So should we also do." Ibid., 40.

10. See Estep, *The Anabaptist Story*, 68.

11. Hubmaier, who supported Christian participation in government and bearing the sword, nonetheless suggests that Christians err in suing in the civil courts over temporal affairs. In his "On the Sword," dated June 24, 1527, Hubmaier specifically addresses 1 Corinthians 6 and Matthew 5:40. In contrast to Sattler, he argues that 1 Corinthians 6 makes clear that Christians are called to judge in civil matters and infers that civil justice requires the coercive force of the sword to back it up. Nonetheless, Hubmaier suggests that litigants err in bringing suit. See Balthasar Hubmaier, "On the Sword," in *Balthasar Hubmaier: Theologian of Anabaptism*, ed. and trans. H. Wayne Pipkin and John Howard Yoder (Scottdale, Pa.: Herald Press, 1989), 503; see also ibid., 502, 507. In his "Justification," Hubmaier picks up this theme in regard to Matthew 5:40: "A Christian does not fight, strike, or kill unless he is a magistrate or commissioned to do it by a proper authority. Otherwise a Christian will surrender his cloak and his coat before he takes the sword. He offers his cheek, indeed, life and limb." Balthasar Hubmaier, "Justification," in *Anabaptism in Outline*, 250.

12. Balthasar Hubmaier, "On Fraternal Admonition," in *Balthasar Hubmaier*, 382.

13. The connection between reconciliation and the work of Christ is then solidified in Hubmaier's "Form for Christ's Supper," which includes a question and answer regarding reconciliation and admonition: "Would you

practice brotherly discipline against your brothers and sisters; make peace and unity among them; and also reconcile yourself with all those who have wronged you; put aside envy, hate, and all evil intentions against one and all; gladly put away all actions and business that give harm, injury, and offense to your neighbor; and have love for your enemy and do good to him; and exclude all those who would not do it, according to the ordinance of Christ, Matthew ch. 18 [v. 17], then each one in particular say: I WILL." Balthasar Hubmaier, "Eine Form des Nachtmahls Christi," in Hubmaier, *Schriften*, 362, translation from Runzo, *Communal Discipline in the Early Anabaptist Communities*, 171.

14. Among other early Anabaptists, former Franciscan monk Leonard Schiemer, writing from prison in late 1527 to Anabaptists in Rattenberg, also rejected litigation. See Leonard Schiemer, "Letter to the Church of God at Rattenberg," in *Sources of South German/Austrian Anabaptism*, ed. C. Arnold Snyder, trans. Walter Klaassen, Frank Friesen, and Werner Packnull (Kitchener, Ont.: Pandora Press, 2001), 79. While Schiemer is a minor voice among the early Anabaptists, he locates forgoing civil suits within the theological context of participation in the cross of Christ in a manner that parallels later Anabaptist reflection on litigation.

15. Clemens Adler, "Das Urteil von dem Schwert, mit unterschiedlichem Gewal dreier Furstentumer: der Welt, Juden und Christen, mit andern anliegenden Sachen," translated and included as an appendix in Peter James Klassen, *The Economics of Anabaptism 1525-1560* (The Hague: Mouton & Co., 1964), 123-24.

16. After the first few years of the Anabaptist movement, a crop of new leaders, such as Pilgram Marpeck, emerged in the developing Anabaptist churches in various countries. In a 1531 letter to Swiss Anabaptists, whom Marpeck believed were being overzealous in their use of the ban, Marpeck takes up a variety of issues, including nonresistance. He makes clear that the church is not to participate in the civil government or, most importantly, its use of the sword. See Pilgram Marpeck, "Judgment and Decision," in *The Writings of Pilgram Marpeck*, 332. With this background, Marpeck reiterates that the church's life is centered on the coming kingdom, not on the present world. See ibid., 343.

This oblique reference to litigation via Matthew 5:40 Marpeck makes explicit, taking up 1 Corinthians 6 itself in his "Exposé of the Babylonian Whore," which Walter Klaassen also dates to 1531. The "Exposé" is unsigned; Klaassen and others attribute it to Marpeck, although that claim is contested. While the proper attribution to Marpeck is not insignificant, the accuracy of this claim is less important for the current project, which is simply tracing early Anabaptist understandings. See *Later Writings of Pilgram Marpeck and his Circle*, vol. 1, *The Exposé, a Dialogue, and Marpeck's*

Response to Caspar Schwenckfeld, trans. Walter Klaassen, Werner Packull, and John Rempel (Kitchner, Ont.: Pandora Press, 1999), 24-48. In this treatise, which is focused on the relationship of the church to secular power, Marpeck argues, "Paul writes to the Corinthians (1 Cor 6[:1-8]) that they have failed Christ because they demanded temporal rights, and that from unbelievers. Is there no wisdom of Christ among you, Paul continues, by which one could admonish the other in patience and love? And even if the least of all the members of the church [Eph 3:8], urges you to the patience and love of Christ (if indeed you were brethren of love and peace) and to judge your own cases, you still insist on doing it before unbelievers. For the brotherhood of Christ is patience and love, does not have nor desires to have either Authority or subjects, but is one in Christ. For where there is no Authority there can also be no subject." Ibid., 37.

While a historical source that must be used with some care, the position of the early Anabaptists can also be discerned by looking to anti-Anabaptist tracts written in this period. Heinrich Bullinger, the heir to Zwingli in Zurich, wrote against the Anabaptists on several occasions. In one such tract, he notes Anabaptist claims and practices, such as, "Christians do not resist violence and do not take recourse to law. They do not use the law courts. Christians do not kill. The punishment used by them is not imprisonment and the sword, but only church discipline." Heinrich Bulllinger, "Der Widertouffern Ursrprung," translated and quoted in Harold S. Bender, "The Pacifism of the Sixteenth Century Anabaptists," *Church History* 24 (1955): 123. When John Calvin responded to Sattler's Schleitheim Confession and, in particular to article 6, highlighted above, he assumed article 6 implied the rejection of the civil courts. Having first addressed the article's explicit rejection of Christians' adjudicating secular disputes (interestingly, via 1 Corinthians 6:2, which states that Christians shall judge the world), Calvin assumes this claim leads to a rejection of litigating civil suits. See John Calvin, "Against the Anabaptists," in *John Calvin Treatises Against the Anabaptists and Against the Libertines: Translation, Introduction, and Notes*, ed. and trans. Benjamin Wirt Farley (Grand Rapids, Mich.: Baker Book House, 1982), 85.

17. Peter Riedemann, *Account of our Religion, Doctrine, and Faith, given by Peter Rideman of the Brother whom Men Call Hutterians*, trans. Kathleen Hasenberg (Rifton, N.Y.: Plough Publishing House, 1970), 112-13.

18. See Estep, *The Anabaptist Story*, 137-38.

19. John Oyer, "Anabaptists, the Law and the State: Some Reflections Apropos North American Mennonites in 1985," proceedings of the Marpeck Academy, March 23, 1985: 5.

20. Significantly, however, as there was not a uniform Anabaptist position on the "state," likewise there was diversity in the understanding of litigation. As noted above, Grebel did not address the topic. Menno Simons did not suggest

that litigation is necessarily problematic. In his travels and writings throughout his native Netherlands and northwest Germany, Simons frequently addressed the ban, its proper institution, and the practice of shunning. See Menno Simons, "A Kind of Admonition on Church Discipline," "A Clear Account of Excommunication," "Instruction on Excommunication," "Instruction on Discipline to the Church at Franeker," "Instruction on Discipline to the Church at Emden," and "Final Instruction on Marital Avoidance," in *The Complete Writings of Menno Simons, c. 1496-1561*, 2d ed., ed. John Christian Wenger, trans. Leonard Verduin (Scottdale, Pa.: Herald Press, 1966). However, no writing of Simons's addresses the use of the civil courts. Further, a confessional statement, directly related to the ban, and traditionally associated with Simons as author, affirms that litigation is permissible: "In the seventh place, as to demanding payment, at law, of just indebtedness, we approve in all cases where no wickedness results therefrom." "The Wismar Articles of 1554," in *The Complete Writings of Menno Simons*, 1042. The Wismar Articles are not without some historical difficulty. Bender notes, "Unfortunately the text in which the resolutions have been preserved is so corrupt that it is impossible to be sure of the original meaning." Harold Bender, "A Brief Biography of Menno Simons," in *The Complete Writings of Menno Simons*, 25.

Another leading Anabaptist bishop present at the meeting in which the Wismar Articles were drafted was Dirk Philips. Like Simons, Philips does not address civil litigation in his writings. See generally Dirk Philips, "The Enchiridion," in *The Writings of Dirk Philips: 1504-1568*, ed. and trans. Cornelius J. Dyck, William E. Keeney, and Alvin J. Beachy (Scottdale, Pa.: Herald Press, 1992), 373-76.

21. The most recent confessional document that has had a significant impact on the Mennonite church in America, the Ris Confession, also reiterates Anabaptist resistance to the use of civil courts. Drafted by Cornelis Ris in 1766 in the Netherlands, this confession took on greater importance in America due to Carl Heinrich Anton van der Smissen appending it to his 1895 history of the Mennonites, with the addition of some further proof texts. It is van der Smissen's English translation that is summarized here. Loewen suggests that this version is the forerunner to the many General Conference Mennonite confessions. See Howard John Loewen, *One Lord, One Church, One Hope, and One God: Mennonite Confessions of Faith in North America, An Introduction* (Elkhart, Ind.: Institute of Mennonite Studies, 1985), 24-25. The Ris Confession takes up the institution of the ban, the role of civil government, and the requirements of nonresistance. In regard to the latter issue, the Ris Confession cites both Matthew 5:40 and 1 Corinthians 6 without specifically addressing the topic of litigation. See Cornelis Ris, "The Ris Confession," trans. Carl Heinrich Anton van der Smissen, 1766, http://www.mhsc.ca/index.asp?content=http://www.mhsc.ca/encyclopedia/contents/

M4637ME.html, 7 February 2005, art. 29. As an apparent alternative to litigation, Ris suggests, "We therefore hold that it is our duty carefully to abstain from the use of all war-like weapons and from the above mentioned hostile resistance; that it is allowed to flee from the evil as much as is in our power (Matt 10:23), to adopt such measures against an enemy that without working to his destruction we may prevent and bring to naught his hostile purposes (Acts 23:6-9), and by means of defensive reasoning and good words (John 18:23; Acts 4:8-13, 19, 20) and manifold kindnesses to bring him to reflect and be at peace (Matt 5:25, 26; Luke 12:58; Gen 21:25-27)." Ibid. The latter citation to Matt 5:25 is to Jesus' suggestion to "come to terms quickly with your accuser while you are on the way to court with him, or your accuser may hand you over to the judge, and the judge to the guard, and you will be thrown into prison" (Matt 5:25).

22. Thieleman J. van Braght, *The Bloody Theater or Martyrs Mirror of the Defenseless Christians Who Baptized Only Upon Confession of Faith, and Who Suffered and Died for the Testimony of Jesus, Their Savior, From the Time of Christ to the Year A. D. 1660*, trans. Joseph F. Sohm (Scottdale, Pa.: Mennonite Publishing House, 1951).

23. See J. C. Wenger, "Publisher's Preface," in *Martyrs Mirror*, 2.

24. Ibid., 1117. As described in chapter 5, this is an accurate restatement of Luther's position.

25. Ibid., 704.

26. Richard K. MacMaster, *Land, Piety, Peoplehood: The Establishment of Mennonite Communities in America 1863-1790* (Scottdale, Pa.: Herald Press, 1985), 203.

27. Theron Schlabach suggests in his review of nineteenth-century Mennonite and Amish life that the proper stance in regard to litigation continued to be debated. Progressive reformers in both America and Canada in the middle of that century argued that litigation with the consent of the church was appropriate. Having noted as much, Schlabach documents the strong rebuke these reformers received from more conservative Mennonites. See Theron F. Schlabach, *Peace, Faith, Nation: Mennonites and Amish in Nineteenth-Century America* (Scottdale, Pa.: Herald Press, 1988), 50-51.

28. See Leland Harder and Kevin Enns-Rempel, "The Henry J. Martens Land Scheme," in *Anabaptist/Mennonite Faith and Economics*, ed. Calvin Redekop, Victor Krahn, and Samuel Steiner (Lanham, Md.: University Press of America, 1994), 199-222.

29. Ibid., 217.

30. This resistance to litigation in practice is consistent with other scholars', such as Oyer's, conclusions: "The Anabaptists and their immediate Mennonite descendants developed and retained a suspicion about the use and practice of law, a negativism that they sustained for centuries. Perhaps the

most poignant illustration of this point comes . . . in seventeenth-century Dutch Mennonite life. Those Mennonites entered every kind of cultural and professional activity: bellestric, painting, hydraulic engineering, commerce, especially medicine—but not law." Oyer, "Anabaptists, the Law and the State," 7. In a footnote, Oyer acknowledges that legal impediments may be a factor in this regard, but he concludes, "That limitation did not restrain them from the practice of medicine during much of the seventeenth century; nor did it prevent those who might have wished to study law from leaving the Mennonite church, as some ethnic Mennonites did when they entered the arts." Ibid., 23, n. 14.

Chapter 8
The Use of the Law

1. Erb argues that Paul's point is not that the Corinthians err in having disputes, but in their taking them to the civil courts. "It is expected that there will arise some matters of disagreement whenever people live in relation." Paul Erb, "Nonresistance and Litigation," *Mennonite Quarterly Review* 13 (1939): 77.

2. Ibid., 79.

3. Ibid., 80-81.

4. Ibid., 173-74.

5. Reinhold Niebuhr, "Fair Employment Practices Act," in *Love and Justice: Selections from the Shorter Writings of Reinhold Niebuhr* (Cleveland, Ohio: The World Publishing Company, 1957), 145, 148, Niebuhr writes, "Justice is partly maintained by balances of power in which the push and shove of competing vitalities in society is brought into some kind of stable or unstable equilibrium." Niebuhr, "Beyond Law and Relativity," in *Faith and History: A Comparison of Christian and Modern Views of History* (New York: Charles Scribner's Sons, 1949), 184.

6. Ibid.

7. Ibid., 189. However, the ethic of love is not wholly irrelevant, for it serves as a judgment on all limited forms of justice: "The question which must be raised is whether the reason by which standards of justice are established is really so pure that the standard does not contain an echo and an accent of the claims of the class or the culture, the nation or the hierarchy which presumes to define the standard. May not the scruple that we ought not enter our own claims in the balances of justice [citing 1 Corinthians 6] represent a profound consciousness of the contingent character of our claims and the taint of interest in the standards by which we regard our claims as justified? One need only consider how every privileged class, nation, or group of history quickly turns privileges into rights, to be stubbornly defended against other claimants in the name of justice, to recognize the importance of this final scruple about our

schemes of justice form the standpoint of Christian love." Ibid., 186. Accordingly, Niebuhr reads 1 Corinthians 6 as a counsel regarding the sinful nature of all claims, but not in any way suggesting a binding ethic for Christian believers.

Nonetheless, Niebuhr at times suggests that forgoing litigation or resolution of disputes within ecclesial settings is salutary or appropriate for individuals. While the main thrust of his argument in "Beyond Law and Relativity" is toward group interactions, Niebuhr appears to consider the ethic of love, while perhaps more achievable, nonetheless, equally inapplicable to individual justice. However, in other contexts, while Niebuhr consistently contends Jesus' ethic of love is unachievable for individuals in interpersonal relationships, he does seem to suggest that this ethic is the goal of such interactions in a manner he does not in regard to groups. Accordingly, Niebuhr suggests that "nothing is clearer than that a pure religious idealism must issue in a policy of nonresistance which makes no claims to be social efficacious. It submits to any demands, however unjust, and yields to any claims, however inordinate, rather than assert self-interest against another. . . . While social consequences are not considered in such a moral strategy, it would be shortsighted to deny that it may not result in redemptive social consequences, at least within the area of individual and personal relationships. Forgiveness may not always prompt the wrongdoer to repentance; but yet it may. . . . Refusal to assert your own interests against another may not shame him into unselfishness; but on occasion it has done so." Reinhold Niebuhr, *Moral Man and Immoral Society: A Study in Christian Ethics*, 2d ed. (New York: Scribner, 1960), 264.

8. Chester K. Lehman, "Biblical Perspectives on Christianity and the State" (paper presented at Mennonite General Conference, Peace Problems Committee Conference on Nonresistance and Political Responsibility, Laurelville, Pa., 21-22 Sept. 1956), Harold and Wilma Good Library, Goshen College, Goshen, Ind., 3.

9. Irvin B. Horst, "Some Principles and Limitations Guiding the Christian Witness to the State" (paper presented at Mennonite General Conference, Peace Problems Committee Conference on Nonresistance and Political Responsibility, Laurelville, Pa., 21-22 Sept. 1956), Harold and Wilma Good Library, Goshen College, Goshen, Ind., 44.

10. Wenger is a key figure in recent Mennonite reflection on litigation. A lawyer in Lancaster, Pennsylvania, and board member of Mennonite Automobile Aid at the time, Wenger presented papers at both relevant conferences as well as publishing on the topic. See Samuel Wenger, "Mennonites and the Law," *Christian Living* 5/2 (1958): 6-8, 33.

11. See generally John D. Burkholder, "The Practical Aspects of Litigation" (paper presented at Mennonite General Conference, Peace Problems Committee Conference on Nonresistance and Political Responsibil-

ity, Laurelville, Pa., 21-22 Sept. 1956), Harold and Wilma Good Library, Goshen College, Goshen, Ind., 21-31. The gist of the responses indicated that suppliers realized good business practice required fair and equitable response to legitimate claims regarding defective goods. Likewise, customers generally responded favorably to a patient approach to bill collection when faced with the personal contact of the Mennonite businessperson regarding the outstanding bill.

The general conclusions of the study regarding Mennonite praxis in the fifties are confirmed by Wenger. In 1958, arguing anecdotally, he concluded, "The record of the church with respect to adverse litigation is surprisingly good. I suspect it is better than on many other characteristic doctrines, as, for example, on the prohibition of entering military service. Out of my twenty years of experience as a lawyer and out of twenty years of observation earlier than that period, I can recall only a sprinkling of legal actions in which a Mennonite has been the aggressive party." Wenger, "Mennonites and the Law," 7.

12. Guy F. Hershberger, "Litigation in Mennonite History" (paper presented at Mennonite General Conference, Peace Problems Committee Conference on Nonresistance and Political Responsibility, Laurelville, Pa., 21-22 Sept. 1956), Harold and Wilma Good Library, Goshen College, Goshen, Ind., 32.

13. See Mennonite Mutual Aid Litigation Problems Study Committee, "Minutes of Meeting," 3 January 1961, Mennonite Mutual Aid, 1945-, Central Correspondence Office Files, 1945-1968 Collection, Mss. 12-6, box 3, entitled "Hochstetler, Ray V., 1959-62, MCC Mutual Aid Conference, 1954-55," Mennonite Church USA Archives, Goshen, Indiana.

14. However, the collection of papers from this conference, as currently found in the library at Goshen College, do not include a final draft of the concluding report, but only a preliminary report, entitled "The Christian and Litigation." This preliminary report, although marked "Confidential: Not for Publication," appears to be the best record of the conclusions of the 1961 consultation group.

15. The statement was the work of the Peace Problems Committee, which used the findings of the Consultation on Litigation Problems, to proceed to a position statement. See Guy Hershberger, Goshen, Indiana, to John Howard Yoder, Goshen, Indiana, 24 April 1963, John H. Yoder (1927-1997) Collection, Hist. Mss. 23/8, entitled "Litigation, 1961-1984," Mennonite Church USA Archives, Goshen, Indiana. The statement itself is important, reaching the following conclusions, among others: "The Christian should live above the law in the sense that Christian love should constrain him to do good unto others beyond what the law requires" and "The ministry of reconciliation which is the Christians primary function must always take precedence over personal considerations of justice, rights, property, and economic gain." "Litigation and The

Use of the Law, A Statement Prepared for Discussion and Possible Adoption by the Mennonite General Conference," n.d., John H. Yoder (1927-1997) Collection, Hist. Mss. 23/8, entitled "Litigation, 1961-1984," Mennonite Church USA Archives, Goshen, Indiana. Most interestingly, the statement concludes with a confession and commitment, which connects litigation with sin: "We also confess that we have sinned, that the divine image has been marred, that we like sheep have gone astray, following each one his own way, looking after his own interests. It is because of this that the good world has been filled with every manner of evil: injustice, frustration, and social maladies; wars and fightings, the spirit of eye for eye, and tooth for tooth, and suits at law." Ibid.

16. See Samuel Wenger, "Classification of Types of Legal Procedures," (paper presented at Mennonite General Conference, Peace Problems Committee Consultation on Litigation Problems, Goshen, Ind., 27-28 July 1961), Harold and Wilma Good Library, Goshen College, Goshen, Ind., 11. Wenger's attempt to distinguish individuals from corporations was rejected by most other participants at the conference. Most insightfully, Paul Peachy located Wenger's distinction in Reinhold Niebuhr's writings, discussed herein, which emphasize a distinction in the applicability of Christian ethics based on individuals and groups.

17. Clayton Beyler, "Scriptural Principles Bearing on Our Litigation Problems and Our Mennonite Practices" (paper presented at Mennonite General Conference, Peace Problems Committee Consultation on Litigation Problems, Goshen, Ind., 27-28 July 1961), Harold and Wilma Good Library, Goshen College, Goshen, Ind., 16. Beyler is here explaining Matthew 5:23-26 and Luke 12:57-59.

18. Ibid., 30.

19. While the significance of the increased emphasis on the language of reconciliation should not be underestimated, it should be acknowledged that the more traditional language of nonresistance remained an important part of the tradition. For example, the "Mennonite Confession of Faith," adopted by the Mennonite General Conference in 1963, rejected litigation solely in the context of nonresistance: "Article 18. Love and Nonresistance—We believe that it is the will of God for His children to follow Christian love in all human relationships. Such a life of love excludes retaliation and revenge. God pours His love into the hearts of Christians so that they desire the welfare of all men. The supreme example of nonresistance is the Lord Jesus Himself. The teaching of Jesus not to resist him who is evil requires the renunciation by His disciples of all violence in human relations. Only love must be shown to all men. We believe that this applies to every area of life: to personal injustice, to situations in which people commonly resort to litigation, to industrial strife, and to international tensions and wars. As nonresistant Christians we cannot serve in any office which employs the use of force. Nor can we participate in military service, or in military training, or

in the voluntary financial support of war. But we must aggressively, at the risk of life itself, do whatever we can for the alleviation of human distress and suffering. Matthew 5:38-48; John 18:36; Romans 5:5; 12:18-21; 1 Corinthians 6:1-8; 2 Corinthians 10:3, 4; James 2:8; 1 Peter 2:23; 4:1." Mennonite General Conference, "Mennonite Confession of Faith," 1963, http://www.mhsc.ca/index.asp?content=http://www.mhsc.ca/index.asp?content=http://www.mhsc.ca/encyclopedia/contents/M4663.html, 7 February 2005, art. 18.

20. In other contexts Yoder will suggest that it is not evident that appeal to the police is always inappropriate. He notes, "The distinction made here between police and war is not simply a matter of the degree to which the appeal to force goes, the number of person killed or killing. It is a structural and a profound difference in the sociological meaning of the appeal to force." John Howard Yoder, *The Politics of Jesus: Vicit Agnus Noster*, 2d ed. (Notre Dame, Ind.: University of Notre Dame Press, 1994), 204. Insofar as the conclusions of *The Use of the Law*, set forth in detail herein, will permit certain forms of litigation that are nonadversarial or which seek justice for the other, but might, nonetheless, ultimately rely on the coercive power of the police to enforce those decision, it would appear that Yoder's suggestion here is not taken up in the most recent reflection of Mennonites on the law. In light of Yoder's own restatement of his understanding of the police function, this omission may be appropriate, although he on several occasions argues for the essential connection between nonviolence and resistance to litigation.

His comments to *The Use of the Law*, in particular addressing the section where the possibility of litigating on behalf of the other is raised, are particularly illuminating. As originally drafted, the section suggested that a Christian may litigate in the instances listed in that section. The language was changed in response to the following comment by Yoder: "With the next section, dealing with acceptable examples, I have some problem precisely because of the predilection of Mennonites to deal with such matters in legalistic terms. You actually say 'may be involved' in a way that sounds like blanket permission. I would rather see us saying 'might be involved.' I am not even sure that in all of these cases it should be assumed that there's no problem, no adversary dimension, or no non-resistant duty simply to accept being taken advantage of. I do not mean to exclude the examples, and the six examples are well chosen. But even these six examples, it seems to me, should be given as 'for instance' suggestions and not as free fire zones." John Howard Yoder, Elkhart, Indiana, to Richard Yordy, St. Jacobs, Ontario, (21 March 1979), John H. Yoder (1927-1997) Collection, Hist. Mss. 23/8, entitled "Litigation, 1961-1984," Mennonite Church USA Archives, Goshen, Indiana.

Marlin Miller raised a similar question in reviewing a 1979 draft of *The Use of Law* at a meeting of Mennonite lawyers: "The degree to which this response [*The Use of the Law*] takes the matter of coercion and the link between the police and the adversary system into account is not immediately clear. The further question would be whether in this response the question of coercion is in effect resolved on the condition that the adversaries in some sense are willing to submit their case to adjudicative process. Or could it be argued that there is an ethically qualitative difference between the police power as linked to the adversary system and military power as exercised in warfare—and that therefore the total rejection of participation in warfare would not necessarily imply complete non-involvement in the adversarial process?" Marlin Miller, "Witnesses to the 'Law of Christ'" (paper presented at Mennonite Lawyers Symposium, Washington, D.C., 25-26 Jan. 1980), on file with author, 20 (my thanks to Professor Alvin Esau at the University of Manitoba for providing a copy of this document). As Yoder's comment above suggests, most likely what would be required for answering these questions would be a more thorough inquiry into the nature of any particular use of the power of the police.

21. John Howard Yoder, "Possible New Procedures for Use in Areas Where Existing Legal Procedures are not Compatible with Scriptural Principle" (paper presented at Mennonite General Conference, Peace Problems Committee Consultation on Litigation Problems, Goshen, Ind., 27-28 July 1961), Harold and Wilma Good Library, Goshen College, Goshen, Ind., 38-40.

22. Ibid., 42. Yoder displayed in his constructive alternatives the manner in which litigation ethics is intimately tied to economic ethics. The tensions Yoder drew between reconciliation, witness, litigation, and wealth were picked up again in a response paper written by Paul Peachey. Peachey located concerns surrounding both violence and litigation in acquisitiveness, citing the following passage from Paul Sabatier's *Life of St. Francis of Assisi*: "The Bishop of Assisi said to Francis one day: 'Your way of living without owning anything seems to me very harsh and difficult.' 'My Lord,' replied he, 'if we possessed property we should have need of arms for its defence, for it is the source of quarrels and lawsuits, and the love of God and one's neighbor usually finds many obstacles therein; this is why we do not desire temporal goods.'" Paul Sabatier, *Life of St. Francis of Assisi* (New York: Charles Scribner's Sons, 1894), 80, quoted in Paul Peachey, "Supplement to Part III of John Howard Yoder's Paper on Litigation" (paper presented at Mennonite General Conference, Peace Problems Committee Consultation on Litigation Problems, Goshen, Ind., 27-28 July 1961), Harold and Wilma Good Library, Goshen College, Goshen, Ind., 48.

23. John Howard Yoder, "Credit Counseling and Refinancing," 15 February 1984, John H. Yoder (1927-1997) Collection, Hist. Mss. 23/8, entitled "Litigation, 1961-1984," Mennonite Church USA Archives, Goshen, Indiana.

24. Mennonite Church General Assembly, *Proceedings: Sixth Mennonite Church General Assembly, August 11-16, 1981, Bowling Green State University, Bowling Green, Ohio* (Lombard, Ill.: Mennonite Church General Assembly, 1981), 9. That task force shared provisional findings with members of the Mennonite Church General Assembly in 1977 and presented a first draft in 1979. After receiving tentative approval with suggested changes in 1979, the final document was approved in 1981. In the Mennonite ecclesial "structure," such statements by the General Assembly have informal authority for the church and take on formal and binding authority when individual Mennonite conferences or congregations confirm them. Denominational archivists have no records of local church adoption. Dennis Stoesz, Goshen, Indiana, email to Richard P. Church, Wingate, North Carolina, 29 December 2004, on file with author. Nonetheless, this lack of formal adoption is often not indicative of the authority given within individual congregations to decisions of the General Assembly.

25. *The Use of the Law: Resume, A Summary Statement & Context of this Statement*, 1981, http://www.mhsc.ca/index.asp?content=http://www.mhsc.ca/encylclopedia/contents/ U78.html, 7 February 2005.

26. Ibid., "A Summary Statement," para. 4.

27. Ibid., "A Summary Statement," para. 6.

28. For example, the summary statement notes, "Since the common norms for the practice of law are designed to serve a pluralistic society, we cannot fully discern God's will apart from specific insights of the Christian faith." Ibid., "A Summary Statement," para. 3.

29. The report cautions about the existence of subrogation clauses in standard insurance contracts. See ibid., "A Summary Statement," para. 4. Likewise, the report suggests that corporate structures may raise additional difficulties in providing counsel, but should not exempt an entity from the concerns surrounding witness in regard to litigation set forth. See ibid., "A Summary Statement," para. 6 ("When members are part of large or corporate entities involved in litigation, the local congregation might not be an adequate source for counsel. In such instances the individual member and the congregation may well seek help from the conference to identify counsel and help in the situation, which would usually include business and professional peers in the church. Managers or business enterprises generally have not had the benefit of direct church support. Effort should be made in the various areas of the church to see that adequate counsel is available to all who desire such counsel"), and para. 7 ("The Christian should resist depersonalization in modern institutional and corporate life rather than using it as justification for the use of adversarial proceedings. It should be recognized that personal feelings, identities, and relationships are significant factors in institutional disputes. The faith and commitment of managers and directors should cause

them to maintain good relationships with persons, conduct corporate affairs with integrity, and seek justice in management decisions").

30. Ibid., "A Summary Statement," para. 1.

31. Ibid., "A Summary Statement," para 2.

32. Ibid., "A Summary Statement," para. 3.

33. Ibid., "A Summary Statement," para. 5. Such guidance is not left at this level of abstraction. The document counsels working with "an appropriate person or committee of the congregation (deacons, elders, pastoral committee, etc.) to identify responsible and trusted counselors." Ibid. In one of several responses to drafts of *The Use of the Law*, Yoder notes in regard to this material, "It is very good to have the accent on IV, the involvement of the congregation. This is one of the original contributions of the study. At the beginning of the second paragraph in this section it might be pointed out that the 'weighty resources for the task' which the congregation has in its midst would include the equivalent of the 'two or three wise men' in 1 Corinthians 6." John Howard Yoder, Elkhart, Indiana, to Richard Yordy, St. Jacobs, Ontario, 23 November 1979, John H. Yoder (1927-1997) Collection, Hist. Mss. 23/8, entitled "Litigation, 1961-1984," Mennonite Church USA Archives, Goshen, Indiana.

34. Mennonite General Assembly, *The Use of the Law*, A Summary Statement, para. 8. More recent Mennonite doctrinal statements affirm this stance. The *Confession of Faith in a Mennonite Perspective*, approved in 1995 by the Mennonite Church General Assembly and the Mennonite General Conference (which merged into the Mennonite Church USA in 2001), provides as commentary to the statement "The Church's Relations to Government and Society": "On a variety of political and social issues, individual Christians need the church to help them discern how to be in the world without belonging to the world (John 17:14-19). The church asks questions such as these: Will this participation in the government or in other institutions of society enable us to be ambassadors of Christ's reconciliation? Or will such participation violate our commitment to the way of Christ and compromise our loyalty to Christ? We ask these questions when we confront issues of military service, office holding, government employment, voting, taxes, participating in the economic system, using the secular courts, pledging allegiance, using flags, public and private schooling, and seeking to influence legislation." Mennonite General Assembly, *Confession of Faith in a Mennonite Perspective*, 1995, http://www.mcusa-archives.org//library/resolutions/1995/1995-23.html, 7 February 2005, comment 3 to art. 23.

35. The document provides, "The church cannot surrender its responsibility to act without weakening the life, witness, and faithfulness of its membership. In this way the Scriptures, the Holy Spirit, and the congregation each contribute to the discernment of the will of God in each situation." Mennonite General Assembly, *The Use of the Law*, "A Summary Statement,"

para. 8. The committee comments prior to the first drafting of *The Use of the Law* also emphasize this point: "Stress the importance of the Christian congregation as the hermeneutic community to bind and loose. The congregation is the link between the words of the Bible and the situation in which they were given and the issues in our situation and discernment of the will of God for our time." Task Force on Litigation, "Minutes," 24-25 November 1978, Carl J. Kreider Collection, Hist. Mss. 2/5, entitled "Litigation, 1976-81," Mennonite Church USA Archives, Goshen, Indiana.

36. The document affirms, "When the counsel [of the church] is for the Christian to accept loss, this could be the occasion for mutual sharing of loss." Mennonite General Assembly, *The Use of the Law*, "A Summary Statement," para. 6.

37. This conclusion is also supported by the direction of Matthew 18 to resolve disputes first in person, then with one or two witness, and finally before the whole church: "Before delay and defensive postures have taken their toll in dispute, the believer should seek face-to-face discussion to hear the concerns of all parties. If this does not result in reconciliation, it is appropriate to seek the help of one or two others. This is a norm when believers, who share a common faith in Jesus Christ as Lord, are involved." Ibid., "A Summary Statement," para 7.

38. See ibid., "A Summary Statement," para. 7-8.

39. Ibid., "A Summary Statement," para. 4.

40. For an introduction to the stance of *Gelassenheit*, or yieldedness, which still predominates in Amish views of the proper relation to the world, and its historical roots in the writings of the medieval Catholic mystics, see Walter Klaassen's "*Gelassenheit* and Creation," *Conrad Grabel Review* 7 (1991): 23-35.

41. See generally John Howard Yoder, *The Christian Witness to the State* (Scottdale, Pa.: Herald Press, 1964, 2002), 8-16, 35-44.

42. See generally Leo Driedger and Donald Kraybill, *Mennonite Peacemaking from Quietism to Activism* (Scottdale, Pa.: Herald Press, 1994), 121-24.

43. Such suits may leave open the possibility that they are coercive while nonetheless nonviolent. If it is noncoercion in lieu of mere nonviolence that is at the heart of the gospel, such distinctions may not be helpful. For a variety of essays taking up the questions surrounding nonresistance versus nonviolent resistance and power, influence, and coercion, see John Richard Burkholder and Calvin Redekop, eds., *Kingdom, Cross and Community: Essays on Mennonite Themes in Honor of Guy F. Hershberger* (Scottdale, Pa.: Herald Press, 1976).

44. The 1972 survey was directed by J. Howard Kauffman and Leland Harder and is summarized in their book *Anabaptists Four Centuries Later: A*

Profile of Five Mennonite and Brethren in Christ Denominations (Scottdale, Pa.: Herald Press, 1975). The 1989 survey was directed by J. Howard Kauffman and Leo Driedger and is summarized in their book *The Mennonite Mosaic: Identity and Modernization* (Scottdale, Pa.: Herald Press, 1991). Portions of the results of both surveys are also found in Leo Driedger and Donald Kraybill's *Mennonite Peacemaking: From Quietism to Activism*. The surveys involved members of the Mennonite Church, the General Conference Mennonites, the Mennonite Brethren, the Brethren in Christ, and the Evangelical Mennonites. The results of both the 1972 and 1989 surveys regarding litigation can be found in Driedger and Kraybill in table 9.1. See ibid., 215. Such diversity of opinion was also noted anecdotally by Marlin Miller in his paper presented at the meeting of Mennonite lawyers in 1980: "In my limited conversations with Mennonite lawyers, I have not found anything approaching a consensus on the relation between the adversary system and a biblical peace witness." Miller, "Witnesses to the 'Law of Christ,'" 13.

45. This chapter can be properly located by considering John Howard Yoder's argument in an essay entitled, "'Anabaptists and the Sword' Revisited: Systematic Historiography and Undogmatic Nonresistants" (in *Zeitschrift für Kirchengeschichte* 85:2 [1974]: 126-39). There Yoder suggests that one's historiographic position will impact the history that one discerns. Among other influences, Yoder suggests that one's historiographic position will impact the construction of one's position in regard to something called "the state." According to him, there is much greater diversity within Anabaptist thought regarding the state than can be discerned in the work of mainstream Anabaptist historians. See Hillerbrand, "The Anabaptist View of the State"; Clarence Bauman, *Gewaltlosigkeit im Täufertum* (Leiden: E. J. Brill, 1968); James Stayer, *Anabaptists and the Sword*, 2d ed. (Lawrence: Coronado Press, 1976).

46. Yoder suggests in regard to Anabaptist historians, "'The State' is assumed to be the same in essence and all times and cultures, so that the ethical issue posed for the Christian by participation in its violence is the same whether we speak of the age of Josiah, of the early church, of Constantine, of Charlemagne, or of Charles V." Yoder, "'Anabaptists and the Sword' Revisited," 127. I could just as well substitute the word *litigation* for *state* in that quotation.

47. Ibid., 128.

Chapter 9
The Practice of Reconciliation

1. A complete argument for the priority of Yoder's ecclesiology is not presented here. These arguments have been made and are worth making, but the present project assumes they are right and proceeds onward to the important task of displaying the connections noted here. Yoder may of course be wrong

about the church or wrong about Anabaptist praxis. Continuing dialogue around each of these questions—even learning a new start is necessary—is always a possibility, but the project is not flawed based solely on the fact it begins these arguments with a view in mind.

2. Yoder notes, "The reference . . . to the early centuries is not made with a view to undoing the passage of time but with a view to properly reorienting our present movement forward in light of what we now know was wrong with the way we had been going before. The truth claims being made by critics of the unfaithfulness into which Christians have fallen through the centuries are therefore not posited upon a vision of some pristine clarity that could be regained by going back to the first century. That is a frequent misconception of what the Protestant Reformation in general and the radical reformation in particular were about. The point is rather that they deny absolute authority to any later epoch, especially to the present, and especially to arrangements which came about in the medieval period through a tacit or explicit relativation of the narrativeness of the incarnation." John Howard Yoder, *The Priestly Kingdom: Social Ethics as Gospel* (Notre Dame, Ind.: University of Notre Dame Press, 1984), 87.

3. See generally Yoder's discussion of "ethics as mission" in "A People in the World," in *The Royal Priesthood: Essays Ecclesiological and Ecumenical*, ed. Michael Cartwright (Scottdale, Pa.: Herald Press, 1998), 79-81. Yoder concludes, "The new Christian community in which the walls are broken down not by human idealism or democratic legalism but by the work of Christ is not only a vehicle of the gospel or only a fruit of the gospel; it is the good news. It is not merely the agent of mission or the constituency of a mission agency. This is the mission." Ibid., 91.

4. Yoder describes this moment as follows, "The present aeon is characterized by sin and centered on man; the coming aeon is the redemptive reality which entered history in an ultimate way in Christ. . . . The seal of the possibility of His will's being done is the presence of the Holy Spirit, given to the church as a foretaste of the eventual consummation of God's kingdom. Thus, although the new aeon is described as coming, it is not only a future quantity. The old has already begun to be superseded by the new, and the focus of that victory is the body of Christ, first the man Christ Jesus, and then derivatively the fellowship of obedient believers." John Howard Yoder, *The Christian Witness to the State* (Scottdale, Pa.: Herald Press, 1964, 2002), 9; see also, Yoder, "Peace Without Eschatology?" in *The Royal Priesthood*, 146-47.

5. Yoder writes, "The church is herself a society. Her very existence, the fraternal relations of her members, their ways of dealing with their differences and their needs are, or rather should be, a demonstration of what love means in social relations. This demonstration cannot be transposed directly into non-Christian society, for in the church it functions only on the basis of

repentance and faith; yet by analogy certain of its aspects may be instructive as stimuli to the conscience of society." Yoder, *The Christian Witness to the State*, 17.

6. John Howard Yoder, "Why Ecclesiology is Social Ethics: Gospel Ethics versus the Wider Wisdom," in *The Royal Priesthood*, 125-26.

7. See Stanley Hauerwas, *The Peaceable Kingdom: A Primer in Christian Ethics* (Notre Dame, Ind.: University of Notre Dame Press, 1983), 55.

8. Locating the church's ethical praxis as the central moment of its witness suggests that the church is something like a Wittgenstinian "form of life," i.e., a unique social and historical location with its similarly unique set of linguistic, institutional, and practical resources. The church is constituted by a unique set of practices (e.g., baptism, communion, the rule of Christ), institutions (e.g., elders and deacons), and linguistic resources (e.g., the Trinity), collectively suggesting a world, the kingdom of Christ, which is visible only in light of these resources. See, e.g., Yoder, *The Priestly Kingdom*, 43 ("Worship is the communal cultivation of an alternative construction of society and of history"); Stanley Hauerwas, "Discipleship as a Craft, Church as a Disciplined Community," *Christian Century* 108 (1991): 884 ("We are Christians not because of what we believe, but because we have been called to be disciples of Jesus. To become a disciple is not a matter of a new or changed self-understanding, but rather to become a part of a different community with a different set of practices"). Accordingly, social location is prior to description, or as suggested by Yoder, "The church precedes the world epistemologically." Yoder, *The Priestly Kingdom*, 11. In another context, Yoder argues, "To celebrate, and to celebrate repeatedly in memory of Jesus, the glory of God as righteous and as sovereign means to cultivate explicitly an alternative consciousness, to maintain a sense of reality running against the stream of the unquestionably accepted commonplaces of the age." Yoder, "Why Ecclesiology is Social Ethics," 123. With this said, what Wittgenstein meant in talking about forms of life is contested. Fergus Kerr notes that something as "vast and internally diverse" as "religion or Catholicism" could not be a form of life. Fergus Kerr, *Theology after Wittgenstein*, 2d ed. (London: SPCK, 1997), 30. I leave open the possibility, however, that the gathered community could constitute a form of life.

Yoder's arguments against "effectiveness" are similarly related to this insight insofar as Yoder is not denying the essential value of effective action by the church, but denying the view of the world that judges "effectiveness" through the short-term lens of immediate power. See Yoder, *The Priestly Kingdom*, 37 ("If Jesus Christ is Lord, obedience to his rule cannot be dysfunctional. Principled or virtuous behavior cannot be imprudent generally, though it may well appear so punctually"). Yoder sets forth a variety of ways in which the minority position may be more "effective." See ibid., 96-99. Further, he argues that principle versus effectiveness is a false dichotomy insofar as another principle always motivates the argument for effectiveness, "so the argument which takes the clothing of 'principles versus effectiveness' really means this principle versus that principle." John Howard Yoder, *Christian Attitudes to War, Peace, and Revolution: A Companion to Bainton* (Elkhart, Ind.: Co-Op Bookstore, 1983), 436-37.

In addition, as noted by Harry Huebner, Yoder's resistance to "effectiveness" is critically tied to his understanding of history. As Huebner describes it, "the church's task is to be a sign of the new, but the realization of the new is a gift from God." Harry J. Huebner, "Moral Agency as Embodiment: How the Church Acts," in *The Wisdom of the Cross: Essays in Honor of John Howard Yoder*, ed. Stanley Hauerwas, et al. (Grand Rapids, Mich.: Eerdmans, 1999), 199. Accordingly, the task of the church is not to make history turn out right, but "to be seen as a moral agent in the same way that Jesus was; that is, the moral significance of Jesus lies not only in his pointing to the nature of the kingdom of God, but also in his embodiment of that to which he pointed." Ibid., 200.

9. This vision of the church is confirmed by Luke. Stephen's death, the first Christian witness in the nonviolent steps of Jesus, is immediately followed by these words, "That day a great persecution arose against the church in Jerusalem; and they were all scattered throughout the region of Judea and Samaria, except the apostles." Acts 8:1 RSV. Persecution spawns dispersion, but that dispersion scatters the church's witness. The echo is clear: "you will be my witnesses in Jerusalem, in all of Judea and Samaria, and to the ends of the earth." Acts 1:8.

10. John Howard Yoder, *The Politics of Jesus: Vicit Agnus Noster*, 2d ed. (Grand Rapids, Mich.: Eerdmans, 1994), 232.

11. Hauerwas makes the same claim regarding Christians' nonparticipation in litigation. See Stanley Hauerwas, "Why the Sectarian Temptation is a Misrepresentation: A Response to James Gustafson," in *The Hauerwas Reader*, ed. John Berkman and Michael Cartwright (Durham, N.C.: Duke University Press, 2001), 104.

12. Yoder, *The Politics of Jesus*, 51.
13. See Yoder, "A People in the World," 86.
14. Yoder, *The Politics of Jesus*, 95.
15. Ibid., 237.
16. Returning to Yoder's comments in the meetings on litigation witness in 1961, several of his summary points should be highlighted, each of which focuses on the relationship of litigation and nonresistance: "A. The basic reason for rejection of litigation is nonresistant love for the neighbor, the enemy [not avoidance of scandal or reduction of conflict with government]. B. The general emphasis of Scripture points in this direction. C. Litigation, resting as it does on ultimate appeal to governmental coercion, is (when used in just

self-defense) morally the equivalent of the direct appeal to the services of the police. . . . The rejection of self-defense by litigation is therefore a part of the general "other-cheek" attitude. . . . I. The recourse to coercion is always a concession to the breakdown of human relations. . . . This is the case when men resort to fists; it is also the case when they resort to the courts. Therefore Christians should be imaginatively on the lookout for more effective, prompt, personal and reconciling ways to meet such situations. This, and not making nonresistance painless, I understand to be the concern of the present conference. K. The New Testament . . . sees the Christian in the broader context of brotherhood. This relates to our problem in numerous ways: (a) The brotherhood is a source of counsel on ethical problems; (b) If a loss is involved in the nonresistant resolution of such a conflict the brotherhood can and should help to bear it; (c) It makes a difference whether the other party is a Christian. If he is, friendly mediation should always suffice (1 Cor 6)." John Howard Yoder, "Possible New Procedures for Use in Areas Where Existing Legal Procedures are not Compatible with Scriptural Principle" (paper presented at Mennonite General Conference, Peace Problems Committee Consultation on Litigation Problems, Goshen, Ind., 27-28 July 1961), Harold and Wilma Good Library, Goshen College, Goshen, Ind., 38-40.

17. Bell argues, "The cross of Christ, as well as the crosses of those who would follow Christ, is not a valorization of suffering but an instance of bearing sin and suffering in order to bear them away." See Daniel Bell, "Sacrifice and Suffering: Beyond Justice, Human Rights, and Capitalism," *Modern Theology* 18 (2002): 351.

18. "But now in Christ Jesus you who once were far off have been brought near by the blood of Christ. For he is our peace; in his flesh he has made both groups into one and has broken down the dividing wall, that is, the hostility between us. He has abolished the law with its commandments and ordinances, that he might create in himself one new humanity in place of the two, thus making peace, and might reconcile both groups to God in one body through the cross, thus putting to death that hostility through it. So he came and proclaimed peace to you who were far off and peace to those who were near; for through him both of us have access in one Spirit to the Father. So then you are no longer strangers and aliens, but you are citizens with the saints and also members of the household of God, built upon the foundation of the apostles and prophets, with Christ Jesus himself as the cornerstone. In him the whole structure is joined together and grows into a holy temple in the Lord; in whom you also are built together spiritually into a dwelling place for God," Ephesians 2:13-22.

19. John Howard Yoder, *Body Politics: Five Practices of the Christian Community Before the Watching World* (Scottdale, Pa.: Herald Press, 2001), 29; see also Yoder, "The Imperative of Christian Unity," in *The Royal Priesthood*, 289-99.

20. Yoder, *Body Politics*, 33.
21. Ibid., 38; see also Yoder, *The Politics of Jesus*, 150-51; Markus Barth, "Jews and Gentiles: The Social Character of Justification in Paul," *Journal of Ecumenical Studies* 5/2 (Spring 1968): 258.
22. Thomas Shaffer, *Moral Memoranda from John Howard Yoder: Conversations on Law, Ethics and the Church between a Mennonite Theologian and a Hoosier Lawyer* (Eugene: Wipf and Stock, 2002), 24.
23. See generally Alasdair MacIntyre, *Whose Justice? Which Rationality?* (Notre Dame, Ind.: University of Notre Dame Press, 1988), on the relationship of different accounts of justice to particular traditions.
24. Thomas Shaffer and Andrew McThenia, "For Reconciliation," *Yale Law Journal* 94 (1985): 1664-65. For more on the relationship of God's law to the gospel, see Markus Barth, "Christ and Law," *Oklahoma Law Review* 12 (1959): 67-85. Contra Luther, Barth argues that law and gospel are only opposites in "the human psyche" not "a basic difference in God himself." Ibid., 69. The law reveals God to humans, reveals to humans who they are, and makes clear that God has not given up on humanity. See ibid. 70-71. Like Shaffer and McThenia, Barth concludes that in God love and justice coincide. See ibid., 71.
25. Shaffer and McThenia, "For Reconciliation," 1665.
26. See Huebner, "Moral Agency as Embodiment," 211, quoting Susan Brooks Thistlethwaite, "Peace and Justice, Not Issues but Identities for the Church (Interview)," *Engage/Social Action* 15 (1987): 33.
27. Oliver O'Donovan, *The Desire of the Nations: Rediscovering the Roots of Political Theology* (Cambridge: Cambridge University Press, 1996), 39.
28. Thomas Shaffer, *On Being a Christian and a Lawyer: Law for the Innocent* (Provo, Utah: Brigham Young University Press, 1981), 139.
29. Ibid.
30. On the relationship of forgiveness and reconciliation, see generally L. Gregory Jones, *Embodying Forgiveness: A Theological Analysis* (Grand Rapids, Mich.: Eerdmans, 1995). Jones begins with the key claim that both divine and human forgiveness are about reconciliation, not the allocation and removal of guilt. Ibid., 5. For an alternative view of the relationship of forgiveness to memory, see Miroslav Volf, *Exclusion and Embrace: A Theological Exploration of Identity, Otherness, and Reconciliation* (Nashville: Abingdon, 1996), 131-40. While Volf is broadly sympathetic to the argument set forth here, he suggests that forgiveness must usher in a kind of forgetfulness insofar as sin cannot be undone. His model is the Old Testament God who "will remember their sin no more" (Jer 31:34). There is much worth considering in Volf's treatment, yet it seems to stray from his own best insight that "the proper context for the interpretation" of biblical texts is "the narrative of the death and resurrection of Jesus Christ." Ibid., 30-31. That event suggests not the forgetting of sin, but the transformation of sin. For a detailed discussion of the

necessity that forgiveness be more than forgetfulness of sin, see John Milbank, *Being Reconciled: Ontology and pardon* (London: Routledge, 2005), 44-60 ("Forgiveness: The Double Waters"). Milbank argues that forgiveness must involve a positive offering of renarration that leads to reconciliation, not the mere denial of sin via a negative forgetting. In lieu of forgetting, Milbank, Hauerwas, and Jones each argue that Christian penance is necessary to reconciliation. See ibid.; Hauerwas, "Punishing Christians," 23; Jones, *Embodying Forgiveness*, 147.

31. See Stanley Hauerwas, "Peacemaking: The Virtue of the Church," in *Christian Existence Today: Essays on Church, World and Living in Between* (Grand Rapids, Mich.: Baker Books, 1988), 89-97.

32. See generally Stanley Hauerwas, "Why Truthfulness Requires Forgiveness: A Commencement Address for Graduates of a College of the Church of the Second Chance," in *The Hauerwas Reader*, 307-17.

33. Yoder notes, "Forgiveness is not a generally accessible human possibility; it is the miraculous fruit of God's own bearing the cost of human rebellion. Forgiveness among us also costs a cross. One can go to one's brother or sister only as God came to us; not counting our trespasses against us. Forgiveness does not brush the offense off with a 'think nothing of it'; it absorbs the offense in suffering love." Yoder, "Binding and Loosing," in *The Royal Priesthood*, 352. See also, Shaffer and McThenia, "For Reconciliation," 1664. With this said, a comment of Yoder's to Shaffer suggests that litigation is not the only impediment to forgiveness: "You seem to me to simplify what you identify as 'the legal order,' as the only power, or the only reason for not forgiving. This seems to me to leave out other reasons generally appealed to in favor of punishment." Shaffer, *Moral Memoranda from John Howard Yoder*, 97.

34. Stanley Hauerwas and Chris K. Huebner, "History, Theory, and Anabaptism: A Conversation on Theology After John Howard Yoder," in *The Wisdom of the Cross*, 402; see also Daniel Bell, "What Gift is Given? A Response to Volf," *Modern Theology* 19 (2003): 278.

35. See John Howard Yoder, "The Spirit of God and the Politics of Men," in *For the Nations: Essays Public and Evangelical* (Grand Rapids, Mich.: Eerdmans, 1997), 229.

36. Yoder, *The Politics of Jesus*, 246; see also John Howard Yoder, "Are You the One Who Is to Come?" in *For the Nations*, 212.

37. Therefore, in counseling the drafters of *The Use of the Law*, Yoder noted, "One of the points to make would be that loving one's enemies is not bad news, imposed by legalistic Mennonite tradition, but is good news, part of the gospel and experience of liberty and reconciliation. Too often the approach to everything having to do with nonresistance has been to feel that it is oppressive rather than a privilege of sharing the nature of God's love in Christ." John Howard Yoder, Elkhart, Indiana, to Richard Yordy, St. Jacobs,

Ontario, 23 November 1979, John H. Yoder (1927-1997) Collection, Hist. Mss. 23/8, entitled "Litigation, 1961-1984," Mennonite Church USA Archives, Goshen, Indiana.

38. Bell details the competitive vision of modern accounts of justice, "predicated not on plentitude but on lack, not the scarcity of created goods." Bell, "Sacrifice and Suffering," 343. As an alternative, he offers a compelling rereading of Anselm's account of atonement on ontological versus economic grounds, displaying the logic of "the plentitude of divine charity." Ibid., 345. This reading collapses the presupposition that there is a difference within the life of God over justice and mercy: "[Justice and mercy] are but two names of the single love of God that desires to draw humanity into communion. Justice and mercy are not opposing logics; rather they share a single end—the return of love, the sociality of all desire, in God." Ibid., 350. For a related argument focusing on the manner in which God's relationship to creation cannot be captured by standard legal accounts of justice, see Herbert Fingarette, "The Meaning of Law in the Book of Job," in *Revisions: Changing Perspectives on Moral Philosophy*, ed. Stanley Hauerwas and Alasdair MacIntyre (Notre Dame, Ind.: University of Notre Dame Press, 1983), 249-86.

39. Bell, "Sacrifice and Suffering," 347.

40. Yoder suggests that justification itself might name "making peace" or "breaking down the wall" between Jew and Gentile. Yoder, *The Politics of Jesus*, 220-21; see also Barth, "Jews and Gentiles: The Social Character of Justification in Paul."

41. See Yoder, "Binding and Loosing," 337. Yoder cites Matthew 5:23-24 in this regard, in which Jesus counsels abandoning worship prior to reconciliation.

42. See generally Gerald Schlabach, "The Christian Witness in the Earthly City: John H. Yoder as Augustinian Interlocutor," in *A Mind Patient and Untamed: Assessing John Howard Yoder's Contributions to Theology and Peacemaking*, ed. Ben C. Ollenburger and Gayle Gerber Koontz (Telford, Pa.: Cascadia Publishing House, 2003), 221-44; John Howard Yoder, "'See How They Go with Their Face to the Sun,'" in *For the Nations*, 51-78; and Jeremiah 29. Yoder notes that in light of Jeremiah, Jesus was saying nothing novel in suggesting the Christians would be resident aliens in the manner of the Jews. What was radical was the early church's inclusion of the Gentiles in this community. See Yoder, "To Serve our God and Rule the World," in *The Royal Priesthood*, 135.

43. See Yoder, *The Priestly Kingdom*, 165; Hauerwas, "Peacemaking," 96.

44. Yoder writes, "[Minority Christian communities] rather called upon the church at large to accept as binding for all Christians the quality of commitment which would in effect lead them all to be separated from the world once again in order to be appropriately in mission to the world." Yoder, *The*

Priestly Kingdom, 85. Yoder suggests that this alternative conflict-resolution process of the church may serve as a model for the wider society. See *Body Politics*, 11. In another example, Yoder notes, "The way the impact of the death of Jesus can enter the social process is not that it does away with punishment, but that it by offers [sic] a paradigm whereby, in one place at one time, the awareness that 'this is too much' can break through. None of these changes opens the new age; each of them partakes in a fragmentary way of the victory of resurrection and Pentecost, offering to others elsewhere, non-coercively, the power to replicate reconciliation." John Howard Yoder, *You Have It Coming: Good Punishment. The legitimate social function of punitive behavior*, 1995, www.nd.edu/~j1yo...gs/punishment/shape.htm (also available from Shalom Desktop Publications), 12 January 1998, chap. 11 ("Back to the Rest of Sociology"). Yoder argues elsewhere that one function of the church is to act as modeling agent of what civil society should be. See Yoder, *The Priestly Kingdom*, 92-94.

Nonetheless, Yoder is clear that the sinful state will not achieve justice, but will always remain sinful. The church in modeling and witnessing to the state is not under the illusion that, for example, once alternative dispute resolution is the norm, the kingdom will have come in some theoretically perfect state. Rather, the church witnesses to injustice and, when one injustice is corrected, moves on to the next. Yoder labels such ad hoc guidance to the state, middle axioms. See Yoder, *The Christian Witness to the State*, 32-33. The idea would appear to be similar to Karl Barth's treatment of the law as exemplary for the civil state. See Karl Barth, *Church Dogmatics*, vol. 4, pt. 2, *The Doctrine of Reconciliation*, trans. G. W. Bromiley (Edinburgh: T&T Clark, 1958), 719-26. Despite the apparent connection Barth draws between the Christian and secular orders, Yoder credits Barth with being the first Protestant theologian since Constantine not to presume that the church can address the wider world as if it were Christian. See Yoder, "Why Ecclesiology is Social Ethics," 108.

45. See Yoder, *The Priestly Kingdom*, 37; "Why Ecclesiology is Social Ethics," 108-9; "Let the Church be the Church," in *The Royal Priesthood*, 170-71.

46. See Yoder, "Why Ecclesiology is Social Ethics," 108.

47. See, e.g., Yoder, "The Otherness of the Church," in *The Royal Priesthood*, 56-57. Yoder notes that the great reversal that followed upon Constantine's conversion was in the visible presence of the church and the lordship of Christ over history: "After Constantine one knew as a fact of experience that Christ was ruling over the world but had to believe against the evidence that there existed 'a believing church.'" Ibid., 57.

48. Yoder notes that the pre-Constantinian church "believed that its Lord was also Lord over the world. . . . This belief in Christ's lordship over the exousiai enabled the church, in and in spite of its distinctness from the

world, to speak to the world in God's name, not only in evangelism but in ethical judgment as well." Ibid., 56.

49. O'Donovan, *The Desire of the Nations*, 150. This tension between the church and the secular judge is the location of the problematic nature of the "Christian emperor" and the right of the bishop to intercede on the behalf of the civilly condemned: "The logic of the convention was, in effect, subversive. It expressed three perceptions: that the task of rulers was to judge; that a Christian ruler should show clemency; and that there was inherent tension between the two obligations." Ibid., 200.

50. Yoder, *The Christian Witness to the State*, 17; see also Yoder, "Let the Church be the Church," 170.

51. Alasdair MacIntyre, *Whose Justice? Which Rationality?* 346.

52. Alasdair MacIntyre, *After Virtue: A Study in Moral Theory*, 2d. ed. (Notre Dame, Ind.: University of Notre Dame Press, 1984), 36-50; MacIntyre, *Whose Justice? Which Rationality?* 334-35.

53. Ibid., 344; see also Alasdair MacIntyre, *Three Rival Versions of Moral Enquiry: Encyclopedia, Genealogy, and Tradition* (Notre Dame, Ind.: University of Notre Dame Press, 1990), 76, in which MacIntyre makes clear the priority of law over rights in the Thomistic tradition.

54. MacIntyre, *Whose Justice? Which Rationality*, 344. In MacIntyre's earlier work, he notes the particular nature of rights language to Western forms of life, see MacIntyre, *After Virtue*, 67-71.

55. Bell, "Sacrifice and Suffering," 335.

56. See generally Alexis de Tocqueville's insightful discussion of American law and lawyers in regard to this matter, in Alexis de Tocqueville, *Democracy in America*, ed. J. P. Mayer, trans. George Lawrence (New York: HarperPerennial, 1969), 263-70. These changes in justice suggest that Thomas Hobbes provides the best description of American political and legal discourse. See generally Thomas Hobbes, *Leviathan*, ed. C. B. Macpherson (London: Penguin Classic, 1982). In other words, modern law is essentially grounded in coercion and violence, for Hobbes is right in suggesting that only coercion and violence can sustain an agonistic community who lack a determinative set of shared values. See generally Robert Cover, "Violence and the Word," *Yale Law Journal* 95 (1986): 1601-29; Max Weber, *Max Weber on Law in Economy in Society*, ed. Max Rheinstein, trans. Edward Shils and Max Rheinstein (New York: Simon and Shuster, 1954), 6. In a related argument, MacIntyre suggests that social structures in an emotivist society must necessarily be manipulative, for any form of persuasion grounded in shared rationality is precluded by emotivism itself. See MacIntyre, *After Virtue*, 23-26. In such a context, effectiveness, i.e., "successful power," becomes the sole criteria for authority. Ibid., 26. MacIntyre goes on to suggest that "the mock rationality" of rights language and utility "conceals the arbitrariness of the will and power at work in its res-

olution." Ibid., 71. This suggestion, which MacIntyre works out in much more detail in regard to the bureaucrat, might go a long way in helping to understand the dissonance in anti-democratic power plays to the Supreme Court cloaked in the language of rights.

57. See Barth, "Christ and Law," 70-71.

58. John Toews argues, "The prevailing paradigmatic interpretation of the term 'law' suggests that *Torah* . . . meant story and stipulation, instruction and law. The Septuagint's use of *nomos* . . . for *Torah* stressed the second half of the original meaning. Torah became law. Torah as story and instruction was lost." John E. Toews, "Some Theses Toward a Theology of Law in the New Testament," in *The Bible and the Law: Occasional Papers No. 3 of Council of Mennonite Seminaries*, ed. William Swartley (Elkhart, Ind.: Institute of Mennonite Studies, 1982), 48-49. In summary, "Torah is grace, not a burden. The covenant is liberation, not servitude." Yoder, *The Priestly Kingdom*, 37.

59. Barth argues, "The imperatives show that God means business when He speaks of salvation. Only when God's holiness is manifested to man as actual limitation, exclusion and prohibition of the ways of unrighteousness, does man become aware of a real alternative to his wicked and miserable ways." Barth, "Christ and Law," 73. In regard to Paul's comments regarding the law, Barth suggests, "Much confusion in the interpretation of Paul's doctrine on law must be attributed to the fact that most often *nomos* in the Pauline epistles is an equivalent of *torah*, while in some cases he uses *nomos* in the wide and ambiguous sense of the Greek term. Depreciatory statements made by him e.g. on the law of sin and death must not be understood as a devaluation of the holy *torah* of God; they treat of 'another' law as Rom. 7:23 clearly reveals." Barth, "Jews and Gentiles: The Social Character of Justification in Paul," 253. Thus, O'Donovan notes, "Authority is the 'the objective correlate of freedom.' That is to say, it evokes free action, and makes free action intelligible." O'Donovan, *The Desire of the Nations*, 30.

60. MacIntyre contrasts Henry II and Becket with Henry VIII and Thomas More: "Henry II and Thomas Becket inhabit a single narrative structure; Henry VIII and Thomas Cromwell on the one hand and Thomas More and Reginald Pole on the other inhabit rival conceptual worlds and tell, as they act and after they act, different and incompatible stories about what they do." MacIntyre, *After Virtue*, 173.

61. Ibid., 174.

62. MacIntyre concludes, "Charity is not of course, from the biblical point of view, just one more virtue to be added to the list. Its inclusion alters the conception of the good for man in a radical way; for the community in which the good is achieved has to be one of reconciliation. It is thus a community with a history of a particular kind." Ibid., 174.

63. See H. Jefferson Powell, *A Community Built on Words: The*

Constitution in History and Politics (Chicago: University of Chicago Press, 2002). In Powell's words, "Hand, like Holmes, made no use of tropes common in romantic accounts of democracy such as 'the popular will' or 'the People.' Democracy in the sense it is practiced in the American constitutional order does not depend on such notions; indeed, its social realism and its commitment to the maintenance of political community through and within sharp political conflict is on a deep level antithetical to the romantic vision of democracy as the great common endeavor of an organic people. Democracy is, instead, 'a political contrivance' enabling people of fundamentally differing views to get by together with as much attention to the general welfare as their disagreements will permit. But it is precisely in the modesty of its claims about the degree of social unity that our constitutionalism expects that Holmes's vision of a community with room for talk but none for command displays what is morally attractive about American constitutionalism." Ibid., 191. Powell concludes, "Constitutionalism is a means for seeking to do justice, not a guarantee that we will have the wisdom or vision to do so." Ibid., 201.

64. MacIntyre, *After Virtue*, 253. MacIntyre nonetheless suggests that it is a real political good that governments sustain the "rule of law." Ibid., 255. Powell rejects MacIntyre's assessment of *Bakke*, contending that the failure to achieve a shared conception of justice does not mean that there is not a shared set of "constitutional principles," be they merely political and procedural. See ibid., 205-10. Nonetheless, Powell's hope to make the crassly political nature of politics, even judicial politics, open remains closely related to Yoder's "defense" of democracy. See generally Yoder, "The Christian Case for Democracy," in *The Priestly Kingdom*, 151-71.

65. This fixation may be more than that; for example, Shaffer suggests as the church assesses the law it must always ask if it was and is still an idol. See Thomas Shaffer, with Mary Shaffer, *American Lawyers and their Communities: Ethics in the Legal Profession* (Notre Dame, Ind.: University of Notre Dame Press, 1991), 205.

66. Yoder notes that the conclusions that follow from the church-world distinction are (1) "Christians ethics is for Christians," and (2) "there may well be certain functions in a given society which that society in its unbelief considers necessary, and which the unbelief renders necessary, in which Christians will not be called to participate." Yoder, "The Otherness of the Church," 62-63. While this position is an uncomfortable one to maintain, I take it Jacques Ellul is right in arguing that this essentially dualistic message is found within the Bible regarding civil order. See Jacques Ellul, *Violence: Reflections from a Christian Perspective*, trans. Cecilia Gaul Kings (London: SCM Press, 1970), 1-2.

67. Nonetheless, Shaffer may be right in noting that in denying the totalizing discourse of the rule of law, Christians are subversive of the law. See Thomas Shaffer, "Faith Tends to Subvert Legal Order," *Fordham Law Review*

66 (1998): 1089-99. Yoder would appear to concur in large measure. See Yoder, *The Priestly Kingdom*, 40; Yoder, *The Politics of Jesus*, 145; Yoder, "The Bible and Civil Turmoil," in *For the Nations*, 84. However, Shaffer notes that Yoder convinced him to change the title of his essay from "Faith Subverts Legal Order" to "Faith Tends to Subvert Legal Order." Shaffer records Yoder's comment: "It is only with a particular 'fallen' definition of what the 'order' has to be recognized as, that the only contribution for the Christian to make is subversion." Shaffer, *Moral Memoranda from John Howard Yoder*, 36. In the light of Romans 13, this is an important corrective, for as O'Donovan repeatedly argues in his book, "Generically, government is legitimated by its judicial function." O'Donovan, *The Desire of the Nations*, 234.

68. In an early book, Shaffer argues that looking from the "bottom up—as if peaceful life in groups were the model," one would see "advocacy as a form of reconciliation." Shaffer, *On Being a Christian and a Lawyer*, 111. While I am willing to acknowledge that advocacy can be a form of reconciliation, I would deny that the vast majority of cases that settle do so based on reconciliation of the parties. Most cases settle because the cost of the lawyer is greater than the cost of the settlement. Settlement is a purely economic decision that has nothing to do with reconciliation, and for that matter little to do with the opposing side itself.

69. See generally Yoder, *Body Politics*. For a closely related discussion of the connections between these practices and forgiveness, see Jones, *Embodying Forgiveness*, 163-204 ("Practicing Forgiveness: Trinitarian Community and the Hope for a New Humanity").

70. See generally Stanley Hauerwas, "Christian Practice and the Practice of Law in a World Without Foundations," *Mercer Law Review* 44 (1993): 743-61; Joseph Allegretti, "Dialogue and the Practice of Law and Spiritual Values: A Christian Perspective on Alternative Dispute Resolution," *Fordham Urban Law Journal* 28 (2001): 997-1006.

71. See Yoder, "Binding and Loosing," 332.

72. Yoder treats the process of binding and loosing in detail in two locations: in a study outline published and revised in multiple versions, concluding with its inclusion in *The Royal Priesthood* and in his short primer on Christian practices, *Body Politics: Five Practices of the Christian Community Before the Watching World*. John Howard Yoder, "Binding and Loosing," in *The Royal Priesthood*, 325-58. This essay was originally published in the Concern Group series under the title "Binding and Loosing." See John Howard Yoder, "Binding and Loosing," *Concern* 14 (Feb. 1967): 2-32. It was then republished two additional times prior to its inclusion in *The Royal Priesthood*. See John Howard Yoder, "Practicing the Rule of Christ," in *Virtues and Practices in the Christian Tradition: Christian Ethics After MacIntyre*, ed. Nancey Murphy, Brad J. Kallenberg, and Mark Thiessen Nation (Harrisburg, Va.:

Trinity Press International, 1997), 132-60, and John Howard Yoder, "Binding and Loosing," in John White and Ken Blue, *Healing the Wounded: The Costly Love of Church Discipline* (Downers Grove, Ill.: InterVarsity Press, 1985), 211-34. These two sources are of great importance insofar as *The Royal Priesthood* version of the binding and loosing article includes revisions made after Yoder's own disciplining and the *Body Politics* version is found in the book in which Yoder sets forth the essential features of the church, of which binding and loosing is one of them. I focus on these two essays as well as Yoder's treatment of "A Reconciling Process" in his essay, "The Hermeneutics of Peoplehood: A Protestant Perspective," found in *The Priestly Kingdom*.

The version in *The Royal Priesthood* includes an additional section (13), "Cavils and Caveats," in which Yoder provides insights into binding and loosing as practiced. The additions appear to be directly influenced by Yoder's own experience of having the ban instituted against him. He emphasizes the need for confrontation of the sinner directly by those that would accuse him, not only to ensure that a power play is not involved but also to allow for clarification of the accusation and its legitimacy. See Yoder, "Binding and Loosing," 357. It is worthwhile to consider in detail the process and outcome of Yoder's own process of being disciplined, for it both informs his understanding of the procedure and exemplifies both the risks and benefits of the church discerning and disciplining. That the process led to the disciplining of the most influential figure in Mennonite life at the time is further testament to the strength of the practices set forth in this chapter. Finally, that Yoder submitted to the process, leading to his reconciliation with his home church a week before his death, is a testament to the power of the process set forth here to lead to reconciliation. With this said, the story is much more complicated than these conclusions.

73. Yoder, "Binding and Loosing," 327.

74. Yoder, *The Priestly Kingdom*, 27.

75. See Yoder, "Binding and Loosing," 330-32. As noted previously, Yoder agrees with Catholic theology on the authority of the church. The disagreement is on what is properly described as "the church." While calling this mandate to speak on God's behalf a "scandal," Yoder is still breaking with his teacher, Karl Barth, here. Barth, remaining closer to the Magisterial Reformers, rejects this view of the church's authority, saying it was more than a scandal, but an impossibility. Barth discounts Matthew 18, rejecting a reading that would construe a correspondence in heaven with decisions of humans via the church here on earth. Such a conclusion reconnects the radical break between God and humans Barth first articulated in his 1921 revised commentary, *The Epistle to the Romans*, thereby confusing the action of humans with that of God. See generally Karl Barth, *The Epistle to the Romans*, 6th ed., trans. Edwyn C. Hoskyns (Oxford: Oxford University Press, 1968). Barth remains as intent on maintaining this distinction in his

few references to Matthew 18 in the Church Dogmatics as he was in first recovering the infinite qualitative difference in *The Epistle to the Romans*. As an alternative, Barth argues that the phrase merely names the participation of the church in the divine project insofar as the church's failure or success opens or closes the doors of heaven. Accordingly, Barth writes, "The solemn connexion with the founding of the community in which it occurs in Matthew 1619 and John 2023, however, makes it probable that primarily and properly it is to be referred to the function of the community in relation to the world. If, it speaks of that which, as the community is at work, either takes place or does not take place in the world and among men, including the members of the community itself. If everything is in order and its work is well done, there must be a great opening, permitting and releasing, i.e., the promise and reception of the forgiveness of sins. If its work is not done or done badly, then contrary to its task the community closes the kingdom of heaven and excludes men from it instead of point them to the door which is open to all. It holds where it should release. The remission which is the content of its witness is kept from men." Karl Barth, *Church Dogmatics*, 4.3.2, *The Doctrine of Reconciliation*, trans. G. W. Bromiley (Edinburgh: T&T Clark, 1962), 861-62.

76. See Yoder, "Binding and Loosing," 335-36. Yoder excludes a variety of other purposes, such as maintaining the purity of the church, avoidance of scandal, etc., that other theologians have suggested are similarly at stake. In Yoder's words, "Reconciliation and restoration is the only worthy motive." Ibid., 335.

77. Yoder writes, "Whether the outcome be the separating of fellowship or its restoration, the process is not one that can be carried on in a limited time and by means of judicial formalities; it demands conversation of a serious, patient, sustained, loving character." Ibid., 352. With this said, the process is not entirely ad hoc. Yoder notes, "The tests of the validity of the process are procedural, having to do with the hearing of several witnesses, subject to correction and change over time." Yoder, *Body Politics*, 27.

78. Yoder argues, "As [Paul] urged the believers in Corinth not to litigate in pagan courts (1 Cor 6:1-8), one of the reasons he gave was that there should be some wise mediator in the midst. That is an application of the same principle." Ibid., 4.

79. In a substantial although informal treatment centered on the work of Rene Girard, Yoder suggests that the place to begin thinking about punishment is from an understanding of its legitimate social function. See Yoder, *You Have It Coming*, chap. 5 ("With and Beyond Girard"). However, Yoder is clear that *legitimate* does not mean redemptive or of the kingdom, which he distinguishes as the cosmic system of gift or grace (vs. the cosmic system of reciprocity or retribution). See ibid., chap. 8 ("Jesus in Relation to the

'Socrates' Section"). Nonetheless, the redemptive work of Christ may have some impact on the order of retribution: "The way the impact of the death of Jesus can enter the social process is not that it does away with punishment, but that it by offers [sic] a paradigm whereby, in one place at one time, the awareness that 'this is too much' can break through. None of these changes opens the new age; each of them partakes in a fragmentary way of the victory of resurrection and Pentecost, offering to others elsewhere, noncoercively, the power to replicate reconciliation." See ibid., chap. 11 ("Back to the Rest of Sociology").

80. The voluntary nature of the practice is ensured by the voluntary nature of the church itself. Yoder notes that the Anabaptist's historical rejection of infant baptism had more to do with the inability to participate in community discernment and discipline than with the infant's age per se. As summarized in chapter 7, Yoder argues that Balthasar Hubmaier made this connection explicit in his early Anabaptist catechism: "Q. But what right has one brother to use this authority on another? A. From the baptismal pledge in which one subjects oneself to the Church and all her members according to the word of Christ." Yoder, "Binding and Loosing," 339-40.

Likewise, Yoder argues for a nonauthoritarian understanding of the practice: "The early Anabaptists were aware of this danger [i.e., an authoritarian vs. redemptive use of discipline], for with their insistence on discipline they coupled Jesus' word: 'the rulers of the Gentiles lord it over them, and their great men exercise authority over them. It shall not be so among you; but whoever would be great among you must by your servant . . . even as the Son of man came not to be served but to serve.' Again the passage relates discipleship and nonconformity; the alternatives are to do as the Gentiles do, or to do as Christ did. One alternative means following Christ; the other means self assertion." John Howard Yoder, "Discipleship and Self-Assertion," *Christian Living* (April 1955): 29. In this regard, contrary to Reinhold Niebuhr, Yoder claims nonviolent action can also be noncoercive. See John Howard Yoder, "The Radical Revolution in Perspective," in *For the Nations*, 100, n. 10.

81. William Cavenaugh argues, "Whereas the discipline of the State seeks to create disciples of Leviathan, the discipline of the Church seeks to form disciples of Jesus Christ, the Prince of Peace. For this reason our discipline will more often resemble martyrdom than military victory." William Cavenaugh, "'A Fire Strong Enough to Consume the House': The Wars of Religion and the Rise of the State," *Modern Theology* 11 (1995): 415; see also Hauerwas, "Punishing Christians," 189. However, this does not mean Christian discipline must be flaccid.

82. Yoder, "A People in the World," 83.

83. Hauerwas suggests, "To be excommunicated is not to be 'thrown out,' but rather to be told that we already [sic] 'outside.'" Hauerwas, "Punishing

Christians," 23. As noted in chapter 6, Calvin argues similarly that excommunication is for the sinner's benefit, calling him back to the church insofar as it names the sinner's unwillingness to repent as her own choice to leave the church. See John Calvin, *The Library of Christian Classics*, vol. 21, *Calvin: Institutes of the Christian Religion*, ed. John T. McNeill, trans. Ford Lewis Battles (Philadelphia: Westminster Press, 1960), 4.11.2, 4.12.10, 1214, 1238.

84. John Howard Yoder, "Church Discipline," *Gospel Herald* (1964): 709; see also O'Donovan, *The Desire of the Nations*, 150.

85. Yoder notes in his first academic article discussing the disciplining of one Andrew Yoder and his subsequent lawsuit against his former church, "When therefore a member severs his relation with the church he at once breaks fellowship with the society, and the institution of the Meidung [i.e. shunning] is merely the formal recognition of that breach, as extending into all of life. From this viewpoint it is immaterial by what means the break came about, for it remains, however it may have happened, that Yoder wanted to leave the group, that the group therefore consistently excluded him, that he was offended because they consistently extended the spiritual breach into the material world, and that he therefore sued the church for not being inconsistent." John Howard Yoder, "Caesar and the Meidung," *Mennonite Quarterly Review* 23 (1949): 90.

86. Yoder, *Body Politics*, 5.

87. Ibid., 2. Yoder notes on several occasions that the roots of the Anabaptist tradition lie not in infant baptism, but in the failure of discipline within Zwingli's Zurich. Accordingly, it was the failure to maintain the church-world distinction via fraternal admonition that Yoder labels as the defining break between the early Anabaptists and Zwingli. As set forth in more detail above, the Anabaptists' position on infant baptism merely followed logically upon this conclusion. See generally Yoder, "Review of Kirchenzucht bei Zwingli," 63.

88. See John Howard Yoder, "The Hermeneutics of the Anabaptists," *Mennonite Quarterly Review* 41 (1967): 291.

89. Ibid., 303.

90. Ibid., 304-5.

91. Ibid., 307.

92. Yoder, *Body Politics*, 8. Here Yoder follows MacIntyre, who argues, "It is through conflict and sometimes only through conflict that we learn what our ends and purposes are." MacIntyre, *After Virtue*, 164. MacIntyre's suggestion here is a part of his larger argument that all rationality is social, discussed below.

93. See generally John Zizioulas, "Communion and Otherness," *Orthodox Peace Fellowship's Occasional Paper* 19 (Summer 1994), http://www.incommunion.org/articles/older-issues/communion-and-otherness,

7 February 2005 and Rowan Williams, "Interiority and Epiphany: A Reading in New Testament Ethics," in *On Christian Theology* (Oxford: Blackwell, 2000), 239-64.

94. Romand Coles, "The Wild Patience of John Howard Yoder: 'Outsiders' and the 'Otherness of the Church'" *Modern Theology* 18 (2002): 318.

95. Stanley Hauerwas, et al., ed., "History, Theory, and Anabaptism: A Conversation on Theology After John Howard Yoder," in *The Wisdom of the Cross: Essays in Honor of John Howard Yoder* (Grand Rapids, Mich.: Eerdmans, 1999), 400.

96. Yoder, "The Imperative of Christian Unity," 292.

97. John Paul Lederach, *Preparing for Peace: Conflict Transformation Across Cultures* (Syracuse, N.Y.: Syracuse University Press, 1995), 18.

98. John Howard Yoder, "Christ, The Hope of the World," in *The Royal Priesthood*, 203; see also, e.g., Yoder, *The Priestly Kingdom*, 94; Yoder, "To Serve our God and to Rule the World," 132, Yoder, "Let the Church be the Church," 172.

99. This discerning is the process I located in *The Use of the Law*, which in no way suggests it was merely restating the "Anabaptist" position, but rather was the collective guidance of the gathering of the body to discern regarding participation in litigation, which guidance was but itself an admonition to discernment within the individual gatherings of the body of Christ.

100. Yoder, *The Priestly Kingdom*, 29.

101. Ibid., 30. Yoder notes that Scripture is "the store par excellence," but worship is also an act of communal memory. Ibid., 31.

102. Ibid., 33.

103. Ibid.

104. See generally Stephen Fowl, *Engaging Scripture: A Model for Theological Interpretation* (Oxford: Blackwell, 1998), 162.

105. Yoder's own description of the Matthew 18 process in light of the standard ethical assumptions of the mainstream churches or modernity is as follows: "It gives more authority to the church than does Rome, trusts more to the Holy Spirit than does Pentecostalism, has more respect for the individual than does liberal humanism, makes moral standards more binding than did Puritanism, and is more open to the new situation than was what some called 'the new morality' a quarter-century ago." Yoder, *Body Politics*, 6.

106. See Joseph Fletcher, *Situation Ethics: The New Morality* (Louisville, Ky.: Westminster John Knox Press, 1966).

107. See C. L. Stevenson, *Ethics and Language* (New Haven, Conn.: Yale University Press, 1944).

108. This story closely follows MacIntyre's account. See MacIntyre, *After Virtue*, 11-22, 64-65; Alasdair MacIntyre, *A Short History of Ethics:*

A History of Moral Philosophy from the Homeric Age to the Twentieth Century (Notre Dame, Ind.: University of Notre Dame Press, 1998), 243-69. In denying the rationality of ethical claims, emotivists follow Mill in his critique of Kant, only disagreeing regarding the convergence of all humanity's preferences on happiness. See John Stuart Mill, "Defense of Hedonism," in *Introductory Readings in Ethics*, ed. William Frankena and John Granrose (Englewood Cliffs, N.J.: Prentice-Hall, 1974), 303.

109. Consider, for example, H. Tristram Engelhardt, who acknowledges the moral discontinuity of rival traditions, yet argues for a public bioethic of autonomy. See generally H. Tristram Engelhardt, *The Foundations of Bioethics* (New York: Oxford University Press, 1986).

110. Yoder, "Why Ecclesiology is Social Ethics," 122.

111. See Franklin Littell, "The Concerns of the Believers' Church," *Chicago Theological Seminary Register* 58 (1967): 14.

112. Yoder, "Why Ecclesiology is Social Ethics," 122.

113. Thus, weak occasionalism is not deductivism (rational extension of a single guiding principle to the situation) or legalism (self-adjudicating rules for all time), because the process (1) relies on and is informed by a variety of modes of reasoning (principles, utility, character, due process), (2) is grounded in a particular understanding of rationality, (3) requires extension, improvisation, and analogical thinking to apply it to the present situation, and (4) is open to revision. Further, Yoder notes, along the lines of Stanley Fish, that the suggestion that there is some nonparticular place in which to stand is simply false. Every location is either a smaller or a wider particularity. See Yoder, *The Priestly Kingdom*, 49.

114. Tom Shaffer concludes a piece in a *Journal of Law and Religion* volume dedicated to his own work, "I wait for the day when [Yoder] will outline his own Christian ethic for lawyers." Thomas Shaffer, "How I Changed My Mind," *Journal of Law and Religion* 10 (1993-94): 301, n. 21.

115. In this regard, the essence of Yoder's advice on the law, as displayed in Shaffer's 2002 *Moral Memoranda from John Howard Yoder*, is to avoid the question "can a Christian be a lawyer?" altogether. According to Shaffer, "The better question, John later said to me, is whether the things a lawyer does in modern America are the things a person who proposes to follow Jesus might do." Shaffer, *Moral Memoranda*, v.

116. Yoder suggests, "We have here an alternative both to individual intuitionism and to completely objective rigidity, in the form of a prescription for a valid, reconciling, decision-making process. That there will be rules, that these will sometimes collide and sometimes need to bend is neither affirmed nor denied, but rather located within a more important question: namely, 'How are you going to go about it?' If you go about it in an open context, where both parties are free to speak, where additional witnesses provide

objectivity and mediation, where reconciliation is the intention and the expected outcome is a judgment that God himself can stand behind, then the rest of the practical moral reasoning process will find its way." Yoder, *The Priestly Kingdom*, 27-28.

117. For two particularly helpful essays on the social and temporal nature of identity as an alternative to the language of agency and the inner self, see Stanley Hauerwas, "Going Forward by Looking Back: Agency Reconsidered," in *Sanctify Them in the Truth: Holiness Exemplified* (Nashville: Abingdon Press, 1998), 93-103, and Rowan Williams, "Interiority and Epiphany."

118. Zizioulas, "Communion and Otherness." It is important to note the coincidence of Eastern Orthodox and Mennonite ecclesiology undergirding this claim. Zizioulas notes that the problem of Protestant ecclesiology is its failure to insist "that the church in her essence is holy and sinless." Ibid. Only this "maximalistic ecclesiology with a maximalistic anthropology" will sufficiently demand not just an "ethics" of "peaceful co-existence," but the "metanoia—repentance" and "new birth" that is the mark of trinitarian community. Ibid.

119. Yoder, *The Priestly Kingdom*, 24.

120. Yoder argues, "This New Testament view of the Church as a unity of ethical commitment might not require believers' baptism; it would at least require bringing a degree of order into the host of mutually contradictory reasons brought forth for baptizing indiscriminately the children of anyone on a church roll, as well as of maintaining on the rolls people who, in awareness of what it would mean, demonstrate no intention of making their ethical decision in the light of the gospel and in the fellowship of the brethren." Yoder, "The Nature of the Unity We Seek," in *The Royal Priesthood*, 229.

121. Yoder, "Sacrament as Social Process: Christ the Transformer of Culture," in *The Royal Priesthood*, 371.

122. Further, identity itself is historically and socially formed. Yoder notes, "Moral obligation is learned, after all, by growing up in historic communities. Our 'knowing' it is prior, in the orders of both knowing and being, to the 'reason' with which we question and clarify it, as well as to the awe and affectivity with which it grasps us." Yoder, *The Priestly Kingdom*, 38.

123. See Richard Hays, *First Corinthians* (Louisville, Ky.: John Knox, 1997), 92-93.

124. See Yoder, "Church Discipline," 334-35.

125. See Jones, *Embodying Forgiveness*, 187.

126. See generally Saint Augustine, *Confessions*, trans. R. S. Pine-Coffin (New York: Penguin, 1961), 10.28-39, 232-48. Yoder concurs, noting that realism about sin means ethical discernment must be communal: "The insights of a Christian community may equally prove instructive to the larger society through the example of sober realism about the temptations of power and the persistence of sin in the life even of the righteous. In spite of their convictions

about the power that is in the gospel for overcoming sin, the early Christians and their faithful successors in all ages have insisted on the need for mutual fraternal admonition and especially for vigilance to be exercised by the entire congregation with regard to the faithfulness of leaders." Yoder, *The Christian Witness to the State*, 18.

127. Here I am arguing along the lines of Augustine and a host of others who would follow him, that the church's call to obedience via its disciplinary process is fundamentally a reconfiguration of how to understand freedom. For Augustine, freedom is the ability to be perfectly obedient to God's will. Thus, the struggle of the *Confessions* is Augustine's competing wills toward sin and God, which are literally tearing Augustine apart. See, e.g., Augustine, *Confessions*, 8.5, 9-10, 164-65, 172-75. Bondage is, as described by Paul, the inability to do the good that I was both created to do and naturally ought to desire to do. See Romans 7:14-25. David Yeago notes that this conception of freedom is grounded in an understanding of the *telos* for human beings in a proper relationship to God: "Only in such a construction of the world, can good governance and the announcement that one has a Lord that reigns be received as good news." David Yeago, "The Office of the Keys: On the Disappearance of Discipline in Protestant Modernity," in *Marks of the Body of Christ*, ed. Carl Braaten and Robert Jenson (Grand Rapids, Mich.: Eerdmans, 1999), 108-12. Yeago contrasts this with modern accounts of freedom as the total lack of governance. See ibid., 110. Discipline, construed Christianly, is the gracious intervention of the church to release me from the bondage of sin, so that I might act freely in obedience to God. See Jones, *Embodying Forgiveness*, 59-64. All of which means that the church's recovery of these practices and the anthropology that makes them intelligible is fundamental to its proclamation of the lordship of Christ as good news.

128. Alasdair MacIntyre, *Dependent Rational Animals: Why Humans Need the Virtues* (Chicago: Open Court, 1999), 107, 156-57.

129. Yoder concurs that Mathew 18 entails that humans are social beings. See Yoder, "Binding and Loosing," 351.

130. This claim is made explicit by Markus Barth: "No man is ever made righteous for himself; justification by faith is a reality only in community with those fellow-men whom God elected for common justification. Fellow-man is neither simply a parallel case nor an appendage of 'my' justification. For fellow-humanity is a presupposition of, a means to, and a proof of, the eternal righteousness promised to me also. There is no personal justification by God without justification of fellow-men by God. And there is no faith in the justifying God without acceptance of the witness given by a neighbor. Briefly: where there is no love there is no faith and no justice." Barth, "Jews and Gentiles: The Social Character of Justification in Paul," 244-45.

131. Yoder notes, "What it means to be the church is to be spoken of

a cause being implemented and not an ontology being realized. Kingdom rather than gnosis is the key mystery." Yoder, "Why Ecclesiology is Social Ethics," 110.

132. In Yeago's words, "This modern notion of religion [as spiritual] was from the start a device for removing Christianity and its dangerous claims about God's dominion from the public realm, and confining their direct implications to an inner sphere of personal spirituality, the inner world of the disengaged self." Yeago, "The Office of the Keys," 113. Similarly, Stephen Fowl argues that Christianity may require a reconfigured assessment of the scope of the public and private. See Fowl, *Engaging Scripture*, 176.

133. Cavenaugh, "'A Fire Strong Enough to Consume the House,'" 414.

134. See Yeago, "The Office of the Keys," 105.

135. Ibid., 110, 113; see generally Charles Taylor, *Sources of the Self: The Making of Modern Identity* (Cambridge: Harvard University Press, 1989), 111-207, for the background story of the turn to the inner.

136. Rereading Old Testament visions of faith, Markus Barth concurs: "Faith is not an intellectual, emotional, or existential act, which each person can effect for himself alone. Rather faith indicates the continual and immovable subordination under God's promise and command, a subordination which becomes real only in the context of the history, liturgy, and the community of Israel." Barth, "Jews and Gentiles: The Social Character of Justification in Paul," 260.

137. Yoder writes, "This statement from Hans Denck has often been looked at as a condensation of the Anabaptist concern for discipline and obedience. The important thing about the correlating of commitment and knowledge is, however, not the emphasis it places upon commitment and obedience, but rather the limitations it places upon knowledge. This has clear and far-reaching implications for what it means when we say that the Bible contains the truth." Yoder, "The Hermeneutics of the Anabaptists," 307.

138. Huebner, "Moral Agency as Embodiment," 193.

139. Ibid., 194.

140. Joel James Shuman, *The Body of Compassion: Ethics, Medicine, and the Church* (Boulder, Colo.: Westview Press, 1999), 119.

Chapter 10
Conclusion

1. David Yeago, "The Office of the Keys: On the Disappearance of Discipline in Protestant Modernity," in *Marks of the Body of Christ*, ed. Carl Braaten and Robert Jenson (Grand Rapids, Mich.: Eerdmans, 1999), 118.

2. John Howard Yoder, "Review of Kirchenzucht bei Zwingli," *Mennonite Quarterly Review* 31 (1957): 71.

3. John Howard Yoder, Elkhart, Indiana, to Richard Yordy, St. Jacobs,

Ontario, 21 March 1979, John H. Yoder (1927-1997) Collection, Hist. Mss. 23/8, entitled "Litigation, 1961-1984," Mennonite Church USA Archives, Goshen, Indiana.

Index

Adekoi, 45-47
Adler, Clemen, 87-88
Allegretti, Joseph, 213n
Alypius, 62-63, 168-69n
Ambrose, 61-62
Anabaptists,
    and Community of goods, 87
    Confessional statements, 85-87, 88-89, 190-91
    and Dispute resolution, 89, 120-22
    and Litigation, 83-107
    and Luther's two kingdom doctrine, 84-85
    and the State, 83-85, 95-96, 186-87n
    and the Sword, 84-85, 186-87n, 189n
    and Withdrawal, 85, 116
Apocalyptic literature, 47-48, 50-53, 157n
Augustine, 10, 21, 23, 57, 59-66, 71, 73-74, 80, 129, 165-66n, 168-73n, 177n, 182n, 220-21n
    and the Bishop's Court, 65-66
    and Dispute resolution, 65-66
    and Justice, 63-64
    and Litigation practice, 64-66
    and Monastic versus lay ethics, 64, 171-72n
    and Punishment, 63-64
    the State, 59-60, 166n, 169-70n
    and Torture, 63, 168n, 169n

Bainton, Roland, 74, 179-80n

Baptism, 53-54, 83-84, 113, 120, 122, 159n, 161n, 203n, 216n
Barrett, C. K., 158n
Barth, Karl, 153n, 209n, 214-15n
Barth, Markus, 149n, 206n, 211n
Bauman, Clarence, 201n
Beck, Connie, 163n
Bell, Daniel, 115-16, 118, 205n, 207n, 208n
Bell, Ryan Brett, 163n
Benjamin, G. Andrew, 163n
Berman, Harold, 174n, 175n
Beyler, Clayton, 98
Binding and loosing, 120-25, 183n, 213-16n
Bishop's court, 60-61, 65-66
Blaurock, Georg, 83, 85-86
Bockmuehl, Markus, 46, 155n
Brace, Paul, 164n
Brazil, Wayne, 164n
Brown, Alexandra, 51, 157n
Brown, Peter, 60, 62, 166-70n, 172-73n
Bullinger, Heinrich, 189n
Bultmann, Rudolf, 50-51, 159n
Burkholder, John, 193-94n, 200n

Calvin, John, 9, 21, 23, 38, 57-58, 72, 73, 74-80, 117, 180-86n
    and the Ban, 77-80, 182-84n
    and Dispute Resolution, 77-80, 184-86n
    and Genevan Consistory, 77-80, 184-86n
    and Litigation, 75-77, 182n, 185-86n

Relationship to Genevan civil authorities, 74-75, 182n
and the State, 75-77, 180-81n
Canon law courts, 17, 58, 67-68, 70
Cavenaugh, William, 130, 216n
Chow, John, 150n
Church,
and Conflict, 15-16
As Discerning community, 122-25
And Discipline, 120-22, 126-31, 216-17n
and Dispute resolution, 49-50, 120-22
Distinction from the world, 43-47, 53-54, 59-60, 116-20
and Nonresistance, 15, 113, 204-5n
and Reconciliation, 15-18, 112-13, 206-7n
Relationship to eschatological community, 110-12, 202n
as Witnessing community, 16-17, 110-12, 202-4n
City of God (Augustine) 59-60, 63-64, 165-66n
Civil Courts, 41, 45-46, 55-56, 62-63, 68, 162-64n, 168-69n
American, 54-56, 162-63n, 164n
and Bias, 41, 45-46, 55-56, 62-63, 162-63n, 164n 168-69n
Corinthian, 41, 45-46
Reformation era, 68
Roman, 62-63, 168-69n
Clark, Andrew, 153-54n, 156n
Cohen, Boaz, 157n
Coles, Romand, 124
Communalism, 128-30
Conference on Nonresistance and Political Responsibility, 93-97
Confession of Faith in a Mennonite Perspective, 199n
Connolly, Hugh, 174-75n

Constantine, 10, 59-61, 63, 165n, 166n, 169-70n, 209n
Constantinism, 38, 106, 112, 116, 124-25, 209-10n
Constitution, 119, 211-12n
Consultation on Litigation Problems, 97-101
Corinth,
Church, 39-44
Courts, 41, 45-46
Strong and Weak, 39-41
Views of the body, 41-44
Council of Arles, 168n

de Tocqueville, Alexis, 210n
Decretum (Gratian), 69, 173n
Defensor civitatis, 63, 169n, 173n
Delcor, Mathius, 158-59n
Denck, Hans, 123, 131, 222n
Dizainiers, 79
Drake, H. A., 58-59, 61, 165-79n
Driedger, Leo, 200-1n

Ellul, Jacques, 212n
Elshtain, Jean Bethke, 59
Emotivism, 126-28, 210n, 219n
Enchiridion (Augustine), 64-65
Enns-Rempel, Kevin, 191n
Epstein, David, 156n
Erb, Paul, 91-93, 102, 192n
Eschatology, 43-44, 47-48, 50-53, 110-12, 149-50n, 157n
and the Church, 43-44, 110-11
Cosmological, 50-53
Existentialist, 50-53
Realized, 50-53, 150n
Essenes, 158-59n
Estep, William, 186-87n, 189n
Eucharist, 16, 69, 120, 128
Evans, G. R., 69, 173-75n
Excommunication, 17, 70, 74-75, 77-78, 122, 183n, 216-17n

Index 227

Exegetical method, 37-39

Failinger, Marie, 186n
Farnsworth, Ward, 162n
Farole, Donald, 164n
Fee, Gordon, 156n
Fletcher, Joseph, 126-27
Forgiveness, 17, 115-19, 121, 206-7n, 213n
Fowl, Stephen, 218n, 222n
Fried, Charles, 143n
Furnish, Victor Paul, 43-44, 152n, 160n

Girolimon, Michael, 181n
Goossen, Rachel Waltner, 25-28, 148n
Götze, Ruth, 179-80n
Gratian, 63, 69, 173
Grebel, Conrad, 33, 85-86, 123, 189n
Gregory of Nazianus, 167n

Haire, Susan Brodie, 164n
Hall, Melinda Gann, 164n
Harder, Leland, 191n, 200-1n
Harries, Jill, 60-61, 66, 167-70n, 173n
Hauerwas, Stanley, 13-14, 19, 124, 143n, 146n, 162n, 203-4n, 207-8n, 213n, 216n, 218n, 220n
Hays, Richard, 27, 38, 47-48, 129, 141n, 150n
Hering, Jean, 153n, 158n
Hershberger, Guy, 194n
Hillerbrand, Hans, 186n, 201n
Hinson, E. Glenn, 168n
Hobbes, Thomas, 119, 210n
Horst, Irvin, 193n
Hubmaier, Balthasar, 86-87, 186-88n, 216n
Huebner, Chris, 115, 207n
Huebner, Harry, 131, 204n, 206n

Individualism, 128-30

Intuitionism, 126, 218n

Jerome, 167n
Jones, A. H. M., 169n
Jones, L. Gregory, 206-7n, 213n, 220-21n
Justice, 63-64, 94-95, 114-19
Justification, 130-31, 208n, 221n

Kant, Immanuel, 117, 126
Käsemann, Ernst, 157n
Kauffman, J. Howard, 200-1n
Keifert, Patrick, 186n
Kelly, J. M., 155n, 163n
Kerr, Fergus, 203
Kingdon, Robert, 77, 79, 181n, 184-85n
Kinman, Brent, 158n
Klaassen, Walter, 186n, 188n, 200n
Kraybill, Donald, 200-1n
Kraybill, Ron, 25-27, 144-46n
Kreider, Carl, 98, 101
Kreider, Robert, 25-28, 148n
Kümin, Beat, 174n

Lampe, G. W. H., 160n
Lancel, Serge, 167n, 169-70n, 173n
Lawyers, 18-19, 55, 97-98, 102, 118, 143n, 163-64n, 210n
Lederach, John Paul, 124, 136
Legal ethics, 18-19, 142-43n, 219n
Lehman, Chester, 193n
Letter to Diognetus, 59
Levinson, Justin, 164n
Litigation,
    as Business, 55
    and Enmity, 54-55, 155-56n, 162n
    on Television, 163n
Littell, Franklin, 219n
Loewen, Howard John, 190n
Luther, Martin, 57-58, 69-74, 84-85, 89, 130, 175-80n, 186-87n

and the Ban, 70, 73-74, 175-76n
and Commerce, 71, 177-78n
and Dispute resolution, 73-74
and Litigation, 70-73, 178-79n
and the State, 57-58, 72-73, 186n
and Two kingdoms doctrine, 73, 84-85

MacIntyre, Alasdair, 19, 117-19, 130, 210-12n, 217-19n
MacMaster, Richard, 90
Manson, T. W., 149n, 154-55n
Manz, Felix, 83, 85-86
Marpeck, Pilgram, 186n, 188-89n
Martensdale, California, 90
Martin, Dale, 39-44, 149-52n, 159n
Martyrs Mirror (van Braght), 89-90
Matthew 18 Process, 120-25, 127, 129, 136, 139, 147n, 165n, 200n, 218n
McGough, Lucy, 162n
McGrath, Alister, 180n
McKee, Elsie Anne, 182-83n
McThenia, Andrew, 114, 206n
Meeks, Wayne, 51-52, 148-51n, 157n, 159-61n
Mennonite Confession of Faith, 195-96n
Mennonite General Assembly, 146n, 199-200n
Mennonite Mutual Aid, 97, 99-101
Mill, John Stuart, 117, 126-28
Miller, Marlin, 196-97n, 201n
Mitchell, Alan, 49-50, 151-52n, 156-60n
Mitchell, Margaret, 53-54, 151n
Monter, E. William, 78
Mueller, William, 180-81n

Niebuhr, Reinhold, 73, 93-95, 104-5, 166n, 192-93n, 195n
and the Ethic of love, 94

and Justice, 94-95, 104-5, 192n
and Litigation, 192-93n
and the State, 93, 166n
and Violence, 94
Nonviolence, 15, 72, 85, 105, 112-13, 124, 196n, 200n

O'Donovan, Oliver, 114, 116-17, 210-11n, 213n, 217n
Odysseos, Paula, 163n
Oyer, John, 89, 191-92n

Paul, 9, 16, 20-21, 39-54, 64-65, 74-77, 114, 116-117, 120, 129, 148-63n, 171n, 192n, 211n, 221n
Peace Problems Committee, 93, 194-95n
Peachy, Paul, 195n
Penitential practice, 68-70, 174-75n
Philips, Dirk, 190n
Political responsibility, 93-97
Possidius, 66, 172n
Powell, H. Jefferson, 14, 119, 211-12n

Quintela, Alberto and Helen, 27-34, 137-38, 147n

Registers of the Consistory of Geneva, 79, 185n
Richardson, Peter, 155n, 161n
Riedemann, Peter, 88-89, 90
Rights, 40, 118, 210-11n
Ris, Cornelius, 190-91n
Roman Catholic Church, 16-17, 142n, 173n, 203n
Rosner, Brian, 154-55n

Sabatier, Paul, 197n
Sabean, David Warren, 185n
Sales, Bruce, 163-64n
Sanctification, 75, 130-31, 172n, 180-81n

Sattler, Michael, 86-87, 189n
Schaefer, Tali, 56
Schiemer, Leonard, 188n
Schlabach, Gerald, 165-66n, 208n
Schlabach, Theron, 191n
Schleitheim Confession, 86-87, 102, 189n
Schwartz v. Schwartz, 162n
Selby, Myra, 164n
Seneca, 46, 159n
Sermon on the Mount, 20, 28, 72-73, 80, 85, 98, 112-13, 176, 180
Sexual relations, 42, 64-65, 152n, 171n
Shaffer, Mary, 142n, 212n
Shaffer, Thomas, 9-11, 18, 114, 142-43n, 206-7n, 212-13n, 219n
Sheehan, Reginald, 164n
Shuman, Joel James, 131, 145n
Simons, Menno, 189-90n
Sirmondian Constitution, 60, 169-70n
Skinner, Quentin, 174n
Smolin, David, 186n
Songer, Donald, 164n
Stayer, James, 201n
Steinmetz, David, 72, 177n, 179-80n
Stevenson, C. L., 218n

The Corinthian Body (Martin), 39-44, 149-52n, 159n
The Politics of Jesus (Yoder), 112-13, 141n, 143-44n, 159n, 196n, 204n, 206-8n, 213n
Theodosius, 60, 63, 166n
Theological method, 19-22
Thiselton, Anthony, 40, 43, 150n, 152n
Toews, John, 211n
Torah, 46, 98, 118, 154-55n, 211n
Trinity, 128-29, 203n, 220n
Troeltsch, Ernst, 74, 180n

Use of the Law, 21, 101-7, 112, 139, 144-46n, 196-200n, 207-8n, 218n

van Braght, Thieleman, 89-90
Vischer, Lukas, 165n
Volf, Miroslav, 206-7n
Volkskirche, 84

Weak occasionalism, 126-28
Weber, Max, 210n
Wendel, Francois, 74, 78, 180-81n, 183-84n
Wenger, J. C., 191n
Wenger, Samuel, 96-97, 193-95n
When Good People Quarrel (Kreider and Goossen), 25-35, 145-48n
Williams, Rowan, 166n, 217-18n, 220n
Winter, Bruce, 38- 45-47, 148-49n, 152-56n, 158n, 164n
Witte, John, 70, 73, 173-77n, 179-80n
Woods, Walter, 173-74n
World, distinction from the church, 43-47, 53-54, 59-60, 116-20

Yeago, David, 130, 138, 145n, 221-22n
Yoder, John Howard, 9-11, 15, 19-22, 29-30, 98-101, 104-6, 109-31, 139, 143-45n, 165-66n, 196-97n, 201-10n, 212-22n
  and Church discipline, 109, 120-22, 213-17n
  and Church-World dualism, 116-20, 208-10n
  and the Church, 109, 110-12, 116-17, 120-25, 202-3n, 208-10n, 212n, 214-15n
  and Conflict, 120-25, 207n, 217n
  and the Consultation on Litigation Problems, 98-101, 204-5n

and Credit counseling/adjustment, 99-101, 197n
and Discernment, 122-25
and Eschatology, 110-12, 202n
and Litigation, 15, 98-99, 204-5n, 207n
and Nonresistance, 15, 29-30, 112-13
and Punishment, 215-16n
and Realism, 111-12, 115, 139, 145n, 203-4n
and Reconciliation, 98-99, 109, 112-13, 202n, 208n
and the State, 104-6, 165-66n, 208-9n, 212n
and the Use of the Law, 196n, 201n, 207-8n

Zizioulas, John, 128, 145n, 217-18n, 220n
Zlotnick, David, 164-65
Zwingli, Ulrich, 83-84, 181-83n, 217n

The Author

Richard P. Church is a healthcare attorney and farmer. He has also served as an assistant professor of religion at Wingate University and as a judicial clerk to Judge John T. Noonan Jr. on the United States Court of Appeals for the Ninth Circuit. He holds both a JD and a PhD in theological ethics from Duke University. His writings have appeared in various journals and magazines, including the *Journal of Law and Religion*, the *Notre Dame Law Review*, and *The Cresset*. With his wife, Kristy, and their 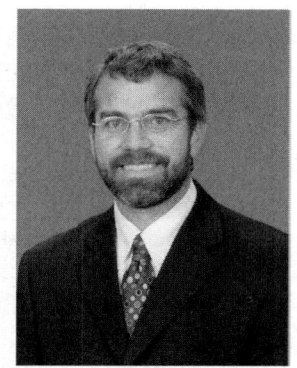 four children, he tends a seventeen-acre diversified farm. He is a member of St. Bartholomew's Episcopal Church in Pittsboro, North Carolina and was born in Oakland, California.

"Challenged by the theological ethics of John Howard Yoder and Stanley Hauerwas, attorney Richard Church began asking why adversarial litigation is seldom questioned in the Christian churches. The result is this carefully constructed argument that followers of Jesus should make reconciliation their highest priority in civil disputes. Inspired by the countercultural stance of the traditional Anabaptist-Mennonite communities, Richard Church introduces a wide range of exegetical and theological perspectives on Christian interaction with secular law courts. His review of major Christian voices—Augustine, Luther, and Calvin—on the understanding and use of 1 Corinthian 6 is informative in itself, even as it serves to highlight the distinctiveness of the Anabaptist-Mennonite efforts at faithful adherence to Paul's admonitions."
—*J. R. Burkholder, professor emeritus, Goshen College*

"Few passages in scripture are as blissfully ignored by Christians than 1 Corinthians 6. We simply do not believe Paul could be seriously stating Christians should not take one another to court. We should be extremely grateful that Richard Church, relying on the best scholarship available, makes it impossible for us to avoid the realization that Paul certainly was serious. Not only does Church help us see how Paul could be serious, but he uses this to help us see that this is a matter of Christians learning to live peaceably in a violent world. Only a person trained as an attorney could have written such an incisive book."
—*Stanley Hauerwas, Duke Divinity School and Duke University School of Law*

"Richard Church has carefully read 1 Corinthians 6 and believes that many forms of litigation render the church's ministry of reconciliation unintelligible. He convincingly tells why dispute resolution is at the heart of the church's witness. He recounts the historical context and theological basis for concerns about litigation that were expressed in every era, from the early church through the Reformation. He believes that maintaining the distinction between the church and the world has helped the Mennonite tradition keep litigation in critical question. This book is a resource for the church, grounded in the cross and embedded with the memory of its history, to discern new ways to resolve disputes."
—*Elvin Kraybill, Gibbel Kraybill & Hess LLP*